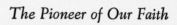

The Pioneer of Our Faith

THE PIONEER
OF OUR FAITH

A New Life of Jesus

by S. Vernon McCasland

McGraw-Hill Book Company

New York   Toronto   London

In Memoriam

Edward Scribner Ames
Shirley Jackson Case
Edgar Johnson Goodspeed
Raymond Thomas Stamm
Harold Rideout Willoughby

Preface

Probably every New Testament scholar hopes sometime to write a life of Jesus. Yet when so many books about Jesus are already available, readers have a right to ask why still another should be published.

The answer is that new points of view now make possible a better understanding of Jesus. The first is that, contrary to the popular view, he lived by faith as other men do, struggling for certainty about God, about his fellow man, about himself; his emotional life was often turbulent. A second insight is that Jesus was constantly studying the Scriptures and, like the Essenes of Qumran—who were his contemporaries—he was seeing fulfillment of the Scriptures in events of his own time. Indeed he was discovering himself in the Scriptures; and because of that self-discovery the Scriptures were the most important external factor in his thought about himself, about the world around him and about God. Recognition of these insights alone would justify another study of the life of Jesus.

But, furthermore, recent psychological and philosophical thought, especially that of Paul Tillich and Martin Buber, on the nature of faith and doubt, and on ideas of good and evil, assists in clarifying the faith and thought of Jesus. And certain concepts from comparative literature aid us in interpreting his colorful language.

Although it has become a vogue to say that the fragmentary and legendary character of the Gospels makes it impossible to write a life of Jesus, my researches have convinced me that the picture of Jesus in the Gospels is essentially reliable. It is true that little information about his childhood and youth has survived, but such a substantial body of the sayings of Jesus has been preserved that we are able to enter with confidence into the world of his mind; and most of the important decisions of his mature life have been recorded. All that this lacks of being a life of Jesus is the interpretation, which is what a scholar must contribute.

A fundamental principle of my study is that an ancient record is entitled to the presumption of authenticity unless there is positive evidence to the contrary. Such evidence might be literary, historical or philosophical, but we have no right to deny the integrity of a saying or tradition unless we can support our denial with proof. While I point out the popular character of some of the biblical material, my purpose is not to show how many legends the Gospels contain, but how much we can say with confidence about the founder of our faith. Nor do I attempt to include everything that I consider authentic. Space does not allow for that. All that I attempt to do is to put together a coherent and intelligible interpretation of Jesus.

The life of Jesus should be seen in a perpendicular as well as in a horizontal dimension. It is not merely a question of the chronological order of events in his life, or where he was born and lived, or where he traveled. Nor is it a question of being able to fill in with historical details the long blank periods in his life left by the Gospels. One may not disregard historical facts, but no amount of uninterpreted information constitutes a life of Jesus, or of any other man. The meaning of a man's life goes beyond events, dates and places. It has to do with his mind, his heart, his soul. It includes what he lives by, his doubts and fears, as well as his faith and hope. A true life of a man will of course reveal his human relationships, but it must also explore the question of his encounters with God.

All this is especially true of Jesus. God is obviously his main preoccupation, the center, the substance of his being. His compassionate grasp of events around him is grounded in his vision of what is above him. His concern for people is matched by his absorption in God. To delineate these qualities in Jesus is to succeed in writing his life; to do less is to fail.

Readers who wish to understand more fully the critical principles which underlie this book should read the chapter in the appendix on "The Sources of Our Knowledge of Jesus." Those persons desiring to refresh or expand their knowledge of the history, literature and religion of the Bible in relation to Jesus are referred to the bibliography.

This book began as the Spring Lectures at the College of the Bible, Lexington, Ky., 1960. The hospitality of President and Mrs. Riley B. Montgomery and of the faculty and students of the college is a cherished memory. Since that time I have completely rewritten and greatly expanded the manuscript; it no longer retains the lecture form. As often before, my wife, Louise, has helped me clarify ideas and style.

All quotations of Scripture are from the Revised Standard Version, copyrighted 1946 and 1952 by the Division of Christian Education of the National Council of Churches, and used by permission.

University of Virginia   *S. Vernon McCasland*

Contents

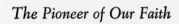

The Pioneer of Our Faith

Our Vantage Point

In the days of Jesus there lived in the city of Jericho a wealthy tax collector named Zacchaeus, who had never seen the great teacher but had heard wonderful things about him. One day when Jesus and his disciples walked down the Jordan valley, on that last and fateful journey from Galilee to Jerusalem, they arrived at Jericho, intending to pass through. Quickly the news spread and the entire population rushed out to watch the famous man go by. But Zacchaeus was such a short man that his view was obstructed by taller people in the crowd. Determined not to miss seeing Jesus, Zacchaeus ran ahead and climbed a tree by the road along which Jesus was to pass. From that vantage point he had a fine view of Jesus and his disciples as they approached. But Jesus also saw the eager Zacchaeus in the tree, and at once recognized his good character. No doubt the curious tax collector was astounded when Jesus called up to him (Luke 19:1–10), "Zacchaeus, make haste and come down; for I must stay at your house today!" Zacchaeus was overjoyed; immediately he became an ardent disciple, and his life was made over by that momentous contact with Jesus.

New Testament Views of Jesus

Ever since the New Testament was written, nearly two thousand years ago, it has been well known that there are many vantage points from which one can get a good view of Jesus. Mark, who wrote the first Gospel, was mainly interested in the great deeds Jesus performed. Matthew and Luke, whose Gospels were revised editions of Mark, showed more interest in Jesus as a teacher. Still later, John presented Jesus as the incarnation of God—as God in the form of a man. His main purpose was to show the religious meaning of Jesus for the people of his time. The Letters of Paul have little interest in the historical facts of the life of Jesus, but present Christ as Lord and Savior. The author of the Letter to the Hebrews—the only New Testament writer to do it—sees Jesus as an eternal high priest serving in a temple in heaven.

Jesus has been a favorite subject of artists, novelists, poets, and musicians as well as historians. Some things about him have been better presented in poems, stories, paintings and music than by historical writings. The accounts of his birth and infancy are of this type, yet they express the Christian faith and belong to our greatest art. Both Matthew and Luke tell of the birth of Christ to a virgin mother in Bethlehem, the city of King David, from whose lineage the Messiah was expected to come. Matthew alone contains the story of the Wise Men of the East who came to see the divine child; the attempt of King Herod to slay the newborn prince; and the flight of Joseph and Mary with the infant to Egypt. Only Luke tells about the shepherds, and how the baby had to be cradled in a manger because there was no room in the inn; only he records the canticles uttered by Zechariah, Simeon and Mary; and only he mentions the singing angels. So we are indebted to Luke for our great tradition of Christmas music.

These birth stories affirm in poetic symbols that Christian faith is based on a miracle; and that miracle is Christ, the man Jesus of Nazareth. He is a miracle because men see God in him. Any event you see God in, whether you consider it natural or supernatural, in ancient times or the present, is a miracle. It is this view of the world which makes the difference between Christians and non-Christians.[1]

The genealogies in Matthew and Luke, each in its own way, trace the ancestry of this marvelous child back to the great kings of the Hebrews, in this way affirming that he has a right to sit on the Messianic throne. Luke carries him all the way back to Adam, the son of God, thus introducing the universality of Christianity. Christians have always believed that God is universal, and that the Messianic Kingdom includes all nations and the whole world.

Here is expressed in unmatched beauty the faith of every generation of Christians: that God reveals himself to the world in this child, not only as the long-awaited Messiah of the Jews, but also as the Savior of all mankind. For the belief which inspired these stories and poems when Jesus was born took root and lived on; and through the dark and tragic days of almost two thousand years that faith has kept Christians singing.

But no less a wonder is the stout affirmation that this same Jesus, whose birth, life, death and resurrection are a continuing miracle, is at the same time in every way a man just as we are.

---

[1] See my article "Miracle." *The Interpreter's Dictionary of the Bible*, the Abingdon Press, Nashville, 1962; also my article "Miracles" in the new revised edition of James Hastings, *Dictionary of the Bible*, Charles Scribner's Sons, New York, 1963.

Presuppositions

Writers begin with certain ideas: they have their interests and presuppositions; they show their religious heritage, they speak the vocabulary of their place and time. They deal with social problems; sometimes they are involved in controversy. This is true of both ancient and modern writers. Each of the New Testament authors has used whatever resources he had at his command: testimony of eyewitnesses, traditions, the Hebrew Scriptures, his own education, the inner light of the Spirit of Christ in his heart, as well as personal presuppositions now lost to view.

The different New Testament conceptions of Jesus may be identified and examined independently and then viewed in comparison with one another. Each indeed reveals some unique light on the life, the person, the meaning of Jesus, and the place he has in the faith of Christians. While all have something important to say, no single view is adequate. Together they reflect what Jesus was, how his immediate disciples understood him, how the early church explained him, what he has been through the centuries, and what he continues to be today.

The Pioneer of Our Faith

The presupposition of this study is that Jesus himself was a man of faith, a religious person. He lived by faith, just as all other religious persons before and after him have lived. He saw God revealed in the natural world, in his moral conscience, in the sacraments of religion, in the sacred Scriptures, in the sense of his own nature and destiny. These apprehensions were insights which grew out of his own experience; they were intuitions of his faith.

Throughout this book it is our intention to analyze the actions and words of Jesus from this point of view. The title of our study is intended to suggest this presupposition: the idea that Jesus himself led the way through that frontier region of life which religious persons call faith. Secular writers may call it insight or intuition, but for biblical people it was response to God's revelation of himself. They also called it vision, which means the kind of sight you attain when you begin to recognize a religious quality in your own life; when your spiritual eyes and ears are opened. Jesus himself was supremely responsive to this wonder of faith; he surrendered himself to its absolute demands; and through it he found a deep and true fulfillment. Any person who understands something of the nature of faith in his own life can begin to understand thhe mystery of Jesus. But unless he does discover this spiritual insight, the most important thing this book attempts to say may remain unintelligible to him.

Hebrews 12:2 provides the title. In this verse the author is addressing Christians under persecution. He calls a roll of persons of great faith in the Old Testament. Beginning with Abel, he lists Enoch, Noah, Abraham, Isaac, Jacob, Sarah and Moses, along with many others who demonstrated faith by heroic loyalty, coming to the climax of his eloquent presentation by naming Jesus in the series. He writes,

> Therefore, since we are surrounded by so great a cloud of witnesses, let us also lay aside every weight, and the sin which clings so closely, and let us run with perseverance the race that is set before us, looking to Jesus the pioneer and perfecter of our faith, who for the joy that was set before him endured the cross, despising the shame, and is seated at the right hand of the throne of God.

Thus the author lists Jesus among persons of outstanding faith, indeed as foremost among them all, a group which will also include Christians he is addressing, provided they remain steadfast under persecution.

The word "pioneer" is derived from an old French term for foot soldier, especially a member of an engineer corps detailed to remove obstructions from roads, dig trenches, make bridges, or effect demolitions. It has come to mean one who goes before, as into a wilderness, preparing the way for others to follow. In our particular passage in Hebrews it refers to an athletic event. The racecourse was familiar to Greeks and Romans all over that world. Greek games brought together famous athletes to compete for prizes. The race alluded to in Hebrews 12:2 involves a team directed by a leader, perhaps a cross-country race. The leader sets the pace and shows his teammates how to run. So this author urges his fellow Christians to lay aside weights and hindrances of every kind and to run the race with determination, setting their eyes on Jesus, their leader, their pioneer.

The importance of this passage in Hebrews is that its author has shown a unique understanding of Jesus. He sees him not as a spectator, nor even as one who will reward those who win, but as himself a runner; as one who for months, perhaps years, has trained himself, running with weights on his legs to develop his muscles; one who knows what it means to feel the stitch in one's side that comes from running, the exhaustion, the sense of imminent collapse; but also as one who knows the exhilaration and freedom that come when a runner gets his second wind and finds himself able to finish the course and win the race.

The Faith of Jesus

Most of what we know about Jesus comes from the brief period of his ministry, when he had already reached full maturity. Luke says he was about thirty years old when his ministry began (3:23). As only one Passover during his ministry is mentioned in the Synoptic Gospels, it may be that not more than one year passed before he was put to death. It seems more probable, however, as the Gospel of John indicates by the number of Passovers mentioned there, that the ministry lasted about three years. In any case, it was a brief period, and from our point of view Jesus was a very young man at the time of his death.

Not much is known about him before that time. Yet there is one revealing episode. Luke tells a story of how Jesus went with his parents to Jerusalem for the Passover when he was twelve (Luke 2:41-52). It was their custom as devout Jews to go every year. Joseph and Mary allowed him to follow his own inclinations during the festival, and when they had completed their religious duties, they started back to Galilee with the other pilgrims. However, missing Jesus, they returned to Jerusalem to search for him, and found him at last in the temple, where he was studying the Scriptures under the guidance of learned teachers. The boy was asking and answering questions, and was surprised when his parents chided him for the worry he had caused them.

This episode is tremendously important, throwing light as it does on the youthful Jesus. Obviously he was an exceedingly precocious child, and had begun to mature at an early age. Most likely along with his parents he participated in all the annual festivals, worshipped in the synagogue, and studied the holy Scriptures whenever he found an opportunity. We may infer that the faith he had as a man was only the mature fulfillment of an experience which had grown steadily in Jesus from childhood. For God surely reveals himself to little children, in ways they can understand, just as he does to those who have arrived at maturity.

The way Jesus lingered behind in Jerusalem engrossed in studying the Scriptures, while his parents set out on the long trek home, was an intimation of the great influence the sacred writings were to exercise over his life. And a recognition of the meaning the Scriptures had for Jesus, and the constant use he made of them in his efforts to understand himself, can throw light on many an otherwise obscure, if not incomprehensible, word or action. In fact Jesus' devotion to the Scriptures is a key to his life scholars have never made full use of; and failure to discover and use this key is an important reason why many have concluded it is impossible to write his life.

His Mature Faith

Jesus is introduced in Mark, the earliest Gospel, as he came with a multitude from Galilee, drawn by the strange words of the prophet John. The Baptizer's message brought to Jesus, as it did to many others of his company, a revelation from God; and from that time on his life took a new course. He entered a new world of the Spirit.

Mark makes it clear from the beginning to the end of his Gospel that, from the time of his encounter with John to his death, the life of Jesus was characterized by a constant struggle to understand the things which were happening to him. For, regardless of the great things Jesus did and the wonderful things he taught, regardless of how he understood himself and what others have believed about him, Jesus himself was first of all a man of faith; and whatever is characteristic of the struggles of other men for faith was also characteristic of him. He knew the conflicts between faith and reason; he knew the agony of doubt, the loneliness that comes when reason shakes a man's confidence in God. At times this loneliness isolated Jesus from his disciples and drove him into solitude. There alone he struggled for clarity and certainty about the will of God for his life. All these points Mark highlights.

Jesus' struggle for faith appears in many ways. The temptation immediately following his baptism is a most notable example. This extraordinary experience must not be passed over as an entirely legendary and therefore insignificant episode. His efforts to overcome uncertainty are especially evident in his habits of prayer. Luke more than any other writer took an interest in the prayers of Jesus. He records that Jesus was praying when he was baptized (3:21). When crowds gathered to hear him and many pressed upon him to be healed, he withdrew into the wilderness to pray (9:18). Only a few days later, when he was praying on a mountain top with Peter, James and John, Luke says (9:28), the transfiguration took place. On another occasion, when he had ceased praying, one of his disciples said, "Teach us to pray" (11:1); then Jesus taught them the Lord's Prayer.

One does not engage in frequent and extended prayer, at times through the night in lonely places, except when he is laboring under burdens, tensions and frustrations, when he is struggling for the very life of his soul. The number of times Jesus engaged in prayer, both with his disciples and alone, is a good reason to suspect, even without further evidence, that, like his disciples all through the ages, Jesus knew what it was to walk alone with doubt.

Nor are we left merely with these instances to infer that the life of Jesus was as familiar with doubt as our own. The prayers he uttered during those last days in Jerusalem are further and unquestionable evidence of the doubt with which he struggled, and of the reality of his inner battle. Mark tells us that on the night of the betrayal, Jesus withdrew to the place called Gethsemane. There he requested his disciples,

"Sit here, while I pray." And he took with him Peter and James and John, and began to be greatly troubled. And he said to them, "My soul is very sorrowful, even to death; remain here, and watch." And going a little farther, he fell on the ground and prayed that, if it were possible, the hour might pass from him. And he said, "Abba, Father, all things are possible to thee; remove this cup from me; yet not what I will, but what thou wilt." And he came and found them sleeping, and he said to them, "Simon, are you asleep? Could you not watch one hour?" (Mark 14:32-37).

Jesus went away again and prayed, saying the same words, but again he came and found the disciples sleeping. A third time he went away and prayed, in utter loneliness, with not a soul to share the agony, to understand the struggle, the uncertainty, which almost overwhelmed him. Three times he uttered an unanswered prayer.

Then followed swiftly the betrayal, the arrest, the flight of the disciples in terror, and the trial before the Jewish court. Early the next day he was condemned by the Romans, and at nine o'clock they crucified him. At noon from the darkness that settled over him, he was heard to cry, "My God, my God, why hast thou forsaken me?" (Mark 15:34). Shortly thereafter he uttered another cry, loud but unintelligible, and died.

Here is a vivid example of the nature of faith. In Gethsemane Jesus identified his will with the will of God when he said with resignation,

"Not what I will, but what thou wilt" (Mark 14:36). But he was still not able to understand; doubt remained with him to the end. Such is the life of faith, both his and ours; it never fully escapes from its doubt. This has always been its nature; and men of faith know that it is still that way today.

In his own life Jesus fully explored the experience of faith. He learned its height and depth; its certainty and uncertainty; its joy and anxiety; its confidence and despair. But he also learned that faith has the capacity to absorb doubt and rise above it. He demonstrated that faith is able to be steadfast, to affirm its intuitions, to live by its own convictions. Out of the agony of his own soul, Jesus found the way; he blazed a trail for all others in search of faith to follow.

Faith and Doubt

Before we can understand what it means to call Jesus the pioneer of our faith, we must know the meaning of faith, also of doubt; we need to comprehend how these attitudes of mind are related to one another, and what they are not, as well as what they are.

Faith is not the same as historical facts, or science, or philosophy. This is not to say that a man of faith is not concerned about history and science and philosophy; yet faith is not the same as any or all of these disciplines. The study of history is not necessarily a religious activity. The facts with which history deals may be discovered by a scholar who has no religious faith. It is an error therefore to assume that faith is the same as historical evidence. This statement is true even of historical passages in the Bible. The mistaken view that faith is the same as historical evidence has caused many people to think that faith is undermined if the historical accuracy of a passage in the Bible is challenged. This is a false conclusion.

In our day the authority of science reigns almost supreme, and men search for scientific authority for their beliefs. If they hear scientific testimony for some belief they will usually accept it. Yet scientific facts are not the same as faith. In itself, science is neither for religion nor against it; it is neutral. Some scientists are not religious persons, some are; those who are religious do not derive their faith from science alone. Nor is faith to be equated with philosophy, nor with facts derived from reason alone. We must not make the mistake of basing our faith solely on philosophical study.

But in a positive sense, what is faith? One of its best known connotations is loyalty; in that sense we speak of keeping faith; we are loyal to a person, to an idea, to truth, to a moral standard, to a religion, to a nation. Commitment is another good element of faith. We may accept an idea or a code of morality in a theoretical sense; we may say we believe in the Ten Commandments or the Golden Rule, but we do not really have faith in these ways of life until we begin to live by them. That is what it means to believe in Christ; we begin to live as Jesus taught men to live; we submit our will to the will of Christ.

Both loyalty and commitment are good meanings of faith in the Bible, especially in the New Testament.

Yet there is another meaning of faith which is more fundamental, and therefore more important, than either of these. Faith is also a form of knowledge: it is one way of understanding things, and it brings a kind of certainty that in some respects transcends history, science and philosophy. Not that faith repudiates these other ways of knowing things, but that it goes beyond them. But what kind of knowledge does faith employ, if it is not history, or science, or philosophy? Here we have to admit that we stand before a mystery; no one can fully explain the nature of faith. According to biblical understanding, faith is a man's response to revelation, which in turn comes from God. Revelation refers to the way God makes himself known to man. Faith therefore involves two aspects of this relationship between God and man. When God reveals himself in any way whatsoever and man responds in acceptance and trust, that response is faith. Such a response is certainty, the greatest certainty man knows; it is therefore the most satisfying kind of knowledge.

This certainty of faith has the nature of a direct apprehension. You can feel it; you apprehend a fact you are so certain of that it needs no further proof. Faith is an immediate awareness; it discerns something that is self-evident. From a psychological viewpoint, we call it intuition. Pascal, a French philosopher, disappointed with his philosophical studies, looking within himself, said the heart has its reasons. In these profound words Pascal was talking about faith as a means of knowing things, the most important things in the world. This again points to the mystery of faith. Even when reason itself has been unable to attain it, the heart brings us certainty. This is the kind of certainty an artist feels or a lover knows. They know when certainty comes, but not how it comes. When we speak of faith as knowledge, that is what we mean.

Paul, the greatest Christian apostle, found the experience of faith a fascinating study. Again and again he wrote eloquently of his certainty of Christ; but when he tried to explain faith and how it comes, the best he could do was to say it is a gift of God (Ephesians 2:8; 3:14–19); and we can do no better than that today. In this way Paul recognized a mystery which defies our efforts to understand it. There is always a deep mystical quality in the certainty that comes to us by faith. Yet, although we do not understand how it is, this means that you come into life with trust in the persons you are dependent on and faith in the things you live by. Thus indeed faith is in us when we are born; it sustains us in childhood and adolescence; and it provides us as adults with the meanings and values that give purpose to life.

Uncertainty

But although faith brings us the greatest certainty we know, it is also true that faith involves an uncertainty. As faith is not achieved by historical evidence, or by science or philosophy, it is therefore unable to demonstrate the truth it holds by means of these studies. So faith always harbors within itself a real possibility of doubt, a doubt planted there by reason. As reason seeks to understand everything in the world by either history or science or philosophy, it tends to be sceptical of any other kind of knowledge. Faith is therefore always vulnerable to attacks of reason; such doubt is inevitable.

The uncertainty we are so often conscious of results from the fact that faith operates partly on a different plane, in a different dimension, from that of reason; and so long as we fail to recognize this and depend on reason alone there is no way the doubt it implants can be removed. This rational doubt should not be denied, and it cannot be safely ignored, but it can be transcended. Even when you are a person of mature faith, you know that time and again, perhaps for long periods, you have to struggle with doubt; you may reach the point of despair; yet somehow you find an uncanny strength to rise above it and go on your way.

Struggle with doubt is such a constant characteristic of faith that it must be regarded as inevitable, as therefore normal, in the religious life. You have two ways of getting knowledge: the intuitive way of faith and the purely rational and scientific way of reason. So long as reason remains in the limited area where it has a right to operate, it causes faith no difficulty; inherently it possesses no natural animosity toward faith. But when you are led to believe that reason is the only way to knowledge, you have given up the true foundation of your spiritual life.

Since man possesses both an intuitive and a rational approach to truth, a competitive struggle between the two is bound to develop from time to time. Out of this struggle between faith and reason for the control of life, doubt arises. Fully understood, however, reason depends on faith. It cannot operate without ideas of order, and law, and causality, which it does not either create or discover, but for which it is indebted to intuitions of the faith which is seemingly born in all of us. As soon as intelligence dawns in us as children, especially as it develops to maturity in our adult life, we find our minds equipped with such ideas as order, law and causality; and we do not know where or how we acquired them. They are clarified and sharpened by academic studies; yet even uneducated people have these same ideas, which are the necessary equipment with which all intelligent minds operate. It is necessary therefore for reason to be self-critical; to be aware of its dependence on the intuitions of faith; and to discipline itself, lest it overstep the boundaries of its proper field of activity.

Once you realize that reason itself is dependent on certain insights of faith, you are better able to recognize and overcome the doubts it creates. The cycle of reason-doubt-faith is a continuing trinity in the spiritual life of intelligent persons. Day after day they have to struggle for their faith. From the beginning of time the religions of mankind have known this fact. But they all testify that men of faith have found it possible to build bridges across the chasms of doubt.

As religion involves the whole of man's personality, it must find a place for both faith and reason, which, in a mature person it always does. Religion has places of honor for history and science and philosophy. There is no necessary conflict between faith and reason. Conflict arises only when there is a misunderstanding of one or the other, when one of these ways of knowing attempts to dominate personality to the exclusion of the other. As we have seen, intelligence has two ways of knowing: one is intuitive, the other is rational; and when faith attains its ideal form, each of these parallel forms of understanding finds a necessary reinforcement in the other.

God's Son

Mark begins his short chronicle of Jesus with a brief but invaluable account of his baptism. His record (1:9–11) is as follows:

> In those days Jesus came from Nazareth of Galilee and was baptized of John in the Jordan. And when he came up out of the water, immediately he saw the heavens open and the Spirit descending upon him like a dove; and a voice came from heaven,
> "Thou art my beloved Son; with thee I am well pleased."

Such terseness is almost beyond the capabilities of modern writers, but in this tiny fragment Mark gives us the oldest record of the event which caused Jesus to become the founder of the Christian religion.

As Mark relates it, when Jesus came up from the water the Spirit descended upon him in the form of a dove; and it was Jesus himself who saw the Spirit come down. For Mark adds that the voice from heaven was directed to Jesus personally: "Thou art my beloved Son." Mark thus calls attention to the intensely personal character of the experience. Neither the prophet John nor the people were aware of the drama in the soul of Jesus. As far as they were concerned, the baptism of Jesus occurred without any unusual incident. Like others who preceded him and came after, Jesus came penitently to receive baptism at the hands of the prophet. Mark then allows Jesus to depart at once into the desert, where the temptation is to begin.

Luke's Version

When Luke (3:21–22) revised Mark's account of the baptism, he rendered it as follows:

> Now when all the people were baptized, and when Jesus also had been baptized and was praying, the heaven was opened, and the Holy Spirit came upon him in bodily form, as a dove, and a voice came from heaven,
> "Thou art my beloved Son; with thee I am well pleased."

Thus Luke has given a reasonably close transcript of what Mark had said. He has preserved enough to let readers see that the experience occurred in the heart of Jesus, giving no indication that others present observed the unusual events. Luke retains Mark's statement that the voice or "manifestation" was directed to Jesus, but does not say that the audience heard it. Luke adds the detail that as Jesus came up from the water he was praying; and in view of the inner character of this experience, Luke's observation is plausible.

Matthew's View

Matthew is famous for the liberties he took with his sources. When he came to this passage in Mark and narrated it for his own Gospel, he completely changed its meaning (3:13–17).

> Then Jesus came from Galilee to the Jordan to John, to be baptized by him. John would have prevented him, saying, "I need to be baptized by you, and you come to me?" But Jesus answered him, "Let it be so now; for thus it is fitting for us to fulfill all righteousness." Then he consented. And when Jesus was baptized, he went up immediately from the water, and behold, the heavens were opened and he saw the Spirit of God descending like a dove, and alighting on him; and lo, a voice from heaven, saying, "This is my beloved Son, with whom I am well pleased."

Matthew reflects the emerging theology of the early church. According to his view, the prophet John recognized Jesus immediately, when he arrived on the scene. At first John refused to baptize him, saying, "I need to be baptized by you"; but when Jesus insisted, John baptized him. When Jesus had been baptized and was coming up from the water, the voice from heaven refers to Jesus in the third person, and does not address him in the second as in Mark; it addresses the prophet and the multitude: "this is my beloved Son." Matthew notes that it was Jesus who saw the heavens opened, but otherwise all of the personal element in the episode has been removed. John and the people are the spectators and participants. The spectacular events are for their benefit, not for Jesus, who is baptized not because he needs to be but to set an example. But in Mark and Luke, the voice is directed only to Jesus. It informs him that he is God's Son, a fact he presumably did not know before.

Matthew very possibly expected that his revision would supersede Mark's account and cause it to be discarded. But what a tragedy for us that would have been: What Mark records as the most revealing single experience in the life of Jesus, in Matthew has been transformed into a spectacle intended to impress others. It throws no light on the great person we should like so much to understand.

John's Interpretation

The most relevant part of John's account occurs in 1:29–34, as follows:

> The next day he saw Jesus coming toward him, and said, "Behold, the Lamb of God, who takes away the sin of the world! This is he of whom I said, 'After me comes a man who ranks before me, for he was before me.' I myself did not know him, but for this I came baptizing in water, that he might be revealed to Israel." And John bore witness, "I saw the Spirit descend as a dove from heaven, and it remained on him. I myself did not know him; but he who sent me to baptize in water said to me, 'He on whom you see the Spirit descend and remain, this is he who baptizes with the Holy Spirit.' And I have seen and borne witness that this is the Son of God."

In this passage hardly a vestige remains of Mark's realistic report of the religious experience in the soul of Jesus when John baptized him. Here the Spirit descends upon Jesus to point him out to John, who up to that time was not acquainted with him, with no intimation of his nature and mission. John had been instructed to be on the watch for this sign. By the descent of the Holy Spirit he was to recognize the Messiah, who was to baptize with the Holy Spirit. John himself had been limited to baptizing in water.

We have noted that, in Matthew, John at first declined to baptize Jesus, feeling his own unworthiness, yet that, when Jesus insisted, John baptized him; and that in Matthew both the baptism and the marvels occurred for the benefit of John and the people, not for Jesus himself. In the Gospel of John this idea is carried much further. Here Jesus is not only represented as being without need of baptism; he does not ask for baptism; and apparently he is not baptized at all. The fourth Gospel's presentation of Jesus as the eternal Word does not lend itself to the feeling that Jesus needed to be baptized. Throughout this Gospel the human nature of Jesus tends to give way in favor of emphasis on his supernatural character, pre-existent and eternal. Jesus is a human manifestation of the infinite Word, the Logos.

The View of Jesus Himself

At the time of his baptism, as Mark interpreted his life, Jesus became a different person. He passed from one level of experience into another; he moved into a new dimension. Informed by the voice from heaven that he was God's Son, Jesus suddenly came to the realization that he possessed a new identity. No longer was he only the carpenter of Nazareth (Mark 6:3); now he realized by the light of a divine illumination that he was the Son of God. This awareness of a divine paternity had come to Jesus as he stepped from the water. The realization occurred in a single instant of time; it was not a gradual development during his youth, nor a memory of childhood. The suddenness of the vision struck Jesus with a confusing shock, and its bewildering mystery drove him alone into the desert, in whose solitude he would seek to penetrate the meaning of what he had seen and heard.

The Vision Jesus Saw

The extraordinary vision Jesus saw has parallels in that of Moses on the mountain hearing God speak from a burning bush; in Amos called from behind his flock to be a prophet; in Jeremiah compelled by an inner fire to speak God's message. There is something like it also in Gautama Buddha as he sat meditating under a banyan tree until illumination came; and one thinks of Mohammed hearing an angel's voice in the cave. Indeed the encounter of Jesus with God's Spirit can be brought within the experience of readers today. The insight of every man, no matter how undistinguished, has something in common with that of Jesus. This spectacular episode in his life is an example of the intuitive understanding the Bible calls faith. It is a realization of the divine with one's whole personality, an immediate awareness of the presence of God.

Men of the East have understood this kind of knowledge better than men of the West, and for this reason they have given the world its religions. Jesus was an Oriental, but his experience can be understood by any person who has apprehended the Spirit of God, whether in the sacraments of the Church, or in the numberless other ways men become aware of God. We can comprehend what happened to Jesus at his baptism only when we realize that the same wonder, although in a small way, has happened or may happen to us. We can understand Jesus insofar as both he and we are persons, for one person can understand another.

Readers today are puzzled by the vision Jesus saw. They feel that such things do not happen now, therefore they did not happen then; they were simply creations of the imagination. We modern westerners tend to associate such things with either a primitive culture or the mentally ill. Even the ill, we are told, do not experience such things unless their mentalities are first shaped by an animistic culture, which believes in invisible spirits residing in natural objects and human personalities.

This approach, however, forces one into the dilemma of saying that Jesus was a primitive or mentally ill, either of which is an utterly untenable alternative. Another way out of the difficulty is to call the Gospel account a mere legend, therefore to be disregarded. But it is more reasonable to look for an interpretation which accepts the integrity of the record.

No biblical scholar of the first rank today would attempt to argue that Jesus was either a primitive or mentally ill. He was nevertheless, a man of the biblical world, more specifically a Jew in a tiny province of the Roman Empire, in the first century A.D. His ideas of man, of spirits and of God were characteristic of his time and his homeland. He thought and spoke in the vocabulary of his age, and his experience of communication with God inevitably assumed forms commonly recognized and accepted by the Jewish culture in which he was born and in which he lived.

We need to perceive that the basic experiences of life remain the same from age to age, but that ways of understanding and describing them are always changing. What our predecessors have said about life may therefore at first be incomprehensible to us, and we may unwittingly reject what they have said as false. Yet more careful study often discovers that the ideas, the phenomena they have recorded are indeed familiar to us, but are set down in a nomenclature and figures of speech difficult for us to understand. Most modern psychology regards as hallucinatory such visions as Jesus saw. But biblical people simply reported that they saw visions and heard voices. We come upon such testimony all the way from Abraham and Moses through the prophets of the Old Testament to Paul and many other early Christians. Records similar to these occur in most of the religions of the world.

However subjective visions may be, it does not follow that they are therefore illusory. Deeper understanding recognizes that biblical accounts of visions are cast in a vocabulary ancient religious persons used to tell others what took place in their souls. They are evidence from that ancient world of what every devout person today feels in his own heart. They testify to the certainty of God and the possibility of communion with him.

How Was Jesus God's Son?

Adoption

The divine sonship that Jesus suddenly realized—the apprehension coming as it did at one instant of time—was in fact sonship in the sense of adoption: God, the Father in heaven, had adopted him, the son of a carpenter, as his own son. Such sonship is a spiritual, not a biological fact. Adoption was a familiar practice in the Roman world of Jesus' day. Roman emperors were especially fond of it. Julius Caesar adopted Octavius to be his successor; Hadrian adopted Antoninus Pius; and Antoninus Pius adopted Marcus Aurelius. Adoption is a wonderful thing. Many a man begets an unwanted son; only a man who really wants a son adopts him. To be adopted by an ordinary man is a compliment to any boy; adoption by an emperor is a rare honor; to be chosen as God's Son, to be able to call him Father, is a privilege, a joy, indescribably precious.

Paul was the first Christian writer to recognize the beauty of adoption. It was his favorite way of expressing what it means to become a child of God by faith. In the Letter to the Galatians (4:4–7), he writes:

> But when the time had fully come, God sent forth his Son, born of woman, born under the law, to redeem those who were born under the law, so that we might receive adoption as sons. And because you are sons, God has sent the Spirit of his Son into our hearts, crying, "Abba, Father." So through God you are no longer a slave but a son, and if a son then an heir.

Paul uses the figure of adoption to express the new Christian sense of sonship again in Romans 8:15 and 8:23. This eighth chapter of Romans—perhaps the most beautiful chapter the great apostle ever wrote—bursts from his lips in the ecstasy, if not the form, of a poem; like a great musical composition, it increases in intensity and power to the end. And the theme about which it moves is the idea of the believer's divine sonship, expressed by the figure of adoption. The believer, Paul says, finds himself inspired by the divine Spirit residing in his heart to call out, "Abba! Father!" an expression which means,

"O God, my Father!"[1] It is this intuition of divine sonship, Paul would have us understand, which for men of faith redeems all the frustrations and tragedies of the world.

A New Birth

The Gospel of John, a half century later, was to discard this picturesque figure of adoption in favor of the biological figure. The author of this Gospel, like Paul, was fascinated by the marvel that occurs in a man's heart when he believes in God. His view is expressed in the famous interview of Nicodemus with Jesus (3:3–8). To this earnest prince of the Pharisees, Jesus said,

> I say to you, "You must be born anew." The wind blows where it wills, and you hear the sound of it, but you do not know whence it comes or whither it goes; so it is with every one who is born of the Spirit.

John has taken the idea of divine sonship from Paul; but he has changed the figure from adoption to birth. He knows there are two ways of acquiring sons: one is to adopt, the other is to beget; and he prefers the latter. In one sense, he goes beyond Paul in his choice of imagery—let no one fail to see that it is imagery we are dealing with here, whether the legal process of a law court or the procreative act of biological generation. The one respect in which John's figure goes beyond Paul's is that whereas adoption is a legal, rational process anyone can understand, birth is enshrined in a mystery which the most profound scientist cannot fully penetrate.

Yet profound though John's figure is, he represents the third generation of the Christian tradition. In the generation before him stood Mark, who has recorded the baptism of Jesus; and before Mark stood Paul, the first Christian to put the new sense of the divine sonship of believers into the records as adoption. It is obvious that Paul and John mean to say the same thing; there is no basic conflict between them; both chose the idea of sonship. It is only that Paul preferred the figure of adoption, while John chose that of a new birth.

The Source of Mark's Information

But how did Mark learn this element of the tradition? According to Mark's own version of the baptism, no one that day except Jesus—

[1] See S. V. McCasland, "Abba, Father," *Journal of Biblical Literature*, vol. LXXII, 1953, pp. 79–91.

neither John nor the multitude—saw the vision or heard the voice.
Mark could not have learned it from John or other persons present,
for they could have no knowledge of the remarkable things Jesus
alone saw and heard.

The Gospels of Mark, Matthew and John, as we have seen, show
the tradition of the baptism of Jesus in three stages. In Matthew and
John the events had no real meaning for Jesus; his baptism was not
a sign of repentance and spiritual renewal; the voice from heaven
brought him no information about himself that he did not already
know. In Mark, however, out of his baptism and the vision which
followed, Jesus for the first time became aware of his divine sonship; his whole life was transformed by the experience.

But how did the information Mark records get into the early tradition? If John did not recognize Jesus when he came for baptism; if the
other persons there did not see or hear what occurred to Jesus; from
whom did the early tradition get the information? In other words, how
did the tradition learn about these things which were seen and heard
only by Jesus himself? By this process of elimination we are forced to
conclude that Jesus has to be the only one who reported these things.
After the period of withdrawal into the desert, after the time of temptation was finished, when Jesus rejoined his friends from Galilee—we
must assume—he reported to them the vision he saw and the words
he heard. Thus the record of the events found their way into the tradition Mark has preserved.

What caused Jesus to conceive of his divine sonship as an adoption?
Does Mark's brief record throw light on that question? Observing the
record closely, we discover that the words Jesus heard are derived from
the Scriptures. Part of it is from Psalm 2:7,

You are my son, today I have begotten you.

Mark quotes only "You are my son," and then bases the remainder
of his quotation on Isaiah 42:1. But Psalm 2:7 is applied to Jesus
without change in Acts 13:33 and in Hebrews 1:5 and 5:5. Moreover, Luke's record of the voice Jesus heard (3:22), according to some
ancient manuscripts, quotes the voice as saying,

You are my beloved Son; today have I begotten you.

This passage of course carries the idea of adoption. The psalm itself
was written for the coronation of some ancient Hebrew king; it was a
Hebrew belief that in a spiritual sense the prince became God's son

when he was crowned. So the idea, and all passages which expressed it, entered into the Messianic thought of early Christians. One can be certain that Jesus was pondering these very Scriptures when he came to John.

The line of Psalm 2:7, "today I have begotten you," also probably explains how the author of the Gospel of John made the transition from the metaphor of adoption to the figure of a spiritual birth. From the idea of "begotten" it was natural to arrive at the concept of a birth; and as the profound transformation Jesus experienced at his baptism, according to Mark, was a result of the coming of the Spirit of God upon him, John drew the inference of a spiritual birth.

A Virgin Birth

The greatest marvel early Christians faced was the amazing personality of Jesus, and they searched the Scriptures daily, fervently believing that in this way they would finally learn the secret of his greatness. So it was that many came to believe that he had no human father and was born of a virgin mother; that he was begotten by the Holy Spirit. The story is recorded in only two of the Gospels: Matthew gives it in 1:18–25, Luke in 1:26–35. There is no trace of it in either Mark or John or in the letters of Paul. But we can see how Matthew or Luke, or some other person on whom they were dependent, arrived at this view: he derived it as an interpretation of the words of Isaiah 7:14, which Matthew quoted as follows:

> Behold, a virgin shall conceive and bear a son,
> and his name shall be called Emmanuel.

This verse was believed by Matthew to be a prophecy of the birth of the Messiah, and from it the inference was drawn that Jesus was born of a virgin. Scholars now know that Isaiah, 700 years before the time of Christ, spoke these words with reference to events of his own time, and that the Hebrew word *'almah* he used meant only a young woman, whether married or unmarried, virginal or not. But when the Hebrew Scriptures (the Old Testament) were translated into Greek, the Greek word *parthenos* chosen to translate the word *'almah* usually meant an unmarried girl, a *virgin* in our sense; and most early Christians read the Old Testament in Greek. In Matthew 1:20 and Luke 1:35 it is stated that the child Jesus was begotten by the Holy Spirit. So this greatly loved story of the virgin mother carries the effort to understand the influence of God's Spirit on man still another step beyond Paul and Mark. It implies that Jesus is God's Son in a biological, procreative sense.

This explanation of who Jesus was gained such a firm hold on the imagination of early Christians that it was soon incorporated into their creeds; and it has been chanted by worshipping congregations across the centuries. Whether we take it as a literal biological fact or a vivid metaphor, the idea of the virgin birth is one of the most sincere tributes ever paid to the character of Jesus.

The Eternal Son

Other early Christians believed Jesus could be understood only on the assumption that he was God's eternal Son. Paul was apparently the first to express this concept which has had such a tremendous influence on subsequent Christian theology. In his letter to the Colossians 1:15–17 he says:

> He is the image of the invisible God, the first-born of all creation; for in him were all things created. . . . He is before all things and in him all things hold together.

This faith was taken up by the author of Hebrews 1:2–3:

> . . . he has spoken to us by a Son, whom he appointed the heir of all things, through whom also he created the world. He reflects the glory of God, and bears the very stamp of his nature. . . .

The Gospel of John opens with the same exalted theme:

> In the beginning was the Word, and the Word was with God, and the Word was God . . . all things were made through him (1:1–3). . . . And the Word became flesh and dwelt among us, full of grace and truth; we have beheld his glory, glory as of the only Son from the Father (1:14).

The Son of Joseph

Yet the sturdy belief that Jesus was a son of Joseph, a carpenter of Nazareth, was never completely forgotten by early Christians. The genealogy of Matthew 1:1–17, which traces the ancestry of Jesus back to David and Abraham, and that of Luke 3:23–38, which traces his lineage all the way back to Adam "the son of God," would be without point except as expressions of the view that Jesus was by flesh and blood the son of Joseph.

This belief is apparently assumed in Mark 6:3, where four of Jesus' brothers are named and his sisters are mentioned. John 1:45 records the words of Philip,

> We have found him of whom Moses and all the prophets wrote, Jesus of Nazareth, the son of Joseph.

In John 6:42 the Jews say,

> Is not this Jesus, the son of Joseph, whose father and mother we know?

The mother of Jesus says in Luke 2:48,

> Son, why have you treated us so? Behold, your father and I have been looking for you anxiously.

Thus the belief that Jesus was the son of Joseph survived in all the Gospels, along with ideas of adoption, of a spiritual birth, and of a virgin birth. Paul too indicates in Romans 1:3 that he also believes Jesus was the son of Joseph:

> . . . the gospel concerning his Son, who was descended from David according to the flesh . . .

It is clear therefore that many early Christians saw no difficulty in believing that Jesus was at the same time both the son of Joseph and the Son of God.

Temptation

Mark reports the temptation of Jesus even more briefly than the baptism, alluding to it in passing as if it were well known in the early church, apparently implying that it was of little importance. He does not seem to place it on a level with the baptism, although he places the two episodes close together. By contrast, Matthew and Luke give far more space to the temptation, thus indicating its importance in the life of Jesus. But a word or phrase in Mark's Gospel often throws more light on the personality of Jesus than much longer passages elsewhere in the early records.

The vividness of Mark's style is illustrated by his account of the temptation (1:12-13):

> The Spirit immediately drove him out into the wilderness. And he was in the wilderness forty days, tempted by Satan; and he was with the wild beasts; and the angels ministered to him.

Using the same word he elsewhere employs for driving out demons, Mark says the Spirit *drove* Jesus out into the wilderness, suggesting that after his baptism Jesus began to act under compulsion. The Spirit of God had come upon Jesus and taken control of him. From this point on to the end of his life, his actions bear a striking resemblance to those great leaders of the Old Testament on whom the Spirit of God is said to have come.

It was Mark's brevity that led Matthew and Luke not many years later to assemble all the new material they could find and publish revised and enlarged editions of his Gospel. But, when one inspects the three Gospels side by side, it becomes obvious that Matthew and Luke did not get their accounts of the temptation from Mark. Yet the identity of the contents and style of the narrative in the two later Gospels makes it certain that their authors used a common source for this passage. Except for minor details, the narratives are identical, though their orders of the temptation are different. Matthew gives the sequence as: (1) the challenge to turn stones to bread; (2) the challenge to leap from a

pinnacle of the temple; (3) the offer of the kingdoms of the world from
a mountain top. In Luke 4:1–13 the order of the second and third
temptations is reversed.

Matthew 4:1–11 preserves the story as follows:

> Then Jesus was led up by the Spirit into the wilderness to be
> tempted by the devil. And he fasted forty days and forty nights
> and afterward he was hungry. And the tempter came and said to
> him, "If you are the Son of God, command these stones to become
> loaves of bread." But he answered, "It is written, 'Man shall not
> live by bread alone, but by every word that proceeds from the
> mouth of God.'"
> Then the devil took him to the holy city, and set him on the pin-
> nacle of the temple, and said to him, "If you are the Son of God,
> throw yourself down; for it is written, 'He will give his angels charge
> of you,' and 'On their hands they will bear you up, lest you strike
> your foot against a stone.'" Jesus said to him, "Again it is written,
> 'You shall not tempt the Lord your God.'"
> Again, the devil took him to a very high mountain, and showed
> him all the kingdoms of the world and the glory of them; and he
> said to him, "All these I will give you if you will fall down and
> worship me." Then Jesus said to him, "Begone, Satan! for it is
> written, 'You shall worship the Lord your God, and him only shall
> you serve.'"
> The devil left him, and behold, angels came and ministered to
> him.

As we have seen in connection with the unusual events which accompanied the baptism of Jesus, so in the temptation! Jesus is the only
person who could have reported what took place. Mark states clearly that
Jesus was driven out into the wilderness, meaning a place without
human habitation of which the lower Jordan Valley offered many.
Aside from animals the only companions Jesus had during the forty days
were Satan, who tried to undermine his integrity, and angels, who then
ministered to him. In the meantime, for forty days and nights he had
gone without food. Jesus was therefore the only human actor, spectator,
and reporter of this series of strange events. Early Christian tradition can
have learned it only from him. The literary style of the story is that
associated with the sayings of Jesus throughout the Synoptic Gospels.
This marks the story as one which Jesus later told his disciples; it reminds us of the parables and allegories so characteristic of Jesus. He
meditated long about his experience, and then with great care put it

into picturesque language which the disciples would never forget. It is true that the longer account in Matthew and Luke adds much to what Mark records, but the fuller story still has an authentic sound.

Fasting

In view of the experience Jesus had undergone in his contact with John the Baptist, it does not seem improbable that he spent forty days and nights fasting. The custom of fasting is deeply rooted in the religions of the Orient. Mahatma Gandhi is the most recent famous example of this practice, but the custom is not unusual among the holy men of modern India; and even in Christianity fasting has had a place from early times down to the present. The eating practices of Lent are the most tangible survival of this ancient Christian rite. Fasting is also one of the pillars of Islam; and any traveler in the Near East soon becomes familiar with their observance of this discipline during the month of Ramadan. Fasting by John's disciples, and also by the Pharisees, is mentioned in Mark 2:18–22; and in the same passage Jesus says the day will come when his disciples will also fast. In Matthew 6:16–18 Jesus cautions his disciples not to make a display of their fasting, with disfigured faces and sad countenances, as hypocrites do, but to anoint their heads, and bathe their faces. Fasting was an established rite in the early church after the time of Jesus. Acts 13:1–3 reports fasting at Antioch, both in worship and in connection with the ordination of Paul and Barnabus as missionaries. This rite also came to have a place in the ritual of casting out demons. Mark 9:29 says, "This kind cannot be driven out by anything but prayer"; but an alternate reading adds, "and fasting."

Jesus once told a story about a Pharisee and a publican, who went up to the place of prayer (Luke 18:9–14). The Pharisee said proudly that he fasted twice each week. The Jewish fast days at the time were Mondays and Thursdays. It was not long before Christians took over this custom; they only changed the days of the week on which they fasted. This is reflected in the quaint injunction in the second-century Christian document called the Didache (8:1), "Let not your fasts be with the hypocrites, for they fast on Mondays and Thursdays; but do you fast on Wednesdays and Fridays."[1] Fasting in Judaism in our time is often associated with high holy days, notably with the Day of Atonement.

[1] Kirsopp Lake, *The Apostolic Fathers*, vol. i, p. 321. The Macmillan Company, New York, 1912. Used by permission.

Moses and Elijah

To what extent Jews in the time of Jesus and before were accustomed to undergo long periods of fasting we do not know, but there are at least two examples of fasts as long as that of Jesus. These are the cases of Moses and Elijah. The long fast of Moses is mentioned in Exodus 34:28:

> And he was there with the Lord forty days and forty nights; he neither ate bread nor drank water. And he wrote upon the tables the words of the ten commandments.

The story of Elijah's fast is related in I Kings 19:1–18. It is a sequel to his contest on Mount Carmel with the prophets of Baal whom he had defeated and slain. This aroused the fury of Queen Jezebel; she vowed she would avenge their blood by killing Elijah. The prophet fled from her rage across the southern border toward Mount Horeb. In the wilderness south of Beersheba, he fell down exhausted and went to sleep. An angel woke him up and gave him food; then a second time the angel came and urged him to eat, for, said he, the journey would be long. Then Elijah "arose, ate and drank, and went in the strength of that food forty days and forty nights to Horeb, the Mount of God."

There are parallels between these experiences of Moses, Elijah and Jesus. The forty days is prominent in all three accounts. Important visions and communications occur in every case. Also the sequence is the same: visions follow fasting, suggesting a connection between the two, a fact often observed and used in the cultivation of the mystical life in various religions. Fasting heightens sensitivity, sharpens perception, opens the personality toward awareness of the divine, induces a state of consciousness in which visions—and revelations—may occur.

Angels

Another point these stories have in common is the role of angels, whose functions, however, are not identical. Exodus 3:1–4:17 tells how an angel of the Lord appeared to Moses in a bush which burned continuously without being consumed. This was on lonely Horeb, the Mount of God, where Elijah also saw his vision. When Elijah had fled from Jezebel, an angel brought him food and gave him a message from the Lord. The Gospels do not say specifically how the angels ministered to Jesus, but it appears that at the end they brought him food.

The Spirit of God

The place of the Spirit of God in these narratives is another parallel, but this is less evident in the story of Moses, the record of whose life is preserved in sources of different ages. Usually it is God himself or an angel who speaks to Moses, but the author of Numbers 11:16-30 has introduced the Spirit into his narrative. Here Moses is instructed to select seventy men to assist him. The Lord says, "And I will come down and talk with you there; and I will take some of the spirit which is upon you and put it upon them; and they shall bear the burden of the people with you." It is further stated, that when the Lord came down and transferred some of the Spirit which was on Moses to the men, they began to prophesy.

The spiritual endowment of Elijah is clear in the story of his marvelous departure from Elisha, the ascent by a whirlwind into heaven (II Kings 2:1-15). Elisha begs Elijah, "I pray you, let me inherit a double share of your spirit." The younger man had his wish fulfilled, and . . . "when the sons of the prophets who were at Jericho saw him over against them, they said, 'The spirit of Elijah rests on Elisha.'"

Satan

The parallel between the stories of Moses, Elijah and Jesus breaks down, however, in the appearance of Satan to Jesus. Satan never appeared to Moses or Elijah. When the records of Moses and Elijah were written, the Hebrews had no belief in Satan; they had their ideas about right and wrong, but they had not arrived at the concept of Satan, an idea which emerged in biblical thought near the end of the Old Testament period.

One comes upon this belief in the Bible first in the Book of Job (1:1—2:9), and again in Zechariah 3:1 ff., in both of which the evil being retains a shadowy nature and is without a name; he is called "the Satan," meaning simply "the Adversary." Already, however, his true nature is indicated; he is a cynic who always doubts the unselfishness and goodness of moral actions. He casts doubt on integrity.

The first time Satan appears in a mature form, with a name of his own —without the definite article—is in I Chronicles 21:1 ff., where he induces David to register all of his people to work in labor battalions and serve in the army, in violation of ancient Hebrew tradition; he gets David into a situation which provokes a national catastrophe.[2]

[2] S. V. McCasland, "'Soldiers on Service,' the Draft among the Hebrews," *Journal of Biblical Literature*, vol. LXII, ii, 1943, pp. 59-71.

The Lord becomes angry at David and sends a pestilence which destroys 50,000 persons; the death angel stands before the gates of Jerusalem, ready to destroy the royal city; and the terrified king is able to save it only by deep penitence and sacrificial rites. In a much earlier account of these same events, II Samuel 24:1 ff., it was Yahweh who got David to register his people, and then turned around and punished him for what he had done. The conflict between the two versions of this matter shows that at the time of David, or soon afterward when II Samuel was written, God himself was believed capable of tricking King David into committing a sin and then punishing him for it. But when the Chronicler wrote, the concept of Yahweh had been so purified that he could no longer do such a thing; so the Chronicler says that Satan caused David to sin, but that God punished him for it.

In the temptation of Jesus, the character of Satan receives development in a new direction. Jews were familiar with the belief that evil spirits of a minor character sometimes appeared to human beings and sought to mislead them, or even gained access into them, assuming control of their personalities and deranging their minds, either temporarily or permanently. But there is no example in Jewish literature before the time of Jesus in which Satan appears to a man face to face and engages him in conversation.

In the story of Job, where Satan makes his longest appearance in the Old Testament, there is no indication that Job or any other human being knew the part Satan was taking in the plot, or were even aware of his existence. The drama of the story lies in Job's challenge of the popular belief that in this life God sends affliction on a man who sins in proportion to his wickedness and rewards a good man in proportion to his uprightness. Job's strength lies in his insight into the question of justice. He knows that he has committed no sin worthy of such calamities; and with great courage he defies the superficial and worn out theology of the time. He does not work out a solution of the problem, but he prepares for the next great advance. Job allows for a large area of mystery in man's apprehension of God.

Nor are we informed that David knew anything about Satan. I Chronicles 21:16 relates that the king saw the angel of the Lord "standing between earth and heaven, and in his hand a drawn sword stretched out over Jerusalem." But we are not informed that the king was given a similar vision of Satan. According to Zechariah 3:1-5, Satan stood at the right hand of the priest Joshua to accuse him before the angel of the Lord; it may be that Joshua was aware of the evil one's presence, but there is no dialogue to demonstrate it. Before the time of Jesus, all references represent Satan as an evil angel, who treats men as puppets, controlling their actions from behind the scenes.

That Satan meets Jesus personally, and openly challenges him, goes beyond the stories of David, Job, and Joshua the priest. The conversation with Jesus shows that Satan has achieved a different role in popular Jewish belief from any previously played by him in the Old Testament. The new concept of Satan presents him in almost a human guise; everything he does and says in the story comes within the realm of human experience. True, he has supernatural power to transport Jesus to the temple and to the mountain top; also he owns the kingdoms of the world; but these assumptions are props, as it were, to make the story possible. Satan acts like a man; one understands his point of view; he has a materialistic philosophy which interprets the Kingdom of God in terms of what the average man desires: food, display and power. This is the common view of the world.

Satan talks with Jesus politely; he is friendly and charming. What the story means to say about Satan is that he has a dull mind; he is unable to grasp spiritual things. He lacks eyes to see and ears to hear. This is the condition of all men who have not heard the Word of God.

Satan and the Serpent

In the contest with Jesus, Satan reminds us not so much of his earlier representations in the Old Testament, as of the serpent in the Garden of Eden. It is true that the serpent is not to be simply equated with Satan. There is no evidence that the serpent has the status of an angel of God, which was always an original element in the character of Satan. Yet the serpent is a representation of evil, as the author of that ancient story conceives it. The serpent has more affinity with Oriental dragons than with angels; he reminds one of the Babylonian Tiamat, slain by Marduk, and the Indian Vritra, killed by Indra; but the serpent of Eden lacked the ferocity of the dragons. Hebrew thought preserves traces of other dragons; Rahab and Leviathan, the sea serpents; and Behemoth and Azazel, dragon and goat monsters of the desert. The serpent of Eden was not identified as Satan by any Old Testament writer; but is so identified for the first time by the author of the apocryphal Wisdom of Solomon 2:24, from the late pre-Christian period. By the time the Revelation of John was written, near A.D. 100, this identification was accepted as a matter of course (12:9; 20:2).

Modern ideas of Satan usually conceive of him with a human torso, wings of an angel, feet and horns of a goat, a barbed serpentine tail, and a trident: attributes drawn from an angel, a dragon, a satyr and Poseidon, god of the sea. But the Gospels give no indication that Satan had any of these features when he met Jesus in the desert. Nor is there evidence that Jesus was frightened; there was no fear or terror; not even any surprise or astonishment when the strange visitor arrived. The reaction of Jesus was like that of Eve to the serpent in the Garden.

Face-to-face conversations with serpents, dragons or Satan are so foreign to the experience of modern persons that they are not conceived as being possible. The suggestion that a person today might engage either a fabulous serpent or Satan in conversation would be judged fantastic. Materialistic science has deprived us of all the dragons and Satans. Even the intrepid comic strip warrior, Alley Oop, has to go back to the third century to find a dragon!

Yet the biblical stories show that neither Eve nor Jesus was perturbed; the serpent and Satan were taken as a matter of course. The equanimity with which Eve talks to the serpent is simply out of this world. Probably no woman since her time has felt such ease in the presence of a serpent, let alone talking to one! The calmness with which Jesus converses with Satan is of the same order. Eve and Jesus take the experiences in their stride; and biblical writers and people who read their books felt the same way. Here are things, they felt, which happen to real people, in real life.

The Deeper Meaning

Some people in our time still believe that these stories about the serpent in the Garden with Eve and about Satan in the desert with Jesus actually occurred as objective historical events. But they usually add that such marvels ceased at the end of the biblical period; and they would not expect them to happen today. This group probably includes most people in our churches.

There are a few persons who believe not only that these things happened as objective events during biblical times, but that such things continue to happen now in a real historical sense. The relatively few persons who hold this view are usually friendly to the idea of demon possession; sometimes they believe in the reappearance of spirits of the dead as ghosts, visible by day and night, especially by night; and it is not uncommon for them to patronize necromancers and mediums, like King Saul, who asked the necromancer of En-Dor to call up the dead prophet Samuel from Sheol.

A third group of persons of our time regards the stories about Eve and the serpent and Jesus and Satan as legends from the past with no historical validity and of no importance today. This group is composed of persons who have gone to college and made some study of the sciences, or read popular books about science, or in some other way have come under the influence of current scientific ideas.

All three of these views fail to understand the biblical stories. The reason for this is that an almost unbridgeable chasm lies between biblical thinking and our own. Many things people of the Bible said have no meaning for us; much of what we say would have had none for them. Their views of geography, history, the natural world, psychology, the earth below, and the heavens above, were different from ours. They lived in a prescientific age. Theirs was a different vocabulary; they used ideas, thoughts, concepts, utterly strange, now unacceptable to us. Where there is such a lack of communication, or of the possibility of it, there is a tendency to say that what the other person reports is not true; that his tradition, his history, is composed of legends, obsolete, now entirely discredited.

The error in this view is that it sees no means of communication between the religious past and the religious present; nor does it make a serious effort to find one. There is no effort to see beyond the words, the vocabulary, the strange, the exotic forms of expression; there is no acceptance of the challenge the ancient writings present.

But we can establish communication in this matter between yesterday and today. We need not deny that the old literatures often contain legends, but we do need to contemplate the possibility that the ancient people of the Bible were talking about things which really happened to them. And once we are alerted to that possibility, we might find the same things happening to us.

Since ancient times an entirely new vocabulary has arisen, a new science, a new philosophy. But human experience from the time of Adam and Eve down to our own day, has remained essentially the same: God is the same God; the world is the same world, and human nature has not changed essentially. In other words, in Adam and Eve we see ourselves; we only use another vocabulary. They are type-people; they are Everyman and Everywoman. And their story, with its elements of beauty and tragedy, is an allegory of all human life.

The reason why Eve was not terrified when the serpent appeared to her is that this was an experience within her own soul; the serpent is the voice of temptation we all know. It is the temptation springing up out of desires with which all of us are born and from which we never escape. We would not be human without these desires. Indeed the events of the Garden of Eden are part of the creation story. Adam and Eve were not fully a man and a woman—they were not fully human —until they experienced temptation; until they discovered conscience; until they learned the meaning of sin; until they were awakened to the fact of their mortality. Only then were they fully created.

Biblical thought holds that desire in itself is neither good nor bad, but that morality is attained only in so far as desire is brought under discipline. Buddhism attempts to bring about complete eradication of desire; but biblical teaching never adopted this extreme view. Christian theology has called innate desire *original sin,* and has gone on to present a bill of particulars under the category of the *cardinal sins;* they are also called the capital sins, the mortal sins, the deadly sins. There are seven cardinal sins: pride, covetousness, lust, anger, gluttony, envy and sloth. These are not popular words with most people in our time. Nevertheless, in their elemental nature every one of them represents a desire which has characterized human personality from the beginning of time. They come to maturity along with personality; as such they are neutral; but they easily lead into *actual* sin. The term *original sin* is an unfortunate designation of these desires, but we can see what the theologians who coined the expression had in mind. The fact that the innate impulses were labeled original sin, although not actual sin, has caused the modern world to repudiate the whole idea, and to fail to grasp the profound truth the obsolete expression carries.

Depth Psychology

The modern school of depth psychology, which stems from Sigmund Freud, gives almost the same picture of personality, although from a secular point of view. Instead of *sin* they use *id* as a designation of innate desire; the *superego* is the restraining power of morality, law, custom; the *ego* is the self, the person, who must choose between the claims of the *id* and the *superego*. This sounds as if Freud had simply adopted a new terminology and taken over what Paul said in the seventh chapter of Romans about the human predicament, in which a man flounders about trying to choose between the *flesh* and the law of God. Freud holds that man is chained by the *id;* Paul laments that he is in bondage to the flesh. This again was essentially the view of Gautama Buddha.

These considerations lay a foundation for understanding the temptation of Jesus. While there is a parallel between the experience of Jesus and that of Adam and Eve, there is also an important difference. The great difference is that Jesus is a historical figure, a real man; his story is not simply an allegory. It is his own personal experience with temptation. Yet because of its accurate delineation of the struggle of Jesus with powerful desires deeply implanted in his being, it is also a true picture, in a general sense, of the struggles of all persons with temptation. The point of identity between Jesus and ourselves is that his body, his mind, his soul, knew the same desires which reside in us; he was tempted at every point just as we are; he also drank this cup to its dregs.

We should not be misled by visions in the stories of Jesus, Moses and Elijah, or even of Adam and Eve. That particular manner of experiencing deep emotional struggles was characteristic of the psychological pattern in which the personalities of biblical people were formed, and in which they moved. We live in an age which rarely projects its inner life in this way, but our attention ought to be directed to the spiritual life itself, not merely to the transitory method of its expression. Let us say clearly that the serpent in Eden is a force forever present within the inner life of every person; and that both Satan and the angels who met Jesus in the desert were elements within himself of which he alone was aware. When Jesus was baptized, as Mark makes clear, Jesus was the only person who saw the heavens opened and the Spirit descending upon him, and who heard the voice of God. If other human beings had been with him in the desert, only Jesus would have known that Satan was there and that angels came to refresh him. Luke (22:43–44) relates that in the midst of the agonizing prayer of Jesus in Gethsemane, an angel appeared and strengthened him, but there is no indication that anyone else present saw the angel. But to deny the essential truth of the incident is only to miss the point; it is failure to understand the nature of religious experience.

From pondering the remarkable story of Adam and Eve, and the tremendous drama of Jesus, alone in the desert struggling with temptation, we begin to rediscover something of the depth lying hidden within our own souls. While it is true that there is a dragon with seven heads deeply hidden in the heart of man, it is also true, according to biblical teaching, that the image of God is implanted in man's soul. If man is terrified at times by the appearance of the dragon, he ought to recall that there is also in his personality a doorway through which angels of God may come.

Fulfillment of Scripture

Once in the Nazareth synagogue Jesus stood up and read the words of Isaiah 61:1–2, beginning (Luke 4:18):

The Spirit of the Lord is upon me because he has anointed me . . .

When he had finished the reading, Jesus amazed those present by saying, "Today this scripture has been fulfilled in your hearing" (Luke 4:21). These men of Nazareth were angered; Jesus had made a blasphemous statement! The claim that this passage had been written for his sake, that it had been fulfilled there that day, was inconceivable.

At first the reaction of these Nazarenes shocks us. They appear to have been so dull, so slow to recognize the nature of this man who had grown up among them. Yet when we consider the situation, we are bound to see that their reaction is not unusual, not unreasonable, for through the centuries many persons have reacted to the words of Jesus just as the Nazarenes did that day.

The Nazarenes were shocked because Jesus appeared to claim an insight into the Scriptures they did not possess. He appeared to set himself above them. They knew him as a man like themselves. What he said implied either superior intellectual insight or a special revelation from God; this the Nazarenes that day could not accept.

I can sympathize with the men of Nazareth because the position I am seeking to establish is that Jesus possessed the same faculties as other men, and therefore knew the same uncertainties, doubts, limitations. If we admit his full humanity, he was not omniscient; he did not possess all knowledge; he was not certain as to what the future would bring. Like all other religious persons, he lived by faith from day to day.

On the other hand, persons who hold the Docetic view that Jesus was divine but not human, with no body of flesh and blood, have no difficulty with these words. They endow Jesus with omniscience; but they also have failed to understand him. They have resolved the difficulty by robbing Jesus of his humanity. Once we take the humanity of Jesus seriously, his words do become a problem. That has been true especially during the last two centuries, when an effort has been made to do full justice to the human nature of Jesus.

The reason for the bewilderment of the men of Nazareth that day, and of many in our own time, is that they failed to recognize that the words of Jesus on that occasion actually throw a light on his personality. They provide us with a key to his life. In these pages of the ancient Scriptures he was penetrating the mystery of his own identity; and the sense of his Messianic destiny was beginning to struggle within him.

Another memorable example of the self-discovery of Jesus in the Scriptures occurs in Luke 22:37, reporting an episode on the night of his betrayal. Jesus was speaking solemnly to his disciples concerning terrible things about to happen:

> For I tell you that this scripture must be fulfilled in me, "And he was reckoned with transgressors"; for what is written about me has its fulfillment.

This particular quotation is from Isaiah 53:12, which makes it evident that toward the end of his life Jesus had been reading the poet's description of the suffering and death of the Servant of the Lord. Accordingly, Jesus had found himself in the Servant. Now he says to his disciples, "What has been written about me has its fulfillment." In other words, the time has come when he is to be reckoned with transgressors; that he is to be accused of crime and be convicted as a criminal. On the basis of his self-discovery in this Scripture, Jesus anticipates his own execution.

In another remarkable passage, one which has its setting in a story about the resurrected Christ, Jesus says,

> These are my words which I spoke to you while I was still with you, that everything written about me in the law of Moses and the prophets and the psalms must be fulfilled (Luke 24:44).

Although tradition attributes this saying to the risen Christ, it was probably first spoken before his death.

The problem of interpreting such sayings of Jesus became more complicated as scholars found dispersed in the early Christian writings numerous quotations from the Old Testament in which not only Jesus first, then the disciples of his time, but also the disciples of the following generation, found particular events, even details of his life.

The next step researchers took was to study the Old Testament passages quoted in their historical contexts in order to determine what the original authors meant. They found that the quoted Scriptures usually related to the time of the writer; that the prophets had no intention to foretell the life of some man of the distant future. In most cases it could be demonstrated that a prophet's words referred to events of his own day and generation.

A third discovery was that in places the Gospels themselves show evidence of having been shaped after the time of Jesus; that the traditions of his life were to some extent formed in the later period; that the faith the disciples attained after the resurrection was sometimes projected backward into the lifetime of Jesus, even incorporated into some of his own sayings. It was concluded by many that this backward projection of the disciples' faith had badly distorted, if not effaced, the picture of the historical Jesus; that the distortion had made it impossible for men of later generations to know the man Jesus as he really was.

This is a far-reaching conclusion. It has such consequences for the integrity of the Gospels and our knowledge of Jesus that it is the privilege, indeed the obligation, of every scholar to be always on the alert, to investigate every approach that might set the problem in a clearer light. It is this problem to which we address ourselves in these chapters.

Is it necessary to deny that Jesus read the Old Testament Scriptures and found himself in them, feeling that what he read was being fulfilled in his life day by day? Is it necessary for us to feel that the New Testament view of Jesus in this respect has been essentially distorted?

As presented in the Acts of the Apostles, the records of the early church are full of references to the study of the Scriptures. Many Old Testament passages are cited which the disciples believed had been fulfilled in Jesus. Nor is this true only of the Acts; the Letters of Paul show the same thing. He was convinced that by reading the Scriptures he could learn about Jesus. The Scriptures appear to have been the main source of Paul's information about Jesus. He relied more on the Scriptures than on tradition; and he had no written Gospels.

We need to bear this fact in mind about all the churches during the years between the death of Jesus and the writing of Mark, the earliest Gospel. During about four decades Christians had to depend on tradition handed down orally and on what they could learn by reading the Old Testament, which was their Bible, their only Scripture. The churches had no specifically Christian Scripture for about a hundred years after the death of Jesus.

The Gospels themselves were not at first regarded as Scripture. Such editorial work as Matthew and Luke performed on Mark—cutting as if with scissors, rearranging, retouching its style, changing statements of fact, etc.—would not have been permitted by the church if Mark had already become Scripture. It was well along in the second century before the Gospels began to attain a place beside the Old Testament as inspired writings. In the New Testament itself, with one single exception, where the word Scripture occurs it means one of the Old Testament writings or all of them together. The exception appears in the picturesque words of II Peter 3:15–16, where Paul's Letters are referred to as Scripture:

> So also our beloved brother Paul wrote to you according to the wisdom given to him, speaking of this as he does in all his letters. There are some things in them hard to understand, which the ignorant and unstable twist to their own destruction, as they do the other scriptures.

But II Peter was not written until about A.D. 150. It does show that by the middle of the second century the Letters of Paul were coming to be considered inspired documents. The New Testament as a whole did not come to be so regarded until about A.D. 200. Until that time Christians read as their only Scripture the Bible they had inherited from the Jews; and when they finally canonized a Scripture of their own, they placed it beside the Old Testament and then read both together. They saw a continuity running through them; the subject binding them together was Christ; the Old Testament spoke of him in prospect, and the New Testament showed that all the ancient predictions had come true.

To a large extent the New Testament came into existence as a result of study of the Old for information about Jesus; there certainly would have been no New Testament unless there had first been an Old. It is this widespread practice of reading the Old Testament for knowledge of Jesus which we leave unexplained if we doubt that Jesus himself first taught his disciples to do it. We would seem to be saying that this industrious practice of the early church was like a child born full-grown, something contrary to nature. In other words, our reconsideration of this practice must seriously take into account the use of the Old Testament by early Christians immediately after the death of Jesus. Where and how can we get further light on this practice? For an answer to this question we turn to the Essenes of Qumran.

Evidence from Qumran

Where did early Christians get their custom of reading the Scriptures, and more especially their practice of looking for information about Jesus in them?

Jesus was a Jew, and the first generation of Christians were Jews of Palestine. Christians continued to be almost exclusively Jews until the missionary work of Paul and others had established churches in Antioch of Syria, and throughout Asia Minor and Greece. Hence, for the present purpose, we may exclude the Gentile churches. Undoubtedly this study of the Scriptures existed in the church before Gentiles were brought into it. So we limit our study to the Jews.

Here, however, we have been under a handicap. Although we have abundant information about Jews of the Old Testament period, until recent years—aside from what we can derive from the New Testament itself—there has been little of a specific character about Jews at the time of Jesus. This deficiency has now been considerably rectified by the discovery in 1947 of the ruins of a Jewish ascetic community on the Wadi Qumran on the west side of the Dead Sea. Probably every reader of newspapers has by this time heard of the Dead Sea Scrolls—old Jewish manuscripts taken from caves in that vicinity. The discovery of the ruins in itself was not unusual; archaeologists know hundreds of sites in Judea and Galilee occupied during the time of Christ. What gives the Qumran discoveries a spectacular character is the great number of contemporary manuscripts recovered from caves in the cliffs of the wadi and other nearby regions. These manuscripts throw a brilliant light on the community located there, providing welcome new information about its religious beliefs and practices.

Archaeologists have concluded that the Qumran community was probably a settlement of Essenes—a Jewish sect not mentioned in either the Old Testament or the New. Yet we already know much about the Essenes from the writings of the Jew Philo of Alexandria, and also from Josephus, a Jew of Palestine, but later of Rome—both contemporaries of Paul's. Philo and Josephus had indicated that the Essenes were of considerable importance in the first century A.D. Some of the Essenes, we knew, lived in isolated, segregated communities, but up to 1947 we had not been fortunate enough to locate one of their settlements. It now appears to be established that the community of Essenes at Qumran existed during the Maccabean period, or at least as early as 100 B.C., flourished throughout the century before Christ, and continued until it was destroyed by the Romans when they put down the Jewish rebellion of A.D. 66–70. The Romans destroyed not only Jerusalem, but also practically every stronghold throughout the land. It was in this wholesale destruction that the Qumran community, after an apparently prosperous existence through most of two centuries, came to its end.

As concerns our present study, the first result of the Qumran discoveries is to demonstrate the tremendous place of the study of the Scriptures at the time. During the elapsed nineteen hundred years, the processes of decay and the ravages of insects, animals and cave robbers have undoubtedly destroyed most of the writings left by that ancient community. Yet in spite of the tragic end of this historic settlement and the obliteration or dispersion of its inhabitants, explorers and excavators have recovered several complete manuscripts intact, and hundreds of fragments of others. With possibly one or two minor expections, fragments of every book of the Old Testament, many of the apocryphal writings, and a number of important otherwise unknown books have been found. Only a people interested in study, indeed of great erudition, could have possessed such a quantity of books in those ancient days. Nothing else in their life could have meant as much to them as their Scriptures.

The Scriptures at Qumran

The place of the Scriptures in the life of Qumran is indicated in a passage from their Manual of Discipline (IQS) 6:3–7, which Millar Burrows translates as follows:

> In every place where there are ten men of the council of the community there shall not be absent from them a priest. Each according to his position, they shall sit before him; and thus they shall be asked for their counsel regarding everything. And when they set the table to eat, or the wine to drink, the priest shall stretch out his hand first to pronounce a blessing with the first portion of the bread and the wine. And from the place where the ten are there shall never be absent a man who searches the law day and night, by turns, one after another. And the masters shall keep watch together a third of

all the nights of the year, reading the book and searching for justice, and worshipping together.[1]

Ten persons of the Qumran faith were enough to constitute a community for study and worship. In every such group, study of the law was to be continuous, day and night. This study involved every member of the group; they took turns in reading, studying and expounding the law. The rule shows that throughout every night, as well as during the day, this studious employment continued, and that every man in the settlement must keep awake one third of the nights of the year engaged in such study. This presumably means that there were three periods or watches every night for this intellectual activity, and that the men of the community engaged by relays in the practice. Each man therefore participated four hours during one watch of the approximately twelve hours from sunset to sunrise with eight hours left for sleep. It was assumed also that during the day, even while he carried out the task of his vocation, a man was to concern himself with meditation on the truths of the Scriptures.

The continuous reading and study of the Scriptures was based on the injunction of Joshua 1:8,

> This book of the law shall not depart out of your mouth, but you shall meditate on it day and night, that you may be careful to do according to all that is written in it; for then you shall make your way prosperous, and then you shall have good success.

Study of the Scriptures was the main concern of residents of the Qumran settlement. Whatever else these people did, whether the ordinary occupations necessary to gain a livelihood, such as agriculture, animal husbandry, keeping bees, etc., these activities must have been purely incidental and secondary; it was the study of the Scriptures which gave meaning to their lonely existence in that forbidding wilderness. The vast quantities of fragments of biblical manuscripts surviving in abandoned caves of that region to this day continue to bear mute testimony to the place the Bible held in the life of that ancient people.

Qumran Interpretations

The reason for this intense preoccupation with study and interpretation of the Scriptures at Qumran was that these people believed that the Scriptures were being fulfilled in their lives. They read the Scriptures

[1] Millar Burrows, *The Dead Sea Scrolls*, The Viking Press, New York, 1955, p. 378. Used by permission.

for light on events through which they were living. Such interpretation of Scriptures with reference to contemporary events is evident in many of the Qumran fragments. Their commentary on Habbakuk applies certain statements in that document to a powerful military people of their time—probably the Romans.

But the most fascinating of all their interpretations of Scripture occurs in their Manual of Discipline (IQS 8:13–14),

> When these things come to pass for the community in Israel, by these regulations they shall be separated from the midst of the session of the men of error to go into the wilderness to prepare there the way of the Lord; as it is written, "In the wilderness prepare the way of the Lord; make straight in the desert a highway for our God." This is the study of the law, as he commanded through Moses, to do according to all that has been revealed from time to time, and as the prophets revealed by his Holy Spirit.[2]

The Scripture quoted in this passage is the famous Isaiah 40:3, A voice cries:

> "In the wilderness prepare the way of the Lord,
>   make straight in the desert a highway for our God."

In this passage, written by the Second Isaiah about 550 B.C. relative to the return of the exiles from Babylonia, the prophet foresees that they will come across the desert, and that the Lord will lead them. He urges his people to prepare in the wilderness a highway for the Lord.

The people of Qumran interpreted this with reference to their own life there in the wilderness of Judah. The region in which Qumran was located was known as the Wilderness. They interpreted their life there as a fulfillment of the ancient prophecy uttered some 500 years before, believing that the community they had set up there in the desert was indeed the way of the Lord, and that the prophecy was finding its actual fulfillment in them.

One of their most remarkable beliefs was that one of their leaders, known as the Teacher of Righteousness, had received a special revelation, enabling him to understand the meaning of Scripture and so to apply it to their own time, indeed to their own community. This belief is expressed in their commentary on Habakkuk. In the comment on Habakkuk 1:5, we come upon this statement,

[2] Millar Burrows, *op. cit.*, p. 382. Used by permission.

... the priest into whose heart God put wisdom to explain all of the words of his servants the prophets, through whom God declared all the things that are coming upon his people and his congregation.[1]

This community therefore believed that the Teacher of Righteousness had been given an inspiration, so that he could see new meanings in the Scriptures and apply them to their own life.

Now let us see what light this reading and interpretation of Scripture at Qumran throws on similar practices among early Christians.

John the Baptist

First we turn to John the Baptist, who based his ministry on the same verse, Isaiah 40:3,

In the wilderness prepare the way of the Lord, make straight in the desert a highway for our God.

Only John does not quote it precisely. Like other first-century persons—including the Qumran writers—he "adapted" it to make it better fit the meaning he saw in it (Mark 1:2–3). First he inserted within the quotation "A voice cries" from the preceding line in Isaiah; second he dropped "God" from the last line, and said simply "his," which referred back to "Lord," a term which could apply more easily to the Messiah, who, John said, was about to appear.

Mark introduces this passage as if he were the one who had recognized that John, and later Jesus, was its fulfillment, but it is more probable that this is John's proclamation, his preaching. In the Gospel of John 1:19–23, this passage occurs,

And this is the testimony of John, when the Jews sent priests and Levites from Jerusalem to ask him, "Who are you?" He confessed, he did not deny, but confessed, "I am not the Christ." And they asked him, "Who then? Are you Elijah?" He said, "I am not." "Are you the prophet?" And he answered, "No." They said to him then, "Who are you? Let us have an answer for those who sent us. What do you say about yourself?" He said, "I am the voice of one crying in the wilderness, 'Make straight the way of the Lord,' as the prophet Isaiah said."

In this extraordinary passage, John denies categorically that he is the Messiah; also that he is Elijah who is expected to precede the Messiah; or that he is the expected prophet. Then when they said, "Who are you?" he said, "I am the voice of one crying. . . ." There is no reasonable doubt

[1] Millar Burrows, *op. cit.,* p. 365

that it was John, not Mark, who read this passage and found in it, not only a prophecy of the coming Messiah, but especially of himself, of his mission, proclaiming the Day of the Lord. In this respect he had gone beyond the community of Qumran. Such self-discovery in the Scripture explains the zeal of John in his vigorous preaching there in the desert.

Here we have the case of a new prophet who quotes the famous lines from Isaiah used by the Qumran community, but giving them a slightly different interpretation. It is clear that John continued the use of Scripture which prevailed at the time at Qumran, and that he also used the very passage on which Qumran based its own existence.

Jesus Interprets the Scriptures

This identification of John with prophetic passages from the Old Testament did not stop with John himself. Every careful reader of the Gospels has noted that this passage from Isaiah, as quoted in Mark 1:2–3, is actually joined together with another quotation from Malachi 3:1. As given in the Revised Standard Version, this passage in Mark reads,

> As it is written in Isaiah the Prophet, "Behold, I send my messenger before thy face, who shall prepare thy way; the voice of one crying in the wilderness: Prepare the way of the Lord, make his paths straight."

Now the first half of this quotation is not from Isaiah. According to the accurate text of Mark, both passages are ascribed to Isaiah, but the first half is ascribed to Isaiah in error. In the later form of the text, such as one reads in the King James Version, an interpolator has sought to eliminate the error from Mark by changing "Isaiah" to "the prophets," but the correct text of Mark makes it appear that Mark blundered by attributing both passages to Isaiah. We may reasonably doubt, however, that Mark was the one who made that error, holding instead that in its original form the Gospel of Mark did not contain the quotation from Malachi at this point. When Matthew and Luke revised Mark at this point, they both omitted the lines from Malachi, erroneously ascribed to Isaiah. They did this without collaboration; that is, they did it independently. The most reasonable explanation is to suppose that the text of Mark they were revising did not contain the error.

The rest of the explanation of the apparent error in Mark is that a later scribe has introduced the passage from Malachi 3:1 at this point. As a matter of fact, Malachi 3:1 occurs in both Matthew and Luke, but in a different position from that in Mark. In identical passages in Matthew and Luke, evidently from a source both knew, known to scholars as Q,[1] the Malachi quotation occurs in Matthew 11:10 and Luke 7:27. Neither Matthew nor Luke identifies the author of the passage, but certainly neither ascribes it to Isaiah. That error, then, must have been made by a later scribe who transferred it to Mark 1:2.

According to the Q document as quoted by Matthew and Luke, it was Jesus who first applied this passage from Malachi to John the Baptist. Jesus said, "This is he of whom it is written," and then quoted the lines from Malachi. The problem is set in a new light as soon as we recognize that it was no other than Jesus who identified John as the messenger mentioned by Malachi, who would come to prepare the way of the Lord. In this respect, Jesus followed in the footsteps of John. After Jesus applied the passage to John, at a later time it occurred to some unknown scribe to lift it out of its original context in the Q material of Matthew and Luke and transfer it to Mark 1:2, where it stands in the text today, and where it expands what Mark had already provided to introduce John the Baptist. In doing this, the anonymous scribe introduced an error. Our concern, however, is only to show how John first, and Jesus after him, read the Scriptures and found in them prophecies being fulfilled in their own time.

Jesus went still further in his scriptural identification of John the Baptist. This occurred on the occasion when John sent messengers from his prison to Jesus, of whose deeds he had heard, to ask if he were really the Christ or whether they should look for another. On that occasion Jesus said some complimentary things about John. After quoting the passage from Malachi 3:1, he went on to say (Matthew 11:14 and Mark 9:13) that John was in fact the prophet Elijah, an identification which is startling to modern persons. How could John be Elijah? Nevertheless, according to both of these Gospels, Jesus made the identification. If we read Malachi beyond 3:1, we shall see that Jesus got the idea from Malachi 4:5–6:

> Behold, I will send you Elijah the prophet before the great and terrible day of the Lord comes. And he will turn the hearts of fathers to their children and the hearts of children to their fathers, lest I come and smite the land with a curse.

The most natural explanation of the use of these quotations from Malachi is to take them at face value, and to recognize that Jesus was

[1] Cf. "The Sources of Our Knowledge of Jesus" in the appendix.

reading Malachi in search of the meaning of the times in which he lived. He was convinced that John was not only "the Messenger," but also "Elijah," who was to prepare the way and to announce the Day of the Lord. This "reading into" is strange to us, but we may be sure that in some sense Jesus felt that the spirit of Elijah was on John; that in this way Elijah lived again.

We need to forget our own bookish way of reading the Bible; to put ourselves back into the first century and to read the Scriptures as the people of Qumran did, as John did, as Jesus did, and as his disciples continued to do after him. It is only in this way that we can understand the personality of Jesus, allowing him to be a man of his own time, reading the Scriptures and finding there not only the events of his own time but also himself. Those first-century people read the Scriptures for light on the very days in which they lived; they fully believed that the prophecies were being fulfilled before their eyes. They had a tremendous sense of the Word of God, spoken directly to their generation through the sacred writings. They were not musty ancient records, not archaic, dead books, but living words, messages from God, illuminating contemporary history, indeed their own lives. The Qumran people saw themselves in the Scriptures; John discovered himself there; Jesus saw John in the holy books; moreover, the most decisive experience of his life was that he found himself there. That is the point of our present study. If we read the Gospels with this in mind, many otherwise incomprehensible actions and sayings of Jesus fall into an intelligible pattern.

It was his self-discovery in the Scriptures which caused Jesus, and only Jesus, to refer to himself as the Son of Man; to speak not as the scribes, but "with authority"; to ride into the Holy City like a crown prince, at the head of a triumphal procession; and, as deadly enemies inexorably closed in about him, in the darkest hour, to have an intimation of ensuing triumph.

The New Age to Come

The new age to come that Jesus and his disciples after him spoke of with such conviction was both a visible historical development and an invisible, inner personal experience. The concept was rooted in the poetry of the ancient Hebrew prophets, but as it traveled down the centuries it incorporated belief in the end of the world and a last judgment from the Persian prophet Zoroaster, an otherworldly metaphysics from Greek philosophy and a mystical knowledge of God from Greek and Oriental mystery cults. Yet its most basic element is the almost universal apprehension of a transcendent world of goodness and beauty. This insight has taken a variety of forms in the different religions of the world, but in one way or another it is common to them all.

A Day of Judgment

The first man of Hebrew tradition to introduce this idea was the prophet Amos about 760 B.C. He apprehends a coming Day of the Lord as a time of judgment. A power from outside this world, Amos says, will suddenly break into the everyday life of the Hebrews, visiting upon them catastrophic punishment for their degenerate personal and social life.

> Woe to you who desire the day of the Lord!
>   Why would you have the day of the Lord?
> It is darkness, and not light;
>   as if a man fled from a lion, and a bear met him;
> or went into the house and leaned
> against the wall, and a serpent bit him.
> Is not the day of the Lord darkness, and not light,
>   and gloom with no brightness in it?
>   (Amos 5:18-20).

About a half century later, Isaiah took up this idea but gave it a different interpretation. He saw it as a time when all nations would come up to Jerusalem to worship God and be so transformed in their moral life that they would abandon their habits of war, discarding all armaments, and live together in peace (Isaiah 2:4):

> and they shall beat their swords into plowshares,
> and their spears into pruning hooks;
> nation shall not lift up sword against nation,
> neither shall they learn war any more.

Micah, a somewhat younger contemporary of Isaiah, copied Isaiah's beautiful poem, and then added his own belief (4:4) that the new age to come would be a time when poverty and famine would be forever banished from the earth:

> but they shall sit every man under his vine and under his fig tree,
> and none shall make them afraid;
> for the mouth of the Lord of hosts has spoken.

Resurrection of the Dead

These prophets lived at the most prosperous period of the two Hebrew kingdoms, but the worst fears of Amos were realized when Israel, the northern kingdom, was destroyed by Assyria in 721 B.C. A little more than a century later, 587 B.C., Judah was destroyed by the Babylonians. Both nations were scattered in exile or living under foreign domination during the following centuries, and knew little of either the peace or the prosperity of which Isaiah and Micah dreamed. Yet the prophets of those desolate centuries never ceased to speak of a new age to come. Most of them expressed the hope that God would finally reassemble the dispersed exiles in their native Palestine and re-establish their nation. Some thought this could be done by military means, but others lost confidence in the ability of Hebrews to break the bonds of their oppressors, so they began to look only to God for deliverance. These prophets concluded that devout people do not always receive in this life the justice they deserve, and began to express the faith that the righteous dead would be called from the graves to get their just recompense. Thus the Day of the Lord became primarily a day of judgment and reward, but not in the sense which Amos meant when he first used the term.

One of the first clear expressions of this new hope occurs in the apocalyptic Book of Daniel about 167 B.C.

> At that time shall arise Michael, the great prince who has charge of your people. And there shall be a time of trouble such as never has been since there was a nation till that time; but at that time your people shall be delivered, every one whose name shall be found written in the book. And many of those who sleep in the dust of the

earth shall awake, some to everlasting life, and some to shame and
everlasting contempt. And those who are wise shall shine like the
brightness of the firmament; and those who turn many to righteousness, like the stars forever and forever (Daniel 12:1–3).

The new element in this passage is the idea of a life after death,
which was foreign to the thought of such prophets as Amos, Isaiah and
Micah. As those former prophets understood it, the Day of the Lord
had to do with events taking place in the present age. Indeed the present
age of history was the only one they knew anything about. They pre-
dicted peace, security, prosperity, or punishment in the form of some
historical disaster of the type nations ordinarily encountered. The deliverance of the people normally foretold was the return of exiles from
Assyria, or Babylonia, or Persia, or some other place of bondage, to their
homeland in Palestine. The deliverance Daniel has in mind is not from
the present evil world; it will take place after death, when there will
at last be a just recompense for all, the righteous entering eternal life
and the wicked everlasting contempt. This new order of things will be
supervised by the angel Michael. Between the earlier prophets and
Daniel a great change in Hebrew religious thought occurred, bringing a
very different conception of the reign of God in a new age to come.

Judgment by Fire

Another new feature of the Day of the Lord, as understood in the late
writings of the Old Testament, was the idea that the final separation
between the righteous and wicked would be accomplished by a judgment of fire.

For behold, the day comes, burning like an oven, when all the
arrogant and all evil doers will be stubble; the day that comes shall
burn them up, says the Lord of hosts, so that it will leave them
neither root nor branch. But for you who fear my name the sun of
righteousness shall rise, with healing in its wings (Malachi 4:1–2).

Belief in a general resurrection of the dead, judgment by fire, rewards in heaven and hell, Satan and his legions of demons, and the
prominent roles of great angels, are ideas which do not occur in the
religion of Moses. The Sadducees—a relatively small and conservative
Jewish sect—were right when they denied that these beliefs were derived from the written law. Nevertheless, at the time of Jesus these
ideas were widely held by the Jews; practically everybody but the
Sadducees believed them.

Jews first became acquainted with these beliefs while they were exiles in Babylonia and Persia, where from about 600 B.C. the religion named after Zoroaster prevailed. This man was one of the founders of mono-theistic religion. He belongs to the group composed of Moses, Jesus and Mohammed; these four have given the world its great monotheisms. Moses was the earliest, Zoroaster next, then Jesus, and finally Mo-hammed. Moses thought of monotheism in nationalistic terms; it was essentially limited to the Hebrews, and was linked with their develop-ment as a nation. Zoroaster, on the other hand, went far beyond Moses in defining his faith largely in moral terms in the present life, but seeing its true fulfillment in an age to come. The Jews therefore during their exile learned much from the religion of Zoroaster to enrich their own faith; and Jesus was in a position to draw wisdom from a culture en-riched by the tradition of Zoroaster as well as of Moses. His teachings about an age to come stem largely from the Zoroastrian strain. This does not mean that Jesus read the books of Zoroaster and then borrowed his ideas. Judaism had already adopted those beliefs before Jesus was born; it may well be that he had never heard of Zoroaster.

Justice

The new faith about an age to come deals more adequately with the concept of justice than the religion of Moses and the subsequent prophets had been able to do. Prophets such as Amos and Isaiah taught that there is a just recompense in this life; that every man receives the reward of either his uprightness or his wickedness in this present world, a view which has been found inadequate, contrary to the facts of life as we know it, by saintly persons all through the centuries. The first great writer to refute and repudiate this doctrine was the author of Job, some four centuries before the time of Christ. The new ideas about an age to come, when every one will finally receive a reward according to his merits, were therefore necessary to correct and supplement the religion of Moses and the prophets who succeeded him. Jesus was in a position to benefit from this long development of Hebrew religion.

The Kingdom of God Jesus proclaimed had little to do with the re-ligious nationalism Moses founded. Jesus was a Jew, and began with the Jews, but his far-ranging vision included all mankind. He also believed in justice, but justice would find its full expression only in the age to come. Therefore his religion included the ideas of resurrection of the dead, final judgment, and eternal rewards for both righteous and wicked.

Modern persons are sceptical about the existence of heaven as a physical place, like an oasis in a desert or an eternal Garden of Eden; and they are doubtful of hell as a real place where wicked people are punished forever in a fire that never burns out. Such doubts are justified. The existence of heaven and hell in a literal sense anywhere in the universe as we know it is difficult to conceive. The concepts also involve physical, moral and theological problems. But to become involved in these problems is to miss the point of the teaching about an age to come. The right approach is to recognize that all the ideas about resurrection, a judgment of fire, heaven and hell, have a symbolical character. They are the language of poetry, like that of Milton and Dante; but they are nonetheless true on that account. We are not to think of literal things and places, but of the ideas expressed. The imagery was conceived to help us grasp the truly moral character of religion. Integrity of character is the most important thing in the world; its value is so great that it lasts forever. Evil, on the other hand, is the worst thing in the world; it faces eternal repudiation and ultimate extinction.

Moreover, these concepts emphasize the importance of man's freedom of will. He has the right and the power to make up his own mind about his conduct, to choose good or evil. Freedom of will is one of the great wonders of life; in this respect man is like God. It is God's greatest gift to man; but he holds him responsible for the use he makes of it. In the exercise of his own freedom man determines his eternal destiny. God creates man in his own image; he loves him and works to bring about his redemption; but he is also man's judge.

These ideas are the foundation and the structure of the faith of Jesus. His story of the wastrel who went out into the world and soon squandered both his money and his moral character, but found a real welcome when he finally came home (Luke 15:11–32), shows how Jesus believes that the love of God follows every human being throughout life, seeking to redeem him, yet never coercing his will. On the other hand, Jesus told the story of the rich man and a beggar lying at his gate, each of whom received his just recompense in the age to come, to illustrate his belief that in the end God requires every man to answer for the way he has lived his life (Luke 16:19–31).

The Kingdom Is At Hand

The expression Jesus used for the age to come was the Kingdom of God, or the Kingdom of Heaven. As "heaven" is a metonym for God, the two phrases mean the same thing. The "Kingdom of Heaven" is found only in Matthew, where it occurs some thirty-two times.

There was a note of urgency in the message of Jesus, both in his own teaching (Mark 1:15) and in that of the disciples he sent out to represent him (Matthew 10:7; Luke 10:9). He warned the people that the Kingdom of God was at hand; the new age was ready to begin; and he called everyone to repentance in preparation for its arrival. At times he used the spectacular language of the apocalyptists to describe the opening of the new age, as, for example,

> But in those days, after that tribulation, the sun will be darkened, and the moon will not give its light, and the stars will be falling from heaven, and the powers in the heavens will be shaken. And then they will see the Son of man coming in clouds of great power and glory. And then he will send out the angels, and gather his elect from the four winds, from the ends of the earth to the ends of heaven (Mark 13:24–27).

What Is the Kingdom Like?

On the other hand, many of the sayings and parables show that Jesus thought of the new age as a social development which would gradually appear in human society. It will have to contend with evil forces, like wheat and weeds growing together (Matthew 13:24–30). Or it grows quietly, secretly, and no man knows how (Mark 4:26–29). It is like a mustard seed, which from a modest beginning gradually fills all the garden where it is planted (Mark 4:30–32). Like yeast worked into a batch of dough, it soon penetrates it all (Matthew 13:33). He compares the new age to a priceless treasure. You will buy a tract of land because you know there is a treasure somewhere in it (Matthew 13:44). You will sell all your possessions to buy one beautiful jewel you have always wanted (Matthew 13:45–46). Thus the Kingdom of God is a new faith, a new hope, bringing a meaning into life never there before.

We need to keep all these passages in mind to understand what Jesus meant by the new age to come. On the one hand, he seems to think of it as a spectacular development; on the other, it is a wonder which quietly develops in a person's inner life. It is a great treasure only you yourself are aware of. This latter approach was given its fullest expression in the Gospel of John, where the apocalyptic ideas of an astounding historical coming of the new age are almost entirely replaced by the belief that eternal life is a present possession. The new age arrives with our discovery of a new quality in life; that here in the midst of all the frustrations and disappointments of the world we may at the same time be citizens of God's Kingdom, which is everywhere there are people whose hearts are prepared by faith to apprehend it (John 6:44–51; 6:53–58; 11:25–26; 17:3).

The Theology of Jesus

Jesus was not a theologian, if by that term we mean one who tries to prove the existence of God or to expound his nature and attributes. It is obvious that he had a profound faith in God; he certainly believed in God's existence and had ideas about what he is like; but the only way we can arrive at those ideas is to infer them from his actions and from sayings of many kinds which in some way refer to God. Any systematic statement we make about the theology of Jesus needs to be considered in that light. It is not a system that Jesus himself put together; it is one we construct in an effort to understand him more fully.

A Presupposition

The most striking thing about the theology of Jesus is that God is a presupposition. He never raises a question of the existence of God; nor is there any recorded conversation in which other persons ask Jesus if he believes in God, or seek to draw him into an argument along this line. Nowhere does he mention what we would call an argument for God's existence. He simply assumes that God exists.

Such an assumption was, indeed, characteristic of biblical thought from earliest times. In a somewhat similar way we assume gravitation, electricity, energy, magnetism and biological principles of heredity; or in a more general sense, we assume the existence of "nature." These ideas are so common among us that we take them as a matter of course; they are fundamental to our thinking about the world and the life in it.

God was as self-evident to Jesus and all other biblical people as ideas about nature are to modern men and women. In both cases, whether God or nature, we are dealing with a fundamental presupposition of thought. If a sceptic were to challenge us to prove the existence of nature, or to explain what nature is, we might find ourselves embarrassed. Jesus and biblical people, likewise, would have been shocked by similar questions about God. Indeed it turns out that these two ideas are in fundamental ways rather similar. If we write nature with a capital letter—Nature—the close relationship between the two ideas immediately appears. In both cases we are talking about the cause of everything else around us. In the Bible God is always more than nature, but anyone who grasps the idea of nature is on his way to an understanding of the concept of God. God always means at least that much; but in most theologies, and especially in the thought of Jesus, he means more than that.

God in the Natural World

Throughout the Gospels one comes upon evidence that Jesus was a profound student of the Scriptures; he was familiar with the Law of Moses, the Prophets, and the Writings. As a matter of course, he held the basic theological beliefs reflected in those writings. The books of Moses begin with Hebrew beliefs about the creation of the world and man. Obviously Jesus held those beliefs. Nevertheless, in all his recorded sayings there is no specific reference to those ancient accounts of creation. On the other hand, several statements of Jesus show that he was intensely aware of the presence of God as the power in and behind nature at the present time. He says of God,

> . . . he makes his sun rise on the evil and and on the good, and sends rain on the just and on the unjust (Matthew 5:45).

This is a brief fragment, yet it reflects the belief of Jesus that God is continuously active in all the familiar processes of nature. All life in our natural world depends on sunshine and rain, but it is God who causes the sun to give illumination and heat. No life of man, animals or vegetation can exist without water, yet it is God who sends the rain. So Jesus sees God constantly operating in all these life-giving processes.

In one of his most beautiful sayings about trusting in the goodness of God, Jesus points to birds of the air and says that God takes care of them (Matthew 6:26). Or he illustrates his belief in God's providence by reference to lilies of the field. Even Solomon on his throne did not equal these (Matthew 6:28–29). It is God who provides the birds with food and gives the lilies their beauty. From such brief sayings we see how deeply the faith of Jesus is rooted in his apprehension of God in all the wonder and beauty of the natural world. He sees God as active now as he was at the beginning of time. Indeed Jesus seems more aware of God's present activity. And this is the way the idea of creation ought to be thought of: God is forever active; his processes go on always. He is like the great generator of an electrical system, which constantly sends out electric current over its lines, providing both light and power wherever the system operates.

Jesus showed his feeling that God was present and discernible in the natural world by withdrawing from human companions from time to time and going out alone, or with a small group, into the world of nature. The story of his temptation is the first illustration of his fondness for being alone with nature (Matthew 4:1–11). Some of the most beautiful stories about Jesus show his love for the Sea of Galilee (Mark 3:7; 4:1; 4:35–41; 5:1; 5:21). He went up into the hills to find quiet (Mark 3:13), or to a mountain top to pray (9:2–13); he withdrew to such a solitude as the mountain retreat of Caesarea Philippi (8:27–30). In these ways Jesus reminds us of Elijah, who also loved the world of nature and was able to apprehend God in deserts, hills and mountains.

The God of the Fathers

The deity Jesus believed in was the God of the Fathers; the God worshipped by the heroes of the Hebrew faith, but especially those known as the patriarchs. Even this idea, so obviously true, appears in the teaching of Jesus in only an incidental way. It comes out in a challenge of his belief in immortality by the Sadducees (Mark 12:24–27):

> Jesus said to them, "Is this not where you are wrong, that you know neither the scriptures nor the power of God? For when they rise from the dead, they neither marry nor are given in marriage, but are like angels in heaven. And as for the dead being raised, have you not read in the book of Moses, in the passage about the bush, how God said to him, 'I am the God of Abraham, and the God of Isaac, and the God of Jacob?' He is not the God of the dead, but the God of the living; you are quite wrong."

The Fathers concerned in this case are Abraham, Isaac and Jacob. Moses is mentioned only as the one who wrote the law: (Mark 1:44; 7:10; 10:3; 12:19, 26). Jesus shows no awareness that Moses was otherwise important. Theologians of our time have tended to place great emphasis on the way God revealed himself to Moses and the Hebrews in their escape from bondage. But Jesus shows no interest in the Exodus; he nowhere mentions it.

Jesus also had an interest in King David. In reply to those who criticized his disciples for plucking grain on the Sabbath, Jesus said,

"Have you never read what David did, when he was in need and hungry, and those who were with him; how he entered the house of God, when Abiathar was high priest, and ate the bread of the presence, which it is not lawful for any but the priests to eat, and also gave to those who were with him?" And he said to them, "The sabbath was made for man, not man for the sabbath; so the Son of man is lord even of the sabbath" (Mark 2:25-28).

Jesus believed that David was inspired by the Holy Spirit to write the Psalms (12:36). His significance to Jesus, insofar as we can tell, was, first, because of the religious precedent he set in eating the shewbread; and, second, as an inspired writer.

To us, on the contrary, the importance of David was military and political. He led the Hebrews in a successful rebellion against the Philistines, and then he united them into a strong nation. During his reign Hebrews began their longest period of political unity. But Jesus makes no reference to this historical importance of David. He does not see this as a revelation of God to the Hebrews.

The way Jesus refers to both Moses and David shows that he had little, if any, interest in the Jews as a nation. Jesus was not trying to start a rebellion against Rome; the religious movement he led was not a political nationalism. He did not think of the Kingdom of God in nationalistic terms.

Is God in Heaven?

Some ideas of Jesus about God can only be taken in a figurative or poetic sense; such is his idea that God resides in heaven, illustrated in the following,

> But I say to you, Do not swear at all, either by heaven, for it is the throne of God, or by the earth, for it is his footstool, or by Jerusalem, for it is the city of the Great King (Matthew 5:34-35).

The imagery of this saying is based on the ancient belief that God is king of the universe, and that his throne is located in a heavenly realm up in the sky. This belief is also illustrated in the first words of the Lord's Prayer, "Our Father, who are in heaven." It is the basis of the saying so popular in Matthew, "the Kingdom of Heaven." In this phrase "Heaven"—as the place of God's residence—is a metonym for God, and should always be capitalized, but most translations have failed to recognize this. In this sense, Heaven simply means God. When the prodigal son returns home from his wandering, and says, "Father,

I have sinned against heaven and before you" (Luke 15:21), "heaven" means God.[1]

This view that God resides in heaven is reflected in the story of the ascension of Christ after his resurrection (Acts 1:9–11). It assumes that Jesus has completed the work he came to do and is now returning to his Father in heaven. But it is doubtful that Jesus himself held this idea in a literal way. There are many of his sayings which show that God is a spirit, equally present everywhere all the time. His conversation with the Samaritan woman at Jacob's well shows this (John 4:5–26). She asked Jesus whether it was right to worship God on Mt. Gerizim near her home, or in Jerusalem where Solomon's temple stood. Jesus replied in essence that it makes no difference where you worship God; God is a spirit accessible everywhere. Again, he said, "Blessed are the pure in heart, for they shall see God" (Matthew 5:8). This is one of Jesus' most significant sayings about God; his residence is everywhere, but especially in the pure heart.

We know, of course, that modern astronomy has made obsolete any view that heaven is up above us. Every twenty-four hours of the day, as we understand it, the earth makes a complete rotation on its axis; so heaven would have to be in all directions at the same time. If a man tried to ascend to heaven, in what direction would he go?

The Sovereign of History

Just as Jesus believed that God is in all the processes of nature, so he believed that he is the sovereign of history. Many of his sayings are in the form of apocalyptic symbolism (Mark 13:1–37; Matthew 24:1–51). He shows the influence of such writings as Daniel and I Enoch. Perhaps more than any other form of biblical writings, the apocalypses stress this particular doctrine. They see history moving forward in a straight line, as it were, toward a culmination. God will bring all nations to judgment; because of their corruption they will be replaced by the new age to come—the Kingdom of God. The dead will be raised, there will be a final judgment, and all persons will be rewarded according to the way they have lived.

These ideas were passed on by Jesus to his disciples. They are reflected in other New Testament books, notably in the Revelation of John, one of the most powerful portrayals of God's control over history ever written. Whatever we think of these apocalyptic ideas that we en-

[1] Cf. S. V. McCasland, "Some New Testament Metonyms for God," *Journal of Biblical Literature*, LXVIII, Part ii, 1949, pp. 99–113.

counter in the Gospels they reflect the profound conviction of Jesus that justice will ultimately prevail, whether in the lives of individual persons or in the long history of nations.

God as a Person

Jesus certainly believed that God is a person. In all of his prayers he addressed God as "Father." In the prayer he taught his disciples to pray, and in his many sayings about prayer, he showed his belief that God is personally responsive to those who approach him. For example he said,

> If you then, who are evil, know how to give good gifts to your children, how much more will your Father, who is in heaven, give good things to those who ask him? (Matthew 7:11).

Some of the sayings of Jesus about persistence in prayer show a sense of humor. His story about a hard-hearted judge is of this type. This judge, who represents God in the parable, had no sympathy for anybody, but a widow came to him with such nagging persistence that he finally granted her request, saying,

> Though I neither fear God nor regard man, yet because this widow bothers me, I will vindicate her, for she will wear me out by her continual coming (Luke 18:4-5).

In another humorous tale God is represented by a man sound asleep at midnight, awakened by a neighbor who has come to borrow bread to feed an unexpected guest. Jesus says,

> I tell you, though he will not get up and give him anything because he is a friend, yet because of his importunity he will arise and give him whatever he needs (Luke 11:5-8).

God's personal care for those who believe in him is illustrated by the shepherd of a hundred sheep, who discovered on folding his flock at night that one was missing. So he returned to the pastures to search for it (Luke 15:3-7). The little story about a woman who swept her house, searching for a lost coin, teaches that God is concerned about every human being, regardless of how insignificant (Luke 15:8-10). The wonderful parable of the prodigal son shows that God considers every person as his son or daughter; that he feels a personal interest in every one of us; that his compassion follows us when we go astray; and that he always rejoices when we return home (Luke 15:11-32).

Impersonality in God

Yet Jesus knows that there is also an impersonality in God. He says that God "makes his sun rise on the evil and on the good, and sends rain on the just and on the unjust" (Matthew 5:45). Here Jesus senses something of what we would call the impersonality of the laws of nature. There is an inexorable quality in nature's forces, which makes them operate without regard to any personal feelings whatever, with no sense of either justice or injustice. This is true of all the laws of physics, chemistry, geology, astronomy, biology, etc. Insofar as God operates through these laws, we see only cold impersonality.

This impersonality of God is manifest also in his role of judge of mankind at the last day. Throughout his teachings, Jesus shows a belief that all men must finally stand before the judgment of God; and when that judgment is rendered, the only consideration is the quality of the moral life a man has lived. The unjust man has gone beyond all sympathy, compassion and mercy, as so clearly shown in the parable of the rich man and Lazarus (Luke 16:19–31). Judgment is pronounced according to the impersonal law itself.

Another way of saying this is that all representations of God as a person are figures of speech; they are metaphors. When we address God as Father, the word does not have the same meaning it has when we speak of our human father. God is not our father in a biological sense. To take that position would imply that God has a sexual character; that he has a wife; that he begets the human race as human parents beget their children. We do not mean this. To have realism in our thinking, we must understand that the figure of personality can never be applied to God literally. When we apprehend God by faith, we always feel that he is a person; but when we analyze that experience by reason, we are bound to see that beyond the metaphor there is also an element of impersonality.

The concept of God involves a paradox, in which the personal and impersonal elements are alternately expressions of one another. What we grasp first by faith as personal becomes impersonal when subjected to reason; but cold impersonality becomes warm and personal in our religious intuitions. It is the common experience of mankind that we all stand together facing the mystery of being, the ultimate forces of which we are composed and with which we are surrounded. But we know what it means to feel a surge of hope and confidence in ourselves in response to the friendliness, goodness and grace we apprehend about us in the world. Attempting to designate this mystery in an adequate way, we choose "father," or, in some religions, "mother," the most precious words in our language. These metaphors are the best we can do in expressing the meaning we feel; but we ought to keep in mind that God is more than simply the male element of creation; he must be the female too. God embodies the qualities of both father and mother of us all; but beyond these metaphors there must still be meanings in God beyond all our language or thought.

Signs from Heaven

The Bible gives a large place to the element of the supernatural, both in the Old Testament and in the New, especially in the Gospels. Stories of miracles belong to one of the deepest elements of religion, the desire for certainty, something which people crave more than anything else in life. This desire is often expressed in the biblical writings by the effort to validate faith from external historical events. The Bible represents God as intervening in what we think of as the order of nature: he causes earthquakes, storms or rain; he dries up the sea or the Jordan River to allow the Hebrews to pass over; he allows Moses to strike water from a rock in the desert, or sends a swarm of quails when the food supply is gone.

Nor was it unusual for biblical accounts to associate miraculous phenomena with prophets. One thinks especially of Elijah and Elisha, but also of many others of the great past of Hebrew history. So when we begin to read the Gospels, it is not surprising to learn that his contemporaries were interested in the things Jesus was able to do. They felt that if Jesus were a prophet, or especially if he were the Messiah, he should be able to demonstrate his nature by specific, unquestionably miraculous deeds. The Gospel of Mark relates (8:11-13) that

> . . . the Pharisees came and began to argue with him, seeking from him a sign from heaven to test him. And he sighed deeply in his spirit, and said, "Why does this generation seek a sign. Truly I say to you, no sign shall be given to this generation." And he left them, and getting into the boat again, he departed unto the other side.

The Sign of Jonah

Mark's account of this episode is the earliest form in which the story of a demand for a sign from heaven occurs, but the same incident is recorded in three other places, twice in Matthew and once in Luke. These different forms of the story show how traditions develop and how, in the course of their development, they are modified. The four versions of the story are in fact three different stages of this tradition:

the first stage is in Mark; the second is in the Q document, reflected in the parallel passages of Matthew and Luke, which agree almost verbatim (Matthew 16:4; Luke 11:29); and the third stage is Matthew's expanded version, found in 12:38–40.

Whereas, according to Mark, Jesus said to his challengers, "No sign shall be given this generation," in Q, as preserved in Luke 11:29, it reads,

> . . . this generation is an evil generation. It seeks a sign, but no sign shall be given to it except the sign of Jonah.

With one exception, the Q tradition preserves the story as it was handed down by Mark: it adds the reference to Jonah, but without saying what the sign of Jonah is.

Let us now examine the third stage of the tradition, Matthew 12:38–40. In this passage Matthew has Jesus say,

> An evil and adulterous generation seeks for a sign, but no sign shall be given to it except the sign of the prophet Jonah. For as Jonah was three days and three nights in the belly of the whale, so will the Son of man be three days and three nights in the heart of the earth.

This added elucidation, identifying the sign as the three days and three nights of Jonah in the belly of the whale, is unique; it does not occur elsewhere in the Gospels. Where Matthew got it, we have no certain way of knowing; presumably he himself added it to the tradition; the saying which lay before him in Q had simply said, "No sign shall be given except the sign of Jonah." He probably began to wonder what that sign of Jonah was and, since he knew the story of Jonah, he assumed that the sign was the three days and nights. At any rate this addition to the tradition seems to have been made about A.D. 85, when Matthew wrote his Gospel. By that time, the belief that the resurrection of Jesus on the third day had been foretold in the Old Testament was well established; and this reference to Jonah is the nearest to a quotation of Scripture in the New Testament in support of the resurrection of Jesus on the third day.

In these three stages of this tradition we see an about-face made concerning signs from heaven. When people asked Jesus for a sign, he first said that no sign would be given. In the second stage Q reports that he said, "No sign except the sign of Jonah"; and according to Q the sign of Jonah appears to be the preaching of repentance: just as

Jonah warned Nineveh, so Jesus preached repentance to his generation. But in Matthew's addition to the tradition—the third stage—Jesus has completely changed his position about signs, and explains the sign in detail.

No Sign Shall Be Given

In view of the interest of people of the biblical period in supernatural signs, the attitude of Jesus on this matter is worth considering. If we were to begin with the tradition in its third stage, as Matthew gives it, we should conclude that he also was greatly interested in supernatural signs and wonders; but the farther back we go toward the early sources the less interest in signs on his part do we find. In the earliest version of this story (Mark 8:12), Jesus sighs deeply and says, "Why does this generation seek a sign?" Jesus seemingly was depressed by the popular interest in signs from heaven. He felt that it showed lack of understanding, that the people had missed the essential element of religion, that they had failed to comprehend what he was talking about. So he says that no sign shall be given.

This attitude of Jesus is shown in various ways. There is a story in Mark 1:40–45 of how Jesus healed a leper. After cleansing the man, he

> . . . sternly charged him and sent him away at once and said to him, "See that you say nothing to anyone, but, go, show yourself to the priest and offer for your cleansing what Moses commanded for a proof to the people."

Another example is the healing of two blind men. "Then he touched their eyes, saying, 'According to your faith, be it done to you,' and their eyes were opened. And Jesus sternly charged them, 'See that no one knows it' " (Matthew 9:30). According to Mark 3:12, Jesus was healing the mentally ill; the demons cried out, "You are the Son of God"; and he ordered them not to make him known.

The story of the transfiguration carries the same idea. Jesus took with him Peter, James, and John, and went up a mountain to pray. In the midst of his prayer he was transfigured before them, and they felt that they were in the presence of God; Moses and Elijah appeared and talked with Jesus. When the experience was over, Jesus led them down the mountain and charged his three disciples not to reveal what had occurred (Mark 9:2–13).

One gets a similiar impression of his disinterest in signs from the attitude of Jesus about his Messianic mission. In the well-known passage in which Peter first confesses that Jesus is the Messiah (Mark 8:30), Jesus instructs his disciples to tell no one that he is the Christ.

Moved by Compassion

Mark, the earliest Gospel, gives the uniform impression that the motive of Jesus' deeds of healing is sympathy for the afflicted. He heals a leper or a blind man, or he relieves the mentally ill, not to give signs from heaven, but out of compassion. Here Jesus is presented as one who loves his fellow men; he sympathizes with them in their problems, and does what he can to relieve them.

The raising of the widow's son at Nain (Luke 7:11–17) illustrates the same point:

> As he drew near to the gate of the city, behold a man who had died was being carried out, the only son of his mother, and she was a widow. And a large crowd from the city was with her. And when the Lord saw her he had compassion on her, and said to her, "Do not weep." And he came and touched the bier and the bearers stood still, and he said, "Young man, I say to you, Arise!" And the dead man sat up and began to speak; and he gave him to his mother.

Again the motive is sympathy. In the sequel, of course, the people regard this as evidence that a prophet has appeared among them, and the reputation of Jesus spreads throughout the country.

This example is the second instance of raising the dead in the Synoptic Gospels. Mark has only the daughter of Jairus (5:35–43); Matthew follows Mark; but Luke adds the account of the widow's son. These are the only records of raising the dead in the Synoptic Gospels. The scarcity of material of this kind in these Gospels is evidence that their authors did not have an excessive interest in signs from heaven.

Luke is outstanding in his presentation of the sympathy of Jesus, using material found in no other Gospel. In 13:10–17, he tells how Jesus healed a woman in a synagogue on the Sabbath. This woman's body had been deformed for eighteen years, so that she could not raise herself up. And "when Jesus saw her, he called to her and said, 'Woman, you are freed from your infirmity.' And he laid his hands upon her, and immediately she was made straight." Leaders of the Jews present denounced Jesus because he had healed on the Sabbath, and he replied in his scathing way,

> You hypocrites! Does not each of you on the sabbath untie his ox or his ass from the manger and lead it away to water it? And

ought not this woman, a daughter of Abraham, whom Satan bound
for eighteen years, be loosed from this bond on the sabbath day?

Jesus was so moved by sympathy for this woman that he defied leaders
of the community in performing the act of healing on the Sabbath.

Luke 17:11–19 reports the sympathy of Jesus for ten lepers. The
main point of this story is that only one of the lepers healed returned
to thank Jesus, and this one was a Samaritan. Jesus often expressed
friendliness for Samaritans, Syrophoenicians, and other neighboring
peoples unpopular with the Jews. The parable of the good Samaritan
(Luke 10:29–37) makes this point: the man who aided the Jew beaten
up by thieves was a Samaritan; *he* was the good neighbor.

Evidence from the Q Document

The Q document, as reconstructed, is at best fragmentary, and hence
we should not expect to find many examples of the sympathy of Jesus
there. Yet even here his compassion stands out. An excellent illustration is the healing of the centurion's servant (Matthew 8:5–13; Luke
7:1–10). We know this is Q because it occurs in parallel form in
Matthew and Luke, and is not found in Mark. The essence of the story
is found in Matthew 8:5–7:

> As he entered Capernaum, a centurion came forward to him, be-
> seeching him and saying, "Lord, my servant is lying paralyzed at
> home in terrible distress." And he said to him, "I will come and
> heal him."

Here again the emphasis is on the immediate response of Jesus to a
situation of distress, and not on signs.

The best example from Q is the temptation of Jesus (Matthew 4:1–
11; Luke 4:1–13). This whole story speaks to the idea that the Messianic Kingdom of Jesus ought to be validated in terms of signs from
heaven. Matthew relates that Satan came to Jesus, who had fasted forty
days and no doubt was very weak, and challenged him, in turn, to
satisfy his hunger by converting stones of the desert into food; to display
his power by leaping from the temple unharmed; and to acquire control over the world by pledging allegiance to Satan. But Jesus con-
sistently refused to be misled by such a stupid notion of the Kingdom
of God.

This great story is unquestionable proof that Jesus refused to give
signs from heaven a place in his Messianic program. The episode was

recorded to correct the superficial belief many people held that the true religion of God's Kingdom must be demonstrated by some kind of external miraculous phenomenon. In this narrative Jesus sets himself in unalterable opposition to that view.

Miracles as Allegories

When we turn to the Gospel of John we enter a new world; here the point of view is entirely different from that of the earlier Gospels. The author definitely emphasizes signs from heaven; they are the great motif of his Gospel; he selects the miracle stories with this idea in mind, attempting to make certain that his stories will be accepted as unquestionable signs from heaven.

At the outset, let us list the signs in this Gospel; there are seven of them, the number seven carrying the biblical idea of completeness. (The draft of fish in 21:1-8 is omitted here because that chapter is an epilogue to the Gospel not included in the original plan.)

1. 2:1-11. The story of turning water into wine at a wedding. The author remarks that this is the first sign Jesus performed.

2. 4:46-54. Healing of an official's son, possibly the same as the centurion's servant in Matthew 8:5-13 and Luke 7:1-10.

3. 5:2-9. Healing of a man lame for thirty-eight years, found only in John, and notable for the length of time the man was lame.

4. 6:4-14. Feeding of the multitude, found also in the other Gospels.

5. 6:16-21. Jesus walks on the sea, found also in the earlier Gospels.

6. 9:1-12. Healing a man blind from birth, found only in John; important here because the man had been blind all his life.

7. 11:1-44. The raising of Lazarus, who had been dead four days; unique in John. It is extraordinary that the other Gospels do not contain it; and we note that John has omitted the raising of the daughter of Jairus and the son of the widow. He gives us only this one example of raising the dead, but what an example!

All the miracles John presents are chosen because of their suitability as signs from heaven. That is especially true of certain cases, notably the man lame thirty-eight years, the man blind from birth, and Lazarus who was dead four days. They were obviously conceived from the point of view that they could not have been natural events; they had to be signs from heaven. The author states his intention in 20:30-31:

> Now Jesus did many other signs in the presence of his disciples which are not written in this book, but these are written that you

may believe that Jesus is the Christ, the Son of God, and that believing you may have life in his name.

Yet this interest in signs from heaven is not the only, nor the most characteristic, motif in this Gospel. Although John gives us these accounts of spectacular miracles in a matter-of-fact way, it is still obvious to a person who considers these signs carefully that something deeper is to be derived from them. Indeed the setting forth of signs from heaven turns out to be a minor theme; on a higher level, the author takes us into a spiritual understanding of the career and personality of Jesus not attained in any of the earlier Gospels. On this level the interest in signs falls away; here the authentication of the spiritual life depends, not on signs of any kind, but upon immediate experience; and we encounter the idea that Christian faith is best described as a new birth, a birth of the Spirit. The proof, the validation, of this spiritual life is direct realization, a mystical sense of union with the Spirit of God, which has come into one's life and transformed it.

In no other Gospel do we find such insight into the real, spiritual nature of Christianity. This spiritual view begins in the first verses of John with an exalted conception of the divine Word, which has existed since all eternity and has now become incarnate in Jesus of Nazareth. This Word of God, also conceived as the Spirit of God, is something which comes into a man's heart and bears immediate testimony to the reality of the spiritual life. That is the magnificent conception of the Gospel of John, which moves on this high plane from beginning to end. This is so evident that one gains a feeling before he has finished the Gospel that, when this author emphasizes signs from heaven, he is using "sign" with a subtle, esoteric meaning. He is talking about something comprehended only by one born of the Spirit. The purpose is not to vindicate the ministry of Jesus and the validity of the spiritual life by objective signs, by miracles which cannot be denied; he has something more profound in mind. This writer intends that his stories should appeal on one level to persons who lack the spiritual insight to penetrate into the deep mystery of Christian faith; but the audience for whom he is more concerned is those with understanding, who have eyes to see spiritual things, and ears to hear.

The story of the water turned into wine is really an allegory. The water is drawn from jars used by Jews for ceremonial purification; that water, so important in the religion of the Jews, under the touch of the Spirit of Christ, is turned into wine. One hardly fails to detect the

irony, the subtle meaning: the plain, tasteless water represents the
spirit of Judaism by contrast with the new faith brought to mankind
by Jesus, comparable to delicious wine.

A similar allegory is obvious in the feeding of the multitude. In the
discussion following this narrative, Jesus refers to it again and again
to illuminate his idea that people should be concerned less with the
food which perishes than with the food which endures to eternal life.
The story comes to its climax in 6:50–51, where Jesus says,

> This is the bread which comes down from heaven, that a man
> may eat of it and not die. I am the living bread that came down
> from heaven. If anyone eats of this bread, he will live forever,
> and the bread which I shall give for the life of the world is my flesh.

Continuing in 6:53–54, he says,

> Truly, truly, I say to you, unless you eat the flesh of the Son of
> man and drink his blood, you have no life in you. He who eats my
> flesh and drinks my blood has eternal life, and I will raise him up
> at the last day.

In the hands of John, the feeding of the multitude becomes a parable
suggesting the mystery of the Christian faith.

An Emerging Theology

By the time this Gospel was written a highly developed theology
had begun to emerge, and it is expressed here in these words of Jesus.
John's use of the miracle of the loaves and fishes is an allegory of the
Lord's Supper. The bread and wine are symbols of the flesh and blood
of Jesus. The story means to say that the real bread which sustains
human beings is not food for the body but food for the soul; it is not
physical bread, but a divine nourishment which can satisfy the eternal
hunger; and this spiritual food is received in the sacrament of the Holy
Communion.

Or take the story of the man blind from birth. At the conclusion of
this episode, Jesus says to the blind man in 9:39, "For judgment I
came into this world, that those who do not see may see, and that those
who see may become blind." This is the point. Of course, on the face
of it, the story says that Jesus healed a man blind from birth, but John
intends it to be an allegory; every human being, in the spiritual sense,
is born blind; he is blind from birth, until his eyes are opened by the
divine light of the Gospel of Christ.

A similar interpretation of the other miracles in this Gospel is possible, in particular the raising of Lazarus. Although this is told as a wonder of astonishing magnitude, the main point is its allegorical application. In the very presence of the tomb, Jesus says to Martha, 11:25–26,

> I am the resurrection and the life. He who believes in me though he die, yet shall he live; and whoever lives and believes in me shall never die.

This possibility of immortality is the central message of the Christian faith, and that is what this Gospel is trying to present. The author is saying that every human being must be raised from the dead. We are dead, he says, in the sense that sin has poisoned us; and it is only the Lord Jesus who can call us forth from the tomb. When we read the story in this light, the idea that the raising of Lazarus is a sign from heaven in the conventional sense sinks into insignificance; it becomes unimportant.

Miracles and Ourselves

We have already anticipated the answer to the question, What value do biblical miracles have for our own faith? Sometimes we speak of the "problem of miracles," and miracles are obviously a problem for many people of our time. They have become a problem because of the popular impression that in order to accept the Christian faith one has to believe that miracles occurred as historical events. Sometimes it is felt that one cannot become a Christian because he does not believe that a particular story actually happened as related. One may feel that he would have to violate the integrity of his conscience to become a Christian.

There are several things that ought to be said concerning this problem of miracles. The most fundamental of all is that the attitude of Jesus shows that Christian faith does not depend on any kind of signs from heaven. Jesus repudiated those who insisted that he give signs, indicating that faith does not depend on spectacular manifestations. This in itself ought to be reassuring to those who are troubled about the difficulty of accepting miracles.

A careful consideration of the nature of the miracle stories themselves is often helpful. Some of the narratives can be accepted as reliable accounts of what happened. I see no reason for doubting that many of the stories of healing occurred essentially as they are recorded. The cases of mental illness referred to as demon possession in the Gospels are so closely parallel to mental illness in our time, sometimes relieved by modern psychiatry, that we are justified in accepting them as accurate. Of course, our physicians do not regard the mentally ill as demon-possessed; they talk about neuroses and psychoses. We laymen are familiar with epilepsy, schizophrenia, the manic-depressive complex, paresis, and other modern names for ancient afflictions. This is the vocabulary of contemporary medical science. In the New Testament mental illness was interpreted on the basis of theories now discarded, but the illnesses were the same as some of those with which we are familiar. Once we recognize that the cases described then were examples of mental illness, but presented as ancient Orientals understood it, we are in a position to see that the Gospel records are reliable.

It is possible that other examples of healing related in the Gospels also really occurred, and that we can accept them as historical events. Our problem arises in those cases without parallel in the experience of medicine at the present time. We do not know any way in which leprosy can be healed instantly; nor do we know how, without medical treatment, to open the eyes of a man born blind; nor how to raise a man dead four days. We cannot feed a multitude with a few loaves and fishes; nor can we walk on water. There are indeed episodes of this kind quite beyond the power of ordinary human beings.

What are we to say about such stories? The first is that no one has a right to deny that God could perform acts of this kind should he choose to do it. God made the world and established its orderly operation at all levels; and the divine being who created all forms of life, and is still creating new forms, can go beyond the orderly processes if he wishes to do it. That is not to assume, however, that all the miracle stories beyond our comprehension represent things God has done; some may be legends. It is also of great importance to recognize that some of these stories were written as allegories; that they were not intended to be viewed as historical occurrences.

Ultimately, after all our rationalizations, we have to leave some questions unanswered. As there is no other evidence than the Bible itself, we have no way of verifying the story. We may decide to accept it because it is in the Bible, but on the other hand a person who does not already believe in the inerrancy of the Bible cannot bring himself to such a decision. This means that the argument goes in a circle. There is no way one can feel certain that biblical miracle stories have actually occurred. As much as we would like to be certain, it is impossible for us to know beyond question that any particular story happened as related.

This might seem to be a tragic situation for modern faith, but such is not the case. Faith in the ancient period or today has always been precisely the same thing: it is an immediate sense of the presence of God. A religious person is one who, deep down in his own heart, senses the existence of God, and feels an intimate relationship with God. He is convinced that God undergirds his life, that God is the source of the goodness, truth and beauty in our world. This experience is just as possible for modern persons as it was for the ancients; the elementary conditions of religion have not changed through the centuries. So today we have the same opportunities for faith as were open to Jesus, to his disciples, and to other ancient men like Moses and Abraham.

Religious faith, century after century and the world over, is a unique kind of assurance which can never be validated by any kind of objective, historical signs from heaven. There would be no point in trying to prove religious faith in a scientific laboratory, by mathematics, or by any kind of historical evidence. Such "proof." always has alternate interpretations. The fact is that religious faith carries its own validation. It brings a kind of certainty to man which grows out of his uncertainty; the uncertainty of reason is transcended. And there is no way by which objective signs from heaven could change this dynamic character of faith. If religion were based on "facts" of this kind, its character would be altered. No longer having faith as its foundation, it would be nothing more than scientific facts and historical information. It would have lost its heart.

No one knew the true character of faith better than Jesus. So from the beginning he turned his back on signs from heaven.

Jews and Gentiles

When Jesus sent out his twelve apostles on their first mission, he charged them, "Go nowhere among the Gentiles, and enter no town of the Samaritans, but go rather to the lost sheep of the house of Israel" (Matthew 10:5–6). As this harsh saying occurs only in Matthew, and has been inserted into the earlier account of this episode as recorded in Mark (6:7–11; cf. Luke 9:2–6), one might question its authenticity. However, its style sounds like that of Jesus and it really contains nothing foreign to his spirit and purpose; but it raises a question of his attitude toward Jews and Gentiles.

Jesus' loyalty to the traditions of his fathers is clearly shown in another of Matthew's unique passages (5:17–19) in which Jesus says,

> Think not that I have come to abolish the law and the prophets; I have come not to abolish them but to fulfill them. For truly, I say to you, till heaven and earth pass away, not an iota, not a dot, will pass from the law until all is accomplished. Whoever then relaxes one of the least of these commandments and teaches men so, shall be called least in the kingdom of heaven; but he who does them and teaches them shall be called great in the kingdom of heaven.

This Matthean passage also has a reactionary sound; some have felt, therefore, that Jesus never uttered the words. Yet it was characteristic of him to use strong language. Hyperbole—overstatement for the sake of emphasis—is one of his most frequently used devices. If we set the passage in the proper light, there appears to be no sound reason for denying it an authentic place in the words of Jesus. Although he criticized prevalent scriptural interpretations set forth by the scribes and Pharisees, he never repudiated the ancient writings themselves. He was one of the most loyal expounders of the Scriptures, however much he might select and expound for his purposes their most humane, progressive and liberal principles.

Jesus was a son of Jewish parents, received a Jewish education, and in his own heart was loyal to the faith of his ancestors. All efforts to understand his sayings and the major decisions of his life must take this fundamental actuality into account. He must be understood on his own terms. We should not think of Jesus as a modern Christian, an heir of Western culture now 2000 years old, looking upon Judaism from the outside. He was a man of his own time, seeing life and religion as a Palestinian Jew of the first century.

Hellenistic Ideas

At the same time, Jesus was aware of new cultural and religious tendencies spreading over that world. Especially after the time of Alexander the Great (336–323 B.C.), Judaism had felt the influence of powerful new forces. In the ancient past, it had been strictly a national religion, limited to Hebrews. But new influences both from within and without were seeking to transform it into a Hellenistic religion, in which the center of interest was no longer the nation but the individual. One of the most prominent features of the Hellenistic Age (about 300 B.C.– A.D. 200) was the collapse of old national religions and the emergence of new faiths designed for individual persons rather than for nations. Jesus lived in the very center of this profound transformation, and we shall understand him better if we keep this in mind. The religions of the Greeks, Romans, Egyptians and Asiatic peoples were undergoing similar developments: they were beginning to have a concern about the nature and destiny of man, seeking not only to deal with the present life but also to throw light on a life to come. As most of the old national boundaries had disappeared, the new culture began to think of mankind as a whole rather than of separate nationalities. A new spirit of universalism was binding all peoples together.

Throughout most of the classic period of the Old Testament, Hebrew religion was almost exclusively concerned with the nation; there was no interest in a hereafter. Death was considered the end of man's existence, except for a shadowy abode in Sheol, into which all persons, righteous as well as wicked, went at death, with no thought of either reward or punishment. But as early as 200 B.C. belief in personal immortality began to appear among the Jews, especially in the apocalyptic writings with their new concept of resurrection of the dead. The Book of Daniel (about 167 B.C.) is one of the first clear expressions of this interest. Jonah, also written in this late period, shows the emergence of a new theological universalism; the author is attempting to show that the God of the Hebrews is also the God of all other nations.

Judaism thus began to develop in the direction of both individualism and universalism, a tendency which finally emerged as Christianity. At the same time, the much older strain of nationalism continued in Judaism and was the dominant element of that faith at the time of Jesus. In the rise of Christianity we are able to see the struggle between these rival forces in Judaism. Nationalism led to a disastrous rebellion against Rome in A.D. 66–70, and another in 132–135. Crushed by military might, Jewish nationalism evolved in a new form and produced the rabbinic religion which survived through the centuries, despite many hardships, and finally became Judaism as we know it today. On the other hand, the tendency toward universalism in Jewish culture, repudiated by the nationalistic main stream of Judaism, took root, gained new strength from Hellenistic sources, and became a central idea in Christianity, which sought to become not a national but a world religion.

The Position of Jesus

Not because he opposed the law and the prophets, but by virtue of the liberal principles he espoused, Jesus found himself at variance with all forms of organized Judaism of his day. He could not possibly go along with the tendency of the Pharisees to surround Jews with a wall of ceremonialism which separated them from other peoples of the time. He could not ally himself with the Sadducees, who limited their faith strictly to the words of the five books of Moses. Loving people and having a compassionate concern for them as they lived their daily lives, he could not enter an isolated Essene community, thus withdrawing himself from all contact not only with Gentiles, but with all other Jews everywhere, including the devout plain people of his native Galilee. Nor could he as a matter of conscience support the Zealot movement, agitating for rebellion against Rome. Jesus was not without concern for these groups; he regarded them all as "lost sheep of the house of Israel." But the progressive insights he brought to religion met with greatest response among the common people, the people of the land, regarded by the aristocratic groups as outcasts. Jesus himself belonged to these plain people; among them he found most of his friends; and with them he felt at home.

When Jesus instructed the Twelve not to go among Gentiles or Samaritans, he was only expressing the faith of his fathers. It was commonly believed that God's covenant was with the Hebrews, and that the coming of his kingdom depended on the loyalty of Jews to that ancient covenant. It was necessary, therefore, for Jesus' followers to carry his message of the imminent kingdom first to the Jews. Everywhere the disciples went they urged their fellow Jews to prepare for that kingdom by repentance; that is, to undergo a moral transformation. Jewish blood, the lineage of Abraham, according to Jesus, in itself was not enough to gain admission. Unless Jews understood this, and undertook a profound personal and social reformation, they would not be ready for the kingdom when it came. Preparation had to begin with the Jews. This explains why Jesus charged the disciples not to go among Gentiles and Samaritans.

Samaritans

The independence with which Jesus was able to view the clannishness of Jews is nowhere more evident than in his dealings with Samaritans. Since ancient times Jews had hated Samaritans. This cleavage between the two groups of Hebrews dated from the earliest days of their history. It was evidenced in the rivalry between the northern and southern tribes in the times of Saul, David and Solomon, eventuating in the division of the kingdom when Solomon died. Never after that did the Hebrews again succeed in becoming a fully united people. Animosity between Jews and Samaritans was bitter all through the centuries, and it survived into the time of Jesus; indeed it still exists in our own time. Samaritans were regarded as a mongrel, a degenerate people. Samaritans, on their side, viewed with scorn claims of Jews that Jerusalem was the only legitimate place of worship, pointing to their own shrine of Shechem, which had a far more ancient Hebrew tradition.

Yet when Jesus wished to formulate his teaching about loving one's neighbor as oneself, he chose a Samaritan as the hero of his great parable (Luke 10:25–37). It was a Samaritan who felt compassion for the man wounded by highwaymen and left by the roadside; he was the good neighbor. On another occasion, Jesus healed ten lepers. Only one of these had the thoughtfulness to return and thank Jesus for his healing; he was a Samaritan (Luke 17:16).

The way Jesus transcended the Jewish prejudice against Samaritans is nowhere shown more clearly than in the episode in which he stops at Jacob's well, located in Samaria, to ask a Samaritan woman for a drink (John 4:1–30). The woman was surprised when Jesus showed friendliness; this was so different from the bitterness most Jews manifested as they passed through Samaritan villages. Jesus took time to engage her in a conversation about the Kingdom of God, showing that his concerns included Samaritans as well as Jews. Here is an example of the universalism of his own spirit.

Romans

As a carpenter in a country town and as an itinerant teacher in an out-lying province, Jesus had little contact with Romans, but at least one of his healings is of a servant of a Roman centurion (Matthew 8:5–13; Luke 7:1–10). This centurion was well known among the Jews at Caper-naum. He admired the Jewish faith; indeed he had built a synagogue in that village (Luke 7:5). No doubt he belonged to the class of God-fearing Gentiles who attended worship services of Jews and admired their faith, although he had not accepted their ceremonials; he had not technically become a Jew. But Jesus said of this unusual man that he had not found such faith even in Israel. This is a fine testimony to the good moral character Jesus and other early Christians found in at least some Romans.

The Roman centurion in charge of the crucifixion of Jesus was at heart a kindly man (Mark 15:39). Simon Peter was to encounter an-other outstanding Roman centurion a few years later at Caesarea; this was Cornelius (Acts 10:1–48). And it was a kindly Roman centurion named Julius who took Paul as a prisoner to Rome (Acts 27:1–3, 43). Jesus was the first of the early Christians to admire good qualities in Romans.

Greeks

One of the most interesting stories in Mark is the encounter of Jesus with the Syrophoenician woman who asked him to heal her daughter (Mark 7:24–30). Mark actually calls her a Greek, and it may be that she was Greek by blood; but the word here may be used simply in the sense of a foreigner, a Gentile.

The only certain reference to contact with Greeks by Jesus is John 12:20–23. According to this passage, among the throngs of pilgrims going up to worship at Jerusalem were some Greeks. Evidently they also belonged to the group of God-fearers who admired the faith of the Jews. This party of Greeks approached Philip, a Jewish disciple from Bethsaida in Galilee with a Greek name, and said to him, "Sir, we wish to see Jesus." When this request was conveyed to Jesus, he was pleased by it, saying, "The hour is come for the Son of Man to be glorified."

In view of the primary responsibility Jesus felt toward the Jews, it is remarkable that so many traditions of incidents involving foreigners have survived. But enough of his friendly contacts with Samaritans, Romans and Greeks have been recorded to show that Jesus, having repudiated the aristocratic pride upper-class Jews felt toward their own common people, had also overcome the bitterness most Jews of his time felt toward foreigners. The Kingdom of God, as Jesus understood it, had plenty of room for Samaritans, Romans and Greeks, as well as for Jews.

Many will come from east and west and sit at table with Abraham, Isaac and Jacob in the kingdom of heaven, while the sons of the kingdom will be thrown into the outer darkness (Matthew 8:11–12).

The Messianic Mystery

One of the strangest paradoxes of the Gospels is the reticence Jesus shows toward his own nature and destiny. It may be that he believed in his Messianic mission from the time of his baptism; but if so, it was his steady policy not to proclaim that belief. Whenever other persons undertook to do it, he charged them to keep silent. There are numerous examples of this: among others, the mentally ill, at the time thought to be demon-possessed, had no hesitation in addressing Jesus as the Holy One of God, that is, the Messiah; but Jesus urged them to be quiet, not to reveal his identity (Mark 1:34).

This reticence of Jesus about his Messianic nature has led some scholar to conclude that he did not believe himself to be the Messiah; he was satisfied, they hold, to consider himself only a teacher and prophet; that after his death the disciples, believing he had risen from the dead, inferred that he was the Messiah, and then projected their new faith back into his life.

But the evidence does not make it necessary to take this negative position. Convincing reasons present themselves why Jesus did not proclaim, or wish others to proclaim, that he was the Messiah. One such reason would be that it would not accomplish his own purpose to proclaim his Messianic character unless the people themselves believed it; and Jesus appears to have felt that they should be allowed to infer his nature and destiny from his teachings and deeds.

There was also the further reason that the word Messiah had dangerous political connotations. Both the Roman procurators of Judea and the sons of Herod the Great—Antipas and Philip—as Roman puppets still ruling other parts of Palestine, kept a constant watch for pretenders to the Jewish throne. To claim the royal title was naturally regarded as a threat against the Romans, who had annexed Palestine to their province of Syria in 63 B.C. Jesus certainly knew that to make a Messianic claim would immediately bring about his arrest and execution. Hence he did not go about making this explosive claim. He had important work to do which the claim would have made impossible.

In time the authorities began to regard Jesus as a dangerous agitator.

This was also true of John the Baptist, the first to become a victim of political enemies. Herod Antipas of Galilee arrested John and beheaded him (Mark 6:14–29). The news of John's death must have caused Jesus to realize even more clearly the necessity to proceed with caution. One can hardly doubt that Herod's suspicious police were also keeping an eye on Jesus.

At the same time, Jewish authorities of Jerusalem were alarmed about the growing influence of Jesus up in Galilee. Mark relates in 7:1 ff. that Pharisees and some of the scribes came from Jerusalem full of concern about the teaching of Jesus and the attitude of his disciples toward the ceremonial law. Throughout chapters 7 and 8, one can see that these hostile investigators from Jerusalem had begun to exert a threatening pressure. Jesus must have sensed that he could no longer safely continue his public career in Galilee; indeed he seems to desire to escape the scrutiny of the Jerusalem spies. The first evidence of this is the excursion he made into Phoenician territory, visiting the regions of Tyre and Sidon (Mark 7:24–30).

No sooner had Jesus returned from Tyre and Sidon, however, than he went on another journey; this time, across the Sea of Galilee, into the Decapolis region of Transjordan, continuing northward into Iturea, territory ruled by Herod Philip. Apparently Jesus was seeking a place where he could be in seclusion with his disciples. He led them all the way up into the foothills of Mount Hermon, one of the sources of the Jordan, arriving at an old shrine of the Greek god Pan, a location which had been rebuilt as a city by Philip and named Caesarea in honor of Augustus Caesar.

There in this picturesque retreat, Jesus for the first time asked his disciples pointedly, "Who do men say I am?" (Mark 8:27), only now raising the question of his Messianic character. Even here he does not phrase his question to give them the answer, yet the question leads his disciples to affirm that he is the Christ. First they say, "Some men think you are John the Baptist; others, Elijah or another of the prophets." But he asked them, "Who do you think I am?" The impetuous Simon Peter promptly assures Jesus, "You are the Christ" (8:29), the first time, according to the Synoptic Gospels, that any disciple of Jesus had ever addressed him as the Christ. It must not be assumed, however, that Peter is the only disciple, perhaps not even the first, to reach this conclusion. On the contrary, it seems probable that Peter, who happens to be more ready of speech than the others, simply puts into words what all of them feel. This incident is presented by Mark as the culmination of the career of Jesus, as the high point in his life up to that time. As usual, however, Jesus immediately charges his disciples to tell no one about him (8:30).

The nature of the question Jesus asked the disciples at Caesarea Philippi makes doubly clear why he led them out of the territory of Herod Antipas into the region over which the more peaceful Herod Philip reigned, where they would not be exposed to the police of the tyrant Antipas or the spies from Jerusalem.

That the high court of the Jews at Jerusalem had authority to institute a dangerous inquisition, and that they were ready to send out their agents to accomplish such a mission, is shown by the determined effort the Sanhedrin made soon after the death of Jesus to stamp out the movement he had started. The court put the fanatical Saul of Tarsus at the head of a special police detail to arrest and imprison the disciples, going as far as Damascus, his first approval of violence having been the stoning of Stephen at Jerusalem (Acts 6-9).

These withdrawals of Jesus from Galilee, the first to Phoenicia, the second into the glens of Caesarea Philippi, show that both he and his disciples were aware of the increasing danger to the entire band, but especially to Jesus. The execution of John the Baptist was certainly a premonition of tragedy which might well befall their own group.

An even more basic reason why Jesus so persistently declined to proclaim his Messianic destiny must have been his realization that he could not accept the role of Mesiah within the meaning commonly held by the people. The popular idea of the Messiah at the time was a crown prince of the royal line of David, who would recover political independence for the Jews. Such a Messiah would have to overthrow the Roman domination of Palestine, which would require a terrible war, such as actually occurred in the revolts of A.D. 66-70 and 132-135, both of which ended in fearful catastrophe for the Jewish people. The Romans crushed the Jews on both occasions. It is unthinkable that Jesus held such a conception of the Messiah or of a new independent Jewish kingdom. No word of his indicates that he desired to incite war with Rome; he was no fanatical revolutionary, no Judas Maccabeus, no Simon Bar-Cochba. Hence his caution in using the term Messiah, lest he mislead the people he was so interested in.

Hebrew Nationalism Reinterpreted

Yet the teachings of Jesus are full of the Kingdom of God, and he constantly warned his listeners that the kingdom was at hand; indeed he urged them to prepare for it. This was the dominant theme of his sayings of many types, including his parables. Any kingdom requires a king; the Kingdom of God requires a Messiah to rule over it, that is, one chosen and anointed by God. The caution Jesus showed in allowing the Messianic title to be associated with himself must not be taken to mean that he had no interest in that exalted title and office, nor that he was unaware of that profound and pervasive Hebrew hope. On the contrary, he knew that this hope was dear to the Jews of the time; that talk about this hope could always find a hearing; that it could quickly lead the Messianic underground, always plotting the overthrow of Roman occupation, to step up their sporadic acts of violence and terrorism, and plunge the people into a foolhardy war of rebellion. From such a disaster Jesus recoiled, and he was unwilling that his own teachings should incite it. Here, then, is the reason for his prudence in dealing with persons who spoke of the burning Jewish hope in a political and military sense. He would not allow himself to be associated with the agitators, the violent Zealots. Hence, too, his care in expressing his personal faith, in explaining his own part in the Kingdom of God.

To get his disciples and the multitude to understand the nature of the kingdom he proclaimed was the most difficult undertaking Jesus ever attempted. The thought patterns of a proud people, cherished for centuries, are hard to change. Against their nationalistic view Jesus posed one at the opposite pole. A careful reading of his words shows that he considered God's Kingdom entirely spiritual, consisting of fellowship with the Father in heaven and a transformed moral life, and having nothing to do with re-establishing a Hebrew state or with war against Rome. Jesus sought to transform the deeply rooted nationalism of the Hebrews into a new Kingdom of the Spirit, intangible, invisible, except as one sees the ideals of Jesus in the new faith, the bright hope, the good life of his followers. The virtues of that kingdom are purity of heart, kindness, humility, and the love of one's neighbor as oneself.

Growth of Certainty

It is probable also that the reticence of Jesus was based partly on his own struggle for clarity as he worked out a complete reinterpretation of the old Hebrew hope. Are we to assume that from the time of his first appearance in public life—from his baptism—Jesus had clearly in mind the details of the course he was going to pursue; that he had fully worked out the reinterpretation of the political and military ideals of the kingdom he would present to the people; that from the beginning he had completely grasped all of his grand and brilliant view of God's Kingdom? It hardly seems possible that this extraordinary reconstruction of the Hebrew hope burst with full clarity on the mind of Jesus in one instant of time. Throughout the Gospels there are indications to the contrary; it is evident that Jesus proceeded on an experimental basis while he was becoming certain in his own mind of the path he would follow. This uncertainty caused him to use restraint, to observe the reactions of others to him. Uncertainty may well be another reason why he led his small band to the solitude of Caesarea Philippi; there safe from hostile spies, he would be able to reassure himself by exploring more fully than ever before the attitude toward him of his most trusted followers. This would explain why Jesus at last asked his disciples without ambiguity, "Who do men say I am?" He desired to know beyond question what was in the mind of his disciples; but he hoped also that what they said would help him to achieve full clarity about himself.

This interpretation of the episode at Caesarea Philippi is reinforced by the sequel to it. That dramatic conversation of Jesus with his disciples enabled him at last to overcome his own uncertainty, to reach a final decision. Immediately he announced that they would go to Jerusalem. Whatever misgivings he had felt up to this time were now gone. This conclusion is not only intrinsically probable from the character of the developing dramatic narrative; it is indicated throughout the story of Jesus by his continued dependence on intimate fellowship with the disciples. The records of the events at Caesarea Philippi show that Jesus was at this time more concerned to banish uncertainty from his own mind than from the minds of his disciples. They have already made up their minds on the question Jesus raises: when he asks the question, the disciples do not hesitate to answer. Without ambiguity, Peter, their spokesman, assures Jesus that they consider him the Messiah. The development of the story shows that this strong certainty of the disciples is what Jesus needs, what he has been waiting to hear.

A Revelation from God

Yet the records of this conversation require careful interpretation. They occur in Mark 8:27–30; Luke 9:18–21; and Matthew 16:13–20. Mark's account is earliest, Luke's and Matthew's being based upon it, following Mark closely up to the point where Peter says to Jesus, "You are the Christ." Here Matthew has inserted at the end of 16:16, ". . . the Son of the living God," an explanatory phrase probably based on the voice Jesus heard at his baptism; but the material Matthew adds in 16:17–19 needs special attention.

And Jesus answered him, "Blessed are you Simon Bar-Jona! For flesh and blood has not revealed it to you, but my Father who is in heaven. And I tell you, you are Peter, and on this rock I will build my church, and the powers of death shall not prevail against it. I will give you the keys of the kingdom of heaven, and whatever you bind on earth shall be bound in heaven, and whatever you loose on earth shall be loosed in heaven."

These verses have long been a problem for scholars. Either the author of the Gospel or some subsequent scribe has undoubtedly added this material to Mark's account from other sources now unknown. It is probable that the author of the Gospel is the one who made the addition. This sort of addition and rewriting is characteristic of Matthew's literary method. He likes to bring together sayings of Jesus of sundry types, in many cases dealing with unrelated themes, grouping them as if Jesus had delivered a continuous sermon or homily on a particular occasion. The Sermon on the Mount (Matthew 5–7) illustrates this practice; and there are no less than four, possibly five, other collections of this type in Matthew. This known tendency of the author, or editor, to bring together what he takes to be related sayings from different contexts and to regroup them as if they had all been said at the same time, throws light on the present passage.

The conclusion of Matthew's insertion, "I will give you the keys of the kingdom of heaven, and whatever you shall bind on earth shall be bound in heaven, and whatever you loose on earth shall be loosed in heaven," is only a slight variant of a saying recorded in Matthew 18:18–20, in a different context, where Jesus addressed it to all the disciples.

Truly, I say to you, whatever you bind on earth shall be bound in heaven, and whatever you loose on earth shall be loosed in heaven. Again I say unto you, if two of you agree on earth about anything they ask, it will be done for them by my Father in heaven. For where two or three are gathered in my name, there am I in the midst of them.

This passage shows that Peter was not given unique authority; that whatever authority was given to him was given to all the disciples. But Matthew has in this case applied the passage specifically to Peter, even changing the Greek pronouns to make it apply to Peter alone, a type of rewriting for which he is well known.[1]

[1] Cf. S. V. McCasland, "Matthew Twists the Scriptures," *Journal of Biblical Literature*, LXXX, ii, pp. 143–148, June 1961.

The saying in Matthew 16:18, "And I tell you, you are Peter, and on this rock I will build my church, and the powers of death shall not prevail against it," sounds characteristic of Jesus. The pun on the name of Peter is a bit of colorful language for which Jesus had such a gift; it has an authentic sound. On the other hand, we have no idea of the source from which Matthew derived it; the fact that it has a playful, humorous quality is ground for grave doubt that it was spoken on this solemn occasion; and for doubt, furthermore, that it was intended to confer on Peter any sort of power not shared by the other disciples. If it was meant seriously, it would sound strange indeed to hear Jesus in 16:23 deliver the stinging rebuke to Peter, "Get behind me, Satan!" It is improbable that Jesus would have solemnly addressed Peter as the foundation of the church in one breath and in the next called him Satan.

But the statement in Matthew 16:17, "Blessed are you, Simon Bar-Jona! For flesh and blood has not revealed this to you, but my Father who is in heaven," not only sounds authentic, whether spoken exactly in this context or not, but is tremendously illuminating of the entire life, the spiritual struggle, and the career of Jesus. According to this remarkable passage, Jesus senses that these words of Peter, recognizing him as the Messiah, are not merely Peter's words, expressing the sentiment of the entire band of disciples, but are nothing less than a revelation from God, who has in this way, through the mouth of Peter, informed Jesus that he is the Messiah, thus finally resolving the problem, banishing all doubt from his mind.

It was Jesus' conviction that God's will concerning his own nature and destiny had at last been clearly revealed to him through Peter's words which caused him finally to set his face toward Jerusalem. His intuition of his position in the Kingdom of God had been clarified and strengthened by the faith of his disciples. The meaning of the climactic conversation at Caesarea Philippi is not merely that the disciples have at last come to believe that Jesus is the Messiah, but that their certainty has banished the uncertainty from his own mind.

Some Titles of Jesus

During his ministry, according to the Synoptic Gospels, Jesus never told anyone that he was the Messiah; he entered upon the Messianic mission but left it to others to divine his true identity. As a result of this policy, he was addressed by various other titles. The Messianic mission did not become clear even to the disciples, not to mention the people generally, until near the end. This has led some scholars to infer that Jesus never felt himself to be the Messiah; that he taught about one to come, but never thought of himself in that role. These scholars conjecture that the Messianic mission of Jesus was created by the disciples after his death, and after they came to believe that he had risen from the dead. They hold therefore that other titles by which he was addressed give the key to his mission and personality.

It is our purpose now to consider some of these titles in relation to the career of Jesus, weighing as far as possible the appropriateness with which each expresses characteristic elements of his life.

Jesus

There is general agreement about the personal name Jesus. His mother's name was Mary, and her husband was Joseph, a carpenter. Mark does not mention the husband's name or refer to him at all. Some think that Joseph died before the ministry of Jesus began, but before A.D. 100, as shown by the birth stories of Matthew and Luke, some early Christians had come to believe that Jesus had no human father. Yet in Matthew and Luke, Joseph is named as the husband of Mary, and the ancestry of Jesus is traced back to the royal house of Judah through the lineage of Joseph. In John 6:42 the Jews say, "Is not this Jesus, the son of Joseph, whose father and mother we know?"

Often in the Gospels the founder of Christianity is designated by the simple name Jesus. In time he was called Jesus the Christ, or Christ Jesus, but this could not have been the usual designation during his lifetime. The secrecy surrounding the Messiahship made that impossible. After he was finally recognized as the Messiah, and when the church was founded on the belief that he had risen from the dead, it became a matter of course to refer to him as Jesus the Christ. This appears as a name in the first chapter of Matthew (1:1, 16, 18) and in other late New Testament writings.

Matthew 1:23 also introduces Emmanuel as the name of Jesus, but it occurs nowhere else in the New Testament. This name in all probability rests entirely on the Messianic Scripture which Matthew quotes from Isaiah. Matthew is interested also in finding an allegory in the name Jesus, "for he will save his people from their sins" (1:21).

The Nazarene

Jesus is often called the Nazarene, which probably means no more than that he was a native of Nazareth. But the word does not always occur in the same form. Mark gives it in Greek as *Nazarenos*. Luke follows him in 4:34 and 24:19 but he uses *Nazoraios* in 18:37; this latter form is general in other New Testament writings. The reason for the difference in etymology is not clear. But Jesus was known as the Nazarene and the disciples at a later time were called Nazarenes.

Rabbi

In all the Gospels Jesus is often addressed as Teacher, which corresponds with the fact that he devoted himself to teaching. There is no cause to doubt the Gospel tradition in this respect. The role of teacher was congenial to Jesus and it was not exclusive of other functions he might wish to assume. Undoubtedly therefore Jesus was often called Rabbi, which in his mother tongue meant Teacher; and occasionally the Gospels have preserved the Semitic word itself. Mark gives this title four times (9:5; 10:51; 11:21; 14:45). There is no conflict between Teacher (Greek, *Didaskalos*) and Rabbi as titles of Jesus, for Rabbi is merely the Semitic word for teacher. Matthew explains this to his readers in 23:7–8. But Jesus was never called *Didaskalos*, simply because he and his own disciples spoke Aramaic, not Greek.

At the same time, this word Rabbi sounded strange to Greek readers, for whom our Gospels were written. Luke, whose Greek style is outstanding, has in every instance substituted other terms more comprehensible to his readers. He has either used *Kyrios*, usually translated Lord, or *Epistates*, Master. Matthew also changes one of Mark's examples of Rabbi to Lord (20:33), but he preserves one case and introduces another (26:49; 26:25).

But the profession of teaching carries with it a certain distinction, and the teacher is held in honor. Jesus could be appropriately addressed as

Lord, the equivalent of Sir, or as Master, terms of address sometimes still applied to teachers in our own time. This analysis holds as well for the Gospel of John, where Rabbi occurs eight times (1:38; 1:49; 3:2; 3:26; 4:31; 6:25; 9:2; 11:8).

Lord

Lord also came to be a title of Jesus, and this is his most frequent title in the Gospels as they have come down to us. It occurs often in Mark (5:19; 7:28; 10:51; 11:3; 11:9; 12:36, 37). Matthew and Luke usually preserve the term as they find it in Mark, but they present new examples in the additional material they take from Q and other sources. Lord appears also in John, but perhaps less often than in the earlier Gospels. So it is evident that the title was used widely in the early Greek churches.

The connotation of Lord is often difficult to determine. Generally it is only a term of polite address, implying nothing more than the honor due a person of eminence. But it has also been used to translate Rabbi probably more often than any other word. But Lord is more ambiguous than Rabbi. No problem is created by its ordinary meaning as a term of courteous address, or as a translation of Rabbi. But it is well known that the Greek word *Kyrios* is used in the Greek translations of the Hebrew Scriptures for *Adonai*, Lord, which means God. *Kyrios* was also a common term for deity wherever the Greek language was spoken. The early church came to apply the word Lord to Jesus in this sense; and this was probably its favorite designation of him as soon as his divinity was recognized. The use of Lord in the sense of deity was thus natural and appropriate. On the other hand, it is improbable that Jesus made claims to deity on his own behalf, or that he was so addressed during his lifetime.

Prophet

Another role in which Jesus has often been cast, especially in recent years, is that of prophet. Scholars who draw the negative conclusion from the Messianic secret in Mark have usually felt that the prophetic function is all that Jesus aspired to and that this activity sufficiently expresses the meaning of his life. It is true that this term is applied to Jesus in the Gospels, but not as often as one might suppose. The fact is that the farther back we go the less frequent it becomes. It occurs six times in John (4:19; 4:44; 6:14; 7:40; 7:52; 9:17). Luke has seven illustrations (4:24; 7:16; 7:39; 9:8; 9:19; 13:33; 24:19). Three of these he took from Mark, the others he adds from his additional sources. Matthew has prophet only three times, (13:57; 21:11; 21:46) one from Mark and two are original (21:11; 21:46). Mark has prophet with reference to Jesus only three times (6:4; 6:15; 8:28). The Q document apparently has preserved not a single case. Thus the decreasing evidence of prophet as we go back through the sources makes it doubtful that this was the usual designation of Jesus, or that this was his own idea of himself, or that it exhausts the meaning of his mission and personality.

The occurrences of prophet in connection with Jesus in Mark are worth noting at this point. There is only one in which Jesus seems to refer to himself as a prophet. This saying was uttered at Nazareth where he had been rejected by his own townsmen. In that connection Jesus said, "A prophet is not without honor, except in his own country, and among his own kin, and in his own house" (6:4). While there seems to be no doubt that Jesus refers to himself here, it should be borne in mind that this is the only such case. This saying is in the form of a proverb whose meaning is perhaps to be taken figuratively rather than literally. Mark's second passage (6:14 ff.) states that Herod Antipas thought Jesus was John the Baptist who had risen from the dead, while others thought he was Elijah or one of the prophets. In answer to his question at Caesarea Philippi, the disciples tell Jesus that some persons believe he is Elijah or one of the prophets (8:28).

It appears from Mark that Jesus referred to himself as a prophet only once, and then only by quoting a proverb; and that the other two references associate him with one of the ancient prophets who would thus be reincarnated in him. Specifically, he was thought to be Elijah, in line with the popular belief that Elijah would reappear before the Messiah came, a belief which still lives in Judaism in our day, perpetuated by the custom of leaving a vacant chair at the *seder* of Passover for Elijah and of opening a door to let him in. But Mark also reports a saying of Jesus in which he states that Elijah has already come and "they did to him whatever they pleased" (9:13), referring to John the Baptist, who had been executed.

So Jesus did not think of himself as Elijah, and it is doubtful that he believed himself to be an incarnation of any of the ancient prophets. That does not exclude the possibility that he exercised certain prophetic functions and that his experience in many respects was parallel to that of the prophets. He did some things which a prophet, a person who believed himself to be no more than a prophet, would have done.

A kinship with the spirit of the ancient prophets is evident in Jesus when he denounces both the rabbis and the priests of his time, in the way he reinterprets the Sabbath law, and in his scorn of the views of the Pharisees about ceremonial purity. In his mind purity is a matter of the heart, having nothing to do with foods and ceremonies. In a similar prophetic spirit he defies the Pharisees in associating with the common people, who are regarded as sinners because they do not keep all the rituals. In fact he finds most of his followers among this very class of plain uneducated people, the people of the land. They are the persons who best understand the simplicity and directness of his words about religion. Here Jesus is among his own kind. He is neither Pharisee, Sadducee, Essene nor Zealot, but a leader who emerges from the people of the land. These people are resentful of the ceremonial burden the aristocratic groups place upon them, and in Jesus they find their champion.

Apocalyptists

As the Old Testament period drew to a close, the Jews brought together and re-edited most of their sacred books, which they now had begun to recognize as divinely inspired and authoritative Scriptures; and they believed that God's will for their lives was completely revealed in these books. So they now lived by the words of books rather than by the words of prophets. The experience of prophecy therefore gradually almost entirely disappeared from Hebrew life. At the time of Jesus it was commonly believed that no true prophet had appeared for two or three centuries. This is one reason why we should not expect to find Jesus regarding himself as a prophet.

One of the most interesting results of the view that all divine truth had been revealed and was now to be derived from the books, and that prophecy as such had ceased, was that the prophetic spirit—which could not be entirely quenched—went underground, producing the type of writing known as an apocalypse, that is, a revelation. The author of such a book was an apocalyptist. Such a prophet had no alternative but to be anonymous and to make known his views by writing. As it was believed that the canon of Scripture was closed, the apocalyptist could only get his book read by publishing it under a pseudonym, usually selecting the eminent name of an ancient worthy, such as Enoch, one of the Patriarchs, Baruch or Daniel, so that his book purported to come from ancient times. The apocalyptic writer, in his prophetic role, had no intention to enter upon any type of public career; and as a writer he was buried under a pseudonym.

Jesus was certainly not a prophet of the apocalyptic type. He was not an anonymous author, secretly writing strange symbolical books according to the apocalyptic custom. He engaged openly in a vigorous career. But that he accepted some of the apocalyptic ideas is altogether probable. He looked for the coming of the Messianic Kingdom in the apocalyptic fashion. God would take the initiative in introducing the divine kingdom and would himself place the Messiah on his throne.[1]

The Messiah

It is true that Jesus was a great teacher and was so recognized in his own time, but the records of his life make it clear that the role of teacher falls short of expressing the full range of his personality. Lord, as we have seen, really belongs to the second stage of the Christian tradition. It came in as the Greek word used to translate the Semitic Rabbi. That Jesus did not regard himself simply as a prophet, whether in the ancient traditional sense or as a later apocalyptist, is even more clearly evident. A critical evaluation of the Gospels does not support the view that he was only another Hebrew prophet; or that to cast Jesus in this role dispels the mystery that surrounds his sense of vocation, or is enough to account for the varied interests and activities encompassed by his splendid life.

So if we would do justice to the versatility of Jesus, to his many-sided career, to his sense of divine mission, to his own mind and heart and faith, it is necessary to look beyond the titles of Rabbi, Lord and Prophet. We must turn to some nobler title; and that title, as we have seen in the previous chapter, according to the earliest sources, is nothing less than the Messiah. But Jesus did not pursue this illustrious appellation; he did not seek the Messiahship or any other position of power and glory, either earthly or heavenly. On the contrary, his study of the Scriptures, his apprehension of God's will for his life, his deepening intuition of his own personal destiny, steadily and finally thrust the Messiahship upon him. For Jesus was gradually realizing with equal clarity that the only path to this exalted position lay through humiliation and defeat.[2]

---

[1] The apocalyptic type of writing is further considered in chapters 18 and 19.
[2] The Son of Man, one of the most interesting titles applied to Jesus, one by which he, but only he, often referred to himself, will be considered in chapters 18 and 19.

The Uncanny One

Step by step we approach an understanding of Jesus, but it would be too much to claim that we ever understand him completely, or that the people of his own time did so. Over and above all the components of his character that we can fit into rational, understandable categories, there still remains an uncanny element. There is about Jesus a strange sense of mystery, actions that bewilder persons around him: an extraordinary grasp of understanding, an unusual ability to do things, a power transmitted by a touch or a glance. He amazes, astonishes, inspires awe, terrifies. There is always a transcending secret that suggests the spiritual, the holy, the divine. In the presence of Jesus, whether in his own time or now, men have sensed the presence of the supernatural. To many he is a luminous person; in him they see God revealed. But for others he is a scandal; he shocks their sense of moral security; their religious certainty is undermined when he blasts away the shallow foundations of traditional faith. So they react in outraged anger and charge that he is in league with Satan, not God. But through all the varied responses of men to his surprising strangeness, Jesus retains his own secret: the core of his personality eludes our prying curiosity; it dwells securely within the citadel of his own mind and heart.

The earliest effort to explain this uncanny element in the life of Jesus is the tradition concerning his baptism by the prophet John. This is recorded for the first time in Mark 1:9–13. Here it is related that when Jesus had been baptized and was coming up from the water, he saw the Spirit of God coming down upon him. Indeed according to this passage, the Spirit came into Jesus, and this was truly one of the high points of his life. Then the Spirit drove Jesus out into the wilderness, where he was tempted by Satan. The Gospel of Luke (4:14) continues from this point by stating that Jesus returned in the power of the Spirit into Galilee. The ancient tradition thus holds that at this point in his life he came under the influence and power of the Spirit of God; that from this point on whatever of strangeness we see in Jesus should be ascribed to that divine source.

John was the first to indicate that Jesus was an extraordinary person.

Even before he had met Jesus he expressed a premonition of his uncanny character:

> After me comes he that is mightier than I, the thong of whose sandals I am not worthy to stoop down and untie. I have baptized you with water; but he will baptize you with the Holy Spirit (Mark 1:7–8).

John was a person of real humility, feeling himself to be only a herald of a greater one to come. This mighty one was to be the Lord of whom the prophet in the wilderness cried:

> Prepare the way of the Lord, make his paths straight (Mark 1:3; Isaiah 40:3).

His Uncanny Authority

As soon as Jesus returned to Galilee, he went into the synagogue of Capernaum on the Sabbath and began to teach:

> And they were astonished at his teaching, for he taught them as one who had authority, not as the scribes (Mark 1:22).

Thus the first time the people themselves expressed astonishment at Jesus, it was his teaching that amazed them. They were fascinated by his independence and originality, and he brought them good news, for he said:

> The time is fulfilled, and the Kingdom of God is at hand; repent, and believe in the gospel (Mark 1:15).

For hundreds of years the Jews had been hoping for the coming of God's kingdom. So they were astonished when Jesus suddenly announced that that kingdom had come.

But this news was delivered with a freedom, a naturalness and an authority which was remarkably different from the legalistic lectures they were accustomed to hear the scribes give. The scribes, who were usually Pharisees, could also be called rabbis, that is, teachers. They were, first, persons who were skilled in writing copies of the Scriptures by hand, but as copyists they were also informed about the Scriptures; so they became scholars and teachers. The term rabbi was not then so well recognized in a professional sense as it was to become two or three centuries later. Of course Jesus had never been a copyist; he was not a scribe in that sense. As an informal teacher without official status, he was more properly called Rabbi.

The most obvious characteristic of the scribe was his lack of independence. He was in bondage first to the written Law of Moses, but second to the tradition of the elders, which was the oral law handed down from generation to generation. This oral tradition was composed of accumulated court decisions; it gradually became more important than the written law itself.

Jesus did not feel himself bound by this tradition of the elders, and was often strongly critical of it. So it was this freedom of Jesus from the burden of tradition which astonished the people of Capernaum that day. They rejoiced at the emergence of a new teacher who had the intelligence and courage to challenge the entrenched position of the powerful scribes. They saw hope of escape from their own bondage to economic exploitation and social humiliation.

The independence of Jesus shows up clearly also in contrast with the ancient prophets, whose characteristic claim of authority was to say, "Thus says the Lord." They had no sense of authority beyond the messages expressly revealed to them by God. Whenever the prophet said, "I say unto you," the "I" meant God. This idiom of the "I" was the way in which God was believed to speak to the people of ancient times in the first person. The role of the prophet was to subordinate himself entirely and to allow God to speak through him.

But on the contrary, Jesus would say, "You have heard that it was said so and so, but *I* say unto you." This is the common idiom of Jesus; and when he says, "I say unto you," he means himself, not God. He thus affirms his own autonomy. It was this sense of autonomy which people saw in Jesus that filled them with astonishment.

Another well-known type of teacher during the latter part of the Old Testament was the sage, the author of wisdom literature. His literary style was proverbs, epigrams, aphorisms, and other homely idioms characteristic of the common people.[1] The wisdom writings are a wonderful literature, but they differ in both substance and the sense of authority from the teachings of Jesus. "I say unto you," so often used by Jesus, is not at home with the sages. The sage draws his teachings from rational principles. Although not technical philosophy, the wisdom books approach more closely to philosophy than any other writings in the Bible. Many of the sayings of Jesus are similar in style to words of the sages, but his sayings have a more personal character; and at the same time Jesus places more emphasis on the theological founda-

[1] Good examples of wisdom writings are Proverbs, Ecclesiastes, Job, Wisdom of Solomon, and the Wisdom of Jesus, Son of Sirach.

tion of morality. The sages show how wise it is to live a moral life, but Jesus points out that it is God's will to do so.

Some of the priests were teachers but their interest was limited almost entirely to the sacrifices and ceremonial rites of the temple; and their instruction was intended primarily for persons in training for the priesthood. The source of the priest's learning was the written word of the five books of Moses, that is, the law, beyond which he would not go. He was even more radical than Jesus in repudiating the oral tradition of the elders, at the cost of discarding many good new insights; and he lacked the freedom and concern for the spiritual heart of religion so characteristic of Jesus.

In Jesus therefore the people of Capernaum had found a teacher of a new type. He did not teach like the scribes, the prophets, the sages, or the priests, but as one having an authority of his own. Never before had they heard a teacher like him. So they were astonished at his words.

An Astounding Healer

The people of Capernaum were also amazed by the ability of Jesus to heal, as shown by the following story:

> And immediately there was in their synagogue a man with an unclean spirit; and he cried out, "What have you to do with us, Jesus of Nazareth? Have you come to destroy us? I know who you are, The Holy One of God." But Jesus rebuked him, saying, "Be silent, and come out of him!" And the unclean spirit, convulsing him and crying with a loud voice, came out of him. And they were all amazed, so that they questioned among themselves, saying, "What is this? A new teaching! With authority he commands even the unclean spirits and they obey him" (Mark 1:23–27).

According to the view of modern psychiatrists, this vividly described case of demon possession would now be diagnosed as the psychosis of hysteria; and the relief of the afflicted man by driving the demon out of him, as done here by a command, in a psychological sense, is the same as the treatment of hysteria by suggestion while the patient is under hypnosis.[1] Other examples of mental illness relieved by Jesus are epilepsy (Mark 9:17–27); a manic-depressive (Mark 5:1–20); and Mary Magdalene, who was relieved of seven demons, but the de-

---

[1] Cf. S. V. McCasland, *By the Finger of God,* the Macmillan Company, New York, 1951, p. 42 ff. This book presents an exhaustive study of demon possession and exorcism in early Christianity from the point of view of modern psychiatry.

scription is too brief for diagnosis (Luke 8:2). Others are alluded to.

As soon as we recognize that demon possession was the ancient concept of mental illness, and replace that picturesque but unscientific vocabulary with the terminology and ideas of contemporary medicine, such narratives from the Gospels acquire a realism which inspires full confidence in their reliability. Undoubtedly Jesus was able to restore many to a normal mental life. Nevertheless he knew that such unstable persons may experience a return of their illnesses. Such a relapse lay behind his story of a demon who collected seven others worse than himself and repossessed a man from whom he had been driven out (Luke 11:24–26).

The Gospels also refer to other types of disease healed by Jesus, but in most cases it is now impossible for us to identify the diseases. So we cannot feel the same measure of confidence in such records as we feel in regard to his relief of demon possession. It is possible, indeed probable, that some of these reports are legendary; they have come out of a popular tradition, which may have exaggerated the number and the kinds of sickness healed by Jesus. Yet it is reasonable to believe that Jesus devoted much of his time to relief of disease, and of many types; and the very fact that so many allusions to his healing activities are made is enough to indicate that he was often successful in bringing relief. It was not his purpose to make a show of these matters, or to attempt to validate his mission or to gain popularity by sensational publicity. His only concern was compassion for all suffering persons; undoubtedly he did whatever he could for them; and his success was so great that those who witnessed what he did were filled with awe. There was something in the power of Jesus that went beyond their power of comprehension.

Yet these compassionate acts of Jesus aroused hostility on the part of some:

> But some of them said, "He casts out demons by Beelzebul, the prince of demons"; while others, to test him, sought from him a sign from heaven. But he, knowing their thoughts, said to them, "Every kingdom divided against itself is laid waste, and house falls upon house. And if Satan also is divided against himself, how will his kingdom stand? For you say that I cast out demons by Beelzebul. And if I cast out demons by Beelzebul, by whom do your sons cast them out? Therefore they shall be your judges. But if it is by the finger of God that I cast out demons, then the Kingdom of God has come upon you" (Luke 11:14–20).

Here the enemies of Jesus do not deny his ability to cast out demons; they charge that he does it by the power of Beelzebul, another name for Satan, the prince of demons. They accuse Jesus of practicing black magic, witchcraft, sorcery or necromancy.[1] But the very existence of this charge in the records is extraordinary testimony to the success Jesus had in relieving the mentally ill; and the reply that Jesus makes is equally significant. It shows that he fully accepts the popular belief in demonology, including Satan as prince of demons. But with devastating logic he refutes the hostile charge: if Satan is divided against himself, how can his kingdom stand? Then with a flashing rejoinder he reveals his own understanding: "But if it is by the finger of God that I cast out demons, then the Kingdom of God is come upon you." Here he shows that according to his belief the coming of God's Kingdom first requires driving out the demons, a view he shares with I Enoch and other contemporary Jewish uncanonical writings.

At one point in his career, some of the friends of Jesus, perplexed by his uncanny authority and power, and no doubt shocked by popular rumors about him, concluded that he had actually lost his mind. So, probably for his own protection, they formed a plot to take him by force, perhaps even to bind him in a straitjacket:

> Then he went home; and the crowd came together again, so that they could not even eat. And when his friends[2] heard it, they went out to seize him, for they said, "He is beside himself" (Mark 3:20–21).

The uncanny atmosphere that surrounded Jesus was so pronounced that it finally isolated him from his own family. There is no evidence that any brother of his was a disciple until after his death and resurrection, when he appeared to James (I Corinthians 15:7), who later became a pillar in the Jerusalem church.[3] According to a tradition in the Gospel of John (19:26), Mary, the mother of Jesus, was present at the crucifixion, but the earlier Synoptic Gospels do not indicate that she was there. The estrangement of Jesus from his family is suggested by the following:

[1] The charge that Jesus is possessed by a demon is also made several times in the Gospel of John (7:20; 8:48; 8:52; 10:20; 10:21).

[2] This is translated "his relatives" by Edgar J. Goodspeed in *The New Testament, an American Translation*.

[3] Galatians 2:9; Acts 15:13.

And his mother and his brothers came; and standing outside they sent to him and called him. And a crowd was sitting about him; and they said to him, "Your mother and your brothers are outside, asking for you." And he replied, "Who are my mother and my brothers?" And looking around on those who sat about him, he said, "Here are my mother and my brothers! Whoever does the will of God is my brother, and sister, and mother" (Mark 3:31–35).

Perhaps the most revealing reaction to the uncanny character of Jesus—because it came with such spontaneity—was that of persons believed to be possessed by demons; and their reaction is certainly not one that we need to look upon with scepticism. In the tense atmosphere of Jewish life, so resentful of the presence of the Romans and so restive under foreign domination, hope never died; and the coming of a divine deliverer and the Kingdom of God was momentarily expected. It is not surprising that the appearance of a person such as Jesus aroused hope in many breasts. Cautious persons, like his disciples, waited hopefully; they knew the dangers. Judiciously they held their peace during his ministry, and even at the end only in private admitted their belief that Jesus was the Messiah. With the demon-possessed, the mentally ill, it was otherwise. In their unbalanced minds they also carried the same expectancy; but unlike their more wary companions, they were aware of no danger from revealing the identity of Jesus; they felt no restraining fear. The burning hope others dared to hold only in secret burst upon their distressed understandings with the certainty of inspired premonitions. Without inhibition or hesitation, but with a different motive, they shouted their identification of Jesus as the Holy One of God (Mark 1:24; 1:34; 5:7–9).

Yet a real understanding of such broken personalities indicates that the so-called "confessions" of Jesus by the possessed persons, as their demonic egos cowered in terror from his commanding voice, were shouts of defiance, for revealing the identity of the exorcist was an effort to strip him of his power. A psychosis is actually a tower of refuge into which the frightened psyche of the mentally ill flees for safety; and he can be dislodged, if ever, only by wisdom and patience and compassion. The success Jesus had with such persons is one of the greatest tributes to him the Gospels record.

So the records of the Gospels show that, with no lack of appreciation or reverence, and quite accurately, Jesus might have been addressed as the Uncanny One. Indeed that is not far from what was meant by the Holy One of God.

The New Certainty

With considerable justification scholars in recent years have pointed out the lack of historical continuity in Mark's account of the life and ministry of Jesus. This character of the Gospel was recognized by the early Christian Papias near the middle of the second century, who wrote,

> Mark, having become the interpreter of Peter, wrote accurately whatever he remembered, not, however, recording in order the things that were said or done by Christ . . .

a remark recorded by Eusebius about A.D. 325 in his *Church History*, iii, 39.

This is an illuminating comment on the Gospel of Mark, but it overstates the lack of order. One can hardly fail to see some historical progression from the beginning to the end of the Gospel; and in places within the story we detect normal movements of Jesus and his disciples from place to place. The episode at Caesarea Philippi and the immediate decision of Jesus to lead his disciples to Jerusalem are one of the best examples of a clear sequence Mark records. The sequence is not only one of movement, involving a sudden departure for Jerusalem; there is at this point a natural and decisive change in the attitude of Jesus, and the about-face logically follows the important conversation he has just held with the disciples. Before this point, Jesus has carefully withdrawn from his dangerous foes in Galilee, first to Phoenicia, then to Iturea, as if seeking to avoid the threatening dangers. Now he casts aside all hesitation; he is no longer afraid; there is no further reason to seek seclusion; and suddenly he determines to go to Jerusalem, the very stronghold of his most deadly enemies. So at once he discloses to the disciples his bold new plan of action.

Mark says (8:31-32),

> And he began to teach them that the Son of man must suffer many things, and be rejected by the elders and the chief priests and the scribes, and be killed, and after three days rise again. And he said this plainly.

That this was a shocking disclosure to the disciples, a premonition they were not ready to accept, is shown plainly by what follows:

> And Peter took him and began to rebuke him. But turning and seeing his disciples, he rebuked Peter, and said, "Get behind me, Satan! For you are not on the side of God, but of men" (8:32–33).

This was a paralyzing blow to Peter; only a short time before, he was the one to affirm the disciples' faith that Jesus was the Messiah; and here Jesus turns upon him with a scathing denunciation.

Jesus and his disciples immediately left Iturea and went through Galilee toward Jerusalem. Mark says (9:30–32):

> They went on from there and passed through Galilee. And he would not have anyone know it; for he was teaching his disciples, saying to them, "The Son of man will be delivered into the hands of men, and they will kill him; and when he is killed, after three days he will rise." But they did not understand this saying, and they were afraid to ask him.

Again, Mark records (10:32–34):

> And they were on the road, going up to Jerusalem, and Jesus was walking ahead of them; and they were amazed, and those who followed were afraid. And taking the twelve again, he began to tell them what was to happen to him, saying, "Behold, we are going up to Jerusalem; and the Son of man will be delivered to the chief priests and scribes, and they will condemn him to death, and deliver him to the Gentiles; and they will mock him, and spit upon him, and scourge him, and kill him; and after three days he will rise.

All three of these sayings about the Son of Man mean essentially the same thing; yet here again there is a definite progression. The first must have been said while they were still in the region of Caesarea Philippi; the second, as they were passing through Galilee; and the third, somewhere on the way down the Jordan Valley, which they followed on their journey to Jerusalem. We do not need to say that they are three variant forms of the same saying. The material has a natural order as Mark presents it. It is clear from the reactions of the disciples that they were astonished and afraid, that they failed to comprehend. What they did grasp was that they were heading into some terrible danger, and this they did not like. Moreover, it is comprehensible that Jesus undertook to explain to his disciples something of the tremendous events of which he had a premonition. The three passages in Mark indicate that

he spent much of the time during the three or four days they were
walking to Jerusalem attempting to explain his new understanding of
himself and his own destiny, now at last clear to him.

The Son of Man Must Suffer

We do not underestimate the difficulty New Testament scholars have
found in accepting the authenticity of the above sayings. There are difficulties of at least four kinds. First is the identity of the Son of Man;
second is the identification of the Son of Man with the Messiah; third,
the identification of Jesus with the Messiah and the Son of Man; and
fourth, his foreknowledge of all the things listed in the above sayings.

So far as Jesus himself is concerned, the difficulties are primarily of a
psychological nature. Assuming as we have done that Jesus was fully
human, possessing all of the limitations both intellectual and otherwise
that other human beings do, how is it possible to believe that he plainly
foresaw the events stated so specifically in these sayings? Is there any
way for us to feel that these words were actually spoken by Jesus?

A new light has been thrown on this problem by the use of the Scriptures in the Essene community at Qumran. As noted in an earlier chapter, the intense preoccupation with study of the Scriptures there as a
means of understanding contemporary historical events was taken over
by early Christians, first by John the Baptist, then by Jesus and the
disciples. Moreover, these Essenes and early Christians were not familiar
with our type of exact historical interpretation of the Scriptures. Our
interest in finding out what the original author of a Scripture meant
was entirely foreign to the men of the time of Jesus. Their sole interest
was in what they found in the Scriptures with reference to their own
time and especially to themselves. Nor were they careful in getting a
strict interpretation even in this respect. Drawing inferences from re-
mote similarities and fragmentary statements taken out of contexts in
ways now unacceptable, they had no hesitation in finding two, three or
even more meanings in the same Scripture, with little or no concern
as to the meaning the original author put into the passage. Once we
realize that Jesus himself followed this pattern of interpretation, first
with reference to John, and then concerning himself, we have a foundation for accepting as authentic the sayings of Jesus quoted above.

In an earlier chapter we have seen that Jesus at last accepted from
his disciples the title of Messiah, and that he was greatly strengthened
in his own faith by their strong assurance. It is clear from the passages
quoted in the present chapter that Jesus used Son of Man with refer-

ence to himself. The first of these sayings follows immediately after the notable conversation of Caesarea Philippi in which the disciples declared their faith that Jesus was the Messiah. On the face of it, this association of passages uses Messiah and Son of Man interchangeably, at the same time identifying both with Jesus. We defer consideration of the Son of Man to the following chapter, for the present only noting that Jesus uses that title in all of the above sayings about himself, thus continuing the identification of himself as the Messiah. Let us now rather ask how Jesus arrived at the view that he, the Messiah, the Son of Man, must be rejected and crucified; that he must die and then be raised from the dead.

Without ascribing superhuman knowledge to Jesus, keeping him within the range of human understanding, is it possible to show how he might have acquired these ideas? Can we find in the Scriptures any passage Jesus may have read which would supply the information expressed in these striking sayings?

To ask this question is at the same time to suggest the reply. There is only one passage in the Hebrew Scriptures which contains the ideas suggested in these problematical sayings. The Scripture in question is the famous Suffering Servant poem in Isaiah 52:13–53:12. Anyone who reads this marvelous poem—keeping in mind the possibility that Jesus himself had often read it, meditated upon it, and wondered what it meant, until finally he, as John the Baptist had done when he pondered Isaiah 40:3, found himself in this ancient Scripture, feeling an identification with the Servant there so vividly described—may see that this poem could be the answer. The entire poem follows:

> Behold, my servant shall prosper,
>> he shall be exalted and lifted up, and shall be very high.
> As many were astonished at him—
>> his appearance was so marred, beyond human semblance,
> and his form beyond that of the sons of men—
> so shall he startle many nations;
>> kings shall shut their mouths because of him;
> for that which has not been told them they shall see,
>> and that which they have not heard they shall understand.
>
> Who has believed our report?
>> And to whom has the arm of the Lord been revealed?
> For he grew up before him like a young plant,
>> and like a root out of the dry ground;

he had no form or comeliness that we should look at him,
    and no beauty that we should desire him.
He was despised and rejected by men;
    a man of sorrows, and acquainted with grief;
and as one from whom men hide their faces
    he was despised, and we esteemed him not.

Surely he has borne our griefs and carried our sorrows;
    yet we esteemed him stricken, smitten by God, and afflicted.
But he was wounded for our transgressions,
    he was bruised for our iniquities;
upon him was the chastisement that made us whole,
    and with his stripes we are healed.
All we like sheep have gone astray;
    we have turned everyone to his own way;
and the Lord has laid on him the iniquity of us all.

He was oppressed, and he was afflicted,
    yet he opened not his mouth;
like a lamb that is led to the slaughter,
    and like a sheep that before its shearers is dumb,
so he opened not his mouth.
By oppression and judgment he was taken away;
    and as for his generation, who considered
that he was cut off out of the land of the living,
    stricken for the transgression of my people?
And they made his grave with the wicked
    and with a rich man in his death,
although he had done no violence,
    and there was no deceit in his mouth.

Yet it was the will of the Lord to bruise him;
    he has put him to grief;
when he makes himself an offering for sin,
    he shall see his offspring, he shall prolong his days;
the will of the Lord shall prosper in his hand;
    he shall see the fruit of the travail of his soul and be satisfied;
by his knowledge shall the righteous one, my servant,
    make many to be accounted righteous;
and he shall bear their iniquities.
Therefore I will divide him a portion with the great,
    and he shall divide the spoil with the strong;

    because he poured out his soul to death,
        and was numbered with the transgressors;
    yet he bore the sin of many,
        and made intercession for the transgressors.

The Ancient Meaning

As this poem stands, the Lord's Servant is not identified; unless we read
it in its context, we have no idea to whom it refers. There have been
many theories as to the identity of the Servant, but the most generally
accepted one is that the Servant was the Hebrew people itself. Written
about 550 B.C. by the anonymous prophet ordinarily referred to as
Second Isaiah, the group of poems beginning in Isaiah 40 deals with the
Jews scattered in many parts of the biblical world, far from home, pov-
erty-stricken, suffering, struggling to find a religious meaning in the
catastrophes which had befallen them. In numerous places this author
clearly identifies the Servant as Israel, or Jacob (42:19, 24; 43:1, 10;
44:1, 2), where there can be no doubt the Hebrew people are meant.
Biblical authors were fond of personification; they often spoke of the
Hebrew nation as if it were a single person.

In the above poem the poet develops a new theory of suffering—the
idea of vicarious suffering, the suffering of an innocent person on behalf
of others. Earlier prophets had said calamities came on the Hebrews because they had broken God's covenant; this prophet is saying God has
permitted the Hebrews to suffer innocently on behalf of other nations,
in order to spread the worship of Yahweh; to bring all nations under the
beneficent rule of the true God. The Hebrew who read the poem was
expected to derive from it a new courage, a new self-respect and hope.

It may be that Jesus understood this ancient meaning as well as we
do. Paul could use the reference to the seed of Abraham in Genesis
12:7 with at least three meanings—one was the ancient meaning; another referred to Christ; a third to Christians of his own time (Romans
9:7; Galatians 3:16; 3:29)—with no feeling that it was improper to
find three meanings in the same passage. This was simply the prevailing
method of interpreting the Scriptures among both Jews and Christians,
the Essenes of Qumran and John the Baptist being good examples.
When Jesus stood up to read in the synagogue at Nazareth, he read
Isaiah 61 in the same way, this time finding himself in it (Luke 4:16–
21).

So it is not improbable that the repeated sayings of Jesus anticipating
his rejections, crucifixion, death and resurrection were logical inferences

drawn from his intense feeling of self-discovery and identification with the Servant of the Lord in the great poem of Isaiah 52:13–53:12.

It is true that in the context of the repeated sayings Jesus makes no explicit reference to the suffering Servant poem; but he does quote from it in Luke 22:37, "For I tell you that this scripture must be fulfilled in me, 'And he was reckoned with transgressors'; for what is written about me has its fulfillment." But we do not need to suppose that every Scripture Jesus meditated on, read or quoted to his disciples has been recorded in one of the Gospels. It is unlikely that the Gospels have preserved more than barest fragments of the great body of the sayings of Jesus and the Scriptures he made use of in teaching his disciples.

It is well known that after the death of Jesus his disciples read this Servant poem in Isaiah 52:13–53:12 with a real sense of understanding; Acts 8:26–35 illustrates this. Yet we are not required to conclude that in the light of their new understanding they rewrote the sayings of Jesus to incorporate their view into his words. The view we have proposed has the advantage that it allows the essential integrity of this element of the Gospel tradition, and especially that it permits Jesus to be a man of his time, to read and understand the Scriptures just as did the Essenes and John the Baptist, and various others, both Jews and Christians.

The Servant poem does not specifically mention crucifixion; nor does it expressly say resurrection from the dead; but it is clear that suffering and death are indicated, with a triumph beyond death, and the "three days" or "on the third day" motif is a common idiom for a brief period of time. Crucifixion was a favorite method both Jewish and Roman rulers used to execute rebels. The Maccabean king Alexander Jannaeus (103–76 B.C.) crucified no less than eight hundred Jewish rebels at one time; and during the rebellion of A.D. 66–70 Romans crucified great numbers of Jews who sought to escape from the doomed city of Jerusalem. Now that Jesus had definitely accepted the Messianic role, and had in mind to challenge the hostile Jewish rulers in their stronghold, with his feeling of self-identification with the suffering Servant, he must have had a clear premonition that crucifixion would be his lot.

These sayings of Jesus may indeed have been made more explicit in the tradition after his death, when his crucifixion was well known. We can allow that as a real possibility. But there is no sufficient reason to doubt that at this stage of his career, on his way up to Jerusalem, Jesus had an intimation of what was going to happen; or that the new meaning he found in this Scripture enabled him to press on eagerly toward the holy city.

The Son of Man

At Caesarea Philippi, Jesus welcomes the assurance of Peter, on behalf of the little band of disciples, that he was the Messiah; he pronounced a benediction on Peter for his courage and insight; and went on to affirm that Peter had not acquired this belief from any man, but as a revelation from God. Nevertheless, even after this manifestation of their confidence by the disciples, Jesus did not permit them to inform others that he was the Christ; and as he had been doing all along, he continued to refer to himself as the Son of Man, by all means one of the most puzzling phrases in our Gospels.

The Son of Man is Jesus' favorite self-designation. In the Gospel of Mark, the earliest Gospel, no less than thirteen times he refers to himself as the Son of Man. The references in Mark are as follows:

1. 2:10, "But that you may know that the Son of man has power on earth to forgive sins . . ."

2. 2:27-28, "And he said to them, 'The Sabbath was made for man, not man for the Sabbath; so the Son of man is Lord even of the Sabbath.' "

3. 8:31, "And he began to teach them that the Son of man must suffer many things, and be rejected by the elders and the chief priests and the scribes, and be killed, and after three days rise again."

4. 8:38, "For whosoever is ashamed of me and of my words in this adulterous and sinful generation, of him will the Son of man also be ashamed, when he comes in the glory of his Father with the holy angels."

5. 9:9, "And as they were coming down the mountain, he charged them to tell no one what they had seen, until the Son of man should have risen from the dead."

6. 9:12, "And he said to them, 'Elijah does come first to restore all things; and how is it written of the Son of man, that he should suffer many things and be treated with contempt?' "

7. 10:33, "Behold, we are going up to Jerusalem; and the Son of man will be delivered to the chief priests and the scribes, and they will condemn him to death, and deliver him to the Gentiles."

8. 10:45, "For the Son of man also came not to be served but to serve, and to give his life as a ransom for many."

9. 13:26, "And then they will see the Son of man coming in the clouds with great power and glory."

10. 14:21, "For the Son of man goes as it is written of him, but woe to that man by whom the Son of man is betrayed!"

11. 14:41, "It is enough; the hour has come; the Son of man is betrayed into the hands of sinners."

12-13. 14:61–62, "Again the high priest asked him, 'Are you the Christ, the Son of the Blessed?' And Jesus said, 'I am; and you will see the Son of man sitting at the right hand of Power, and coming with the clouds of heaven.' "

The Q document was probably as old as Mark. In the Q passages quoted by Luke, the Son of Man is used ten times (Luke 6:22; 7:34; 9:58; 11:30; 12:8; 12:10; 12:40; 17:24; 17:26; 17:30). In his parallel to Luke 6:22, in 5:11 Matthew has written "my" in place of Luke's "of the Son of man." The parallel to Luke 12:8 occurs in Matthew 10:32 as "I." Either Matthew has deleted "Son of man" twice or Luke has inserted it into the Q tradition.

In addition to the ten occurrences of the Son of Man in the material Luke has taken from Q, there are five more examples in unique sayings of Luke (18:8; 19:10; 21:36; 22:48; 24:7), giving a total of some fifteen examples in Luke.

Matthew has seven examples of the Son of Man from Q (8:20; 11:19; 12:32; 12:40; 24:27; 24:37; 24:44). Elsewhere, in his independent material, Matthew has another nine passages (10:23; 13:37; 13:41; 16:13; 16:28; 19:28; 24:39; 25:31; 26:2).

Thus there are at least thirty-seven separate occurrences of Son of Man in the first three Gospels, counting parallels but once. There are thirteen in Mark; at least eight in Q; nine independent examples in Matthew; and seven in Luke. Matthew has dropped the expression from Mark 8:31, and possibly from Q as preserved in Luke 6:22 and 12:8. Luke has dropped it from Mark 9:9; 9:12; 10:45; and 14:41, altogether four times; and he may have added the expression to Q in 6:22 and 12:8. Otherwise there is no evidence that Luke has inserted the title into the sayings of Jesus. On the other hand, Matthew has inserted the expression in taking over Mark 8:27; 9:1; 10:29; and 14:1. As noted above, he has dropped the title from Mark 8:31, and possibly from Q material in Luke 6:22 and 12:8.

One conclusion from this summary of references to the Son of Man in the first three Gospels is that their authors show a reasonable fidelity to the sources they used. Matthew and Luke have preserved essentially what lay before them in Mark and Q. Luke dropped more passages than he added; Matthew certainly added four; he clearly dropped one, and possible three. Luke presents five new examples from his unique material; and Matthew adds eight in sayings peculiar to him. The authors of the Synoptic Gospels have not substantially changed what they found in the tradition before them; and there is no stratum of tradition in these Gospels to which the Son of Man is unknown.

The Gospel of John

A similar conclusion is to be drawn from a study of the Gospel of John, where twelve examples of the Son of Man occur (1:51; 3:13; 3:14; 5:27; 6:27; 6:53; 6:62; 8:28; 9:35; 12:23; 12:34; 13:31). Thus John confirms the uniformity of usage in regard to this title of Jesus in the Gospel literature showing that the Son of Man is not peculiar to any particular section or fringe of the early Christian tradition, but is central in all the surviving records. Usually so different from the Synoptic Gospels, with respect to the Son of Man John treads on common ground with his predecessors.

As the four Gospels are thought to represent four different regions of the ancient church, their agreement in using the Son of Man as a title indicates that this phrase was the accepted usage in widely separated communities. The phrase did not grow up and survive only in some obscure corner or sect of the Christian world, as some have contended. The title found a secure place in the tradition very early; in fact it must have belonged to the story of Jesus from the beginning.

Outside of the four Gospels, the phrase occurs only one time, the sole example being in the words of Stephen before the priests, as related in Acts 7:55-56,

> But he, full of the Holy Spirit, gazed into heaven and saw the glory of God, and Jesus standing at the right hand of God; and he said, "Behold I see the heavens open, and the Son of man standing at the right hand of God."

The phrase "*a* son of man" is found in Hebrews 2:6; Revelation 1:13; and 14:14; but beyond the four Gospels *the* Son of Man occurs only in the above mentioned Acts 7:55-56. The Son of Man is foreign to the language of Paul and, with this one exception in Acts, to the vocabulary of the other New Testament writers; the same is true of the early church Fathers. They are familiar with the expression in the Gospels, yet they do not use it except in quoting the words of Jesus.

It is clear therefore that the Son of Man is at home only in the language of Jesus. This explains why the phrase does not occur in Paul and elsewhere outside the Gospels. Paul believes that the Spirit of Jesus inspires him, but, with the exception of two or three allusions (I Corinthians 7:10; 7:25; 11:23–24), he does not quote any of the sayings of Jesus. Presumably for the same reason other New Testament writers are silent with reference to this title; the lone case of the dying Stephen is the exception which proves the rule.

Problems Raised

Ever since scholars began to make a careful study of the Gospels they have been raising difficult questions about the Son of Man. As Jesus uses the phrase, what does it mean? Does it always have the same meaning for him? Does it occur elsewhere in the Bible? If found in other parts of the Bible, what is its usual meaning?

Does this phrase occur in other Jewish literature? Can it be equated with the Messiah? How are we to understand the statement of Jesus that the Son of Man has power on earth to forgive sins? How is the Son of Man lord of the Sabbath? One of the most baffling ideas expressed by Jesus is that the Son of Man sits at the right hand of Power, and will be seen coming on the clouds of heaven. Some scholars have thought that Jesus used this phrase with reference to another person, not referring to himself; that the Son of Man referred to a popular belief of the time about a divine or semi-divine being who was to come, but that Jesus did not identify himself with this heavenly figure. Another theory holds that Jesus never used this phrase, either witth reference to himself or another, but that the words have been inserted into his reported sayings by the imaginative church after his death.

As this title has puzzled so many readers of the Gospels through the centuries, are we to suppose the disciples of Jesus knew what he meant when he so frequently used the term? Did the Jewish enemies know what he was talking about? Did the police sent by Herod Antipas understand this strange expression? Did the Pharisees and scribes from Jerusalem recognize it? If Jesus did habitually use this expression, and as a self-designation, why did the disciples never use it, either in addressing him or in conversations among themselves? If they heard him use this phrase, but did not understand it, why did they not, at least somewhere in the Gospels, show an indication that they did not understand? Why did they not ask Jesus what it meant? It can hardly be adequate to say they were too shy to ask him; they did not hesitate to ask about other things they did not comprehend. Neither the disciples, the multitude, nor the enemies appear to be confused by it. They all take it in their stride.

What we want to know most of all is what the words meant to Jesus. Where did he get them, and why did he choose to use them? Are we able to use them as a key to his own faith, to his understanding of himself? If we are to see Jesus as the pioneer of our faith, is this strange phrase a bit of evidence to be used to good purpose? The insight that Jesus was himself a man of faith, that he was a profound student of the Scriptures, and that he was steadily finding himself more and more in those sacred writings, seems to be the right approach to these uncertainties.

A second insight which follows as a necessary corollary is that Jesus must be allowed to be a man of his time; he thought, felt and believed as other men of his time did. We must not continue to make the mistake of assuming that Jesus looked upon the world as a man of the twentieth century.

Once some of the obsolete forms of thought have been removed and the meanings restated in terms we can understand, the ideas and faith of Jesus have a wonderful universality. Yet he lived in a world of apocalyptic symbols, poetic imagination, Messianic hopes—religious faith expressed in exotic concepts of oriental fiction, demons and angels —now strange, if not unacceptable to modern persons. These were the common ideas of his Jewish culture; and he accepted them without question, just as we take over the ways of thought prevailing in our own world. When we fully grasp this truth about Jesus, allowing him to belong to his own time as we belong to ours, much of the mystery surrounding the Son of Man will vanish, and so naturally that we hardly realize it.

Apocalyptic Symbols

The Son of Man, a title Jesus applies to himself in the third person some forty-nine times in the Gospels, is a phrase he draws from the apocalypses, a type of literature popular among the Hebrews at the end of the Old Testament period. The best examples of this litertaure are Ezekiel and Daniel in the Old Testament; I Enoch from the apocryphal and pseudepigraphic writings never accepted into the biblical canon; and the Revelation of John from the New Testament.

Readers of our time often fail to understand the apocalypses because they find this type of writing unfamiliar and uncongenial. Apocalyptic writings are not to be thought of as historical records, and their language was never intended to be taken as literal matter of fact. The key to understanding the apocalypses is to recognize that they are fiction, and of a fantastic character, at times not entirely unrelated to science fiction.

Fiction is of many types, and writers of fiction usually avoid actual, historical occurrences, preferring to create characters not identified with any living persons. Realistic authors of fiction portray conditions and persons true to life and nature; other writers prefer imaginative themes not corresponding to any reality known to their readers. Thus we have *Gulliver's Travels, Pilgrim's Progress* and *Alice in Wonderland,* all of which are both entertaining and serious pieces of writing. Fables, parables and allegories of various kinds are known in most cultures. Science fiction, popular even in the comics, is another type of writing with a large following. Alley Oop and the time machine, permitting him the excitement of diverse types of space travel, is a comic strip created long before men learned to fly into outer space. However fantastic the cartoonist's concepts and plots, they are understandable to children and adults alike, and are even conversed about seriously, the fantastic becoming accepted, almost normal, when the fantasy appeals to a culture.

Most of the great poetry of the world also belongs to fiction. The epics of Homer, the plays of Shakespeare, and the works of Dante and Milton are clearly in this category. It must not be supposed, therefore, when we classify a writing as fiction, that we thereby depreciate it or cast reflection on it. Fiction may be beautiful; it is often entertaining; sometimes it is highly instructive; it is certainly one of the most effective ways of communicating between author and reader.

An author of fiction may of course deal with historical characters in what we call historical fiction. Some of the plays of Shakespeare are of this type; novelists and dramatists sometimes choose historical characters and real places and events for their otherwise imaginative themes. Yet the outstanding characteristic of fiction is that the authors are free to take liberty with the persons they write about; they make them do and say whatever they choose to have them do and say, and send them any place they wish them to go. It is also possible for an author to cast himself as one of the characters. A novelist may tell his story in the first person. The author of a comic strip may put himself into his drawings. The novelist can make his people do all sorts of things not possible for persons in ordinary life. He can place Robinson Crusoe on a desert island or send Alice into Wonderland; he can dispatch some brave warrior to a distant planet, causing him to ride the wind, a cloud, a sunbeam or a flying saucer. All such literary devices we need to keep in mind as we read the apocalyptic literature of the biblical period, and all terminology drawn from apocalypses into ordinary speech. The Son of Man, as Jesus used the term, can only be understood and appreciated in this setting. Seen in this light, the term never fails to retain something of the poetic beauty, the awe and the mystery of the apocalypses it was drawn from.

Its Primary Meaning

Long before the Son of man achieved its spectacular role in the apocalypses, it had established itself in the plain speech of the people, popular especially in their poetry. The device by which Hebrew poetry is recognized is parallelism. A verse may have two, three, four or more lines. The theme is stated in the first line, and either the same idea rephrased, or its opposite, or a supplementary thought, follows in the subsequent lines. In such poetic contexts, if "man" is used in the first line, it is common to find "son of man" in the second. The following lines from Psalm 8:4 are a good illustration:

> What is man that thou art mindful of him,
> and the son of man that thou dost care for him?

In this couplet "the son of man" obviously means the same as "man." In a technical sense, "son of man" is a metonym for "man," meaning mankind; that is, it is a figure of speech using one attribute or thing associated with an object as a symbolical or poetic name for the object itself. Elsewhere this same idiom occurs in Psalms 80:17; 144:3; 146:3; Numbers 23:19; Job 25:6 and Isaiah 51:12; 56:2.

As an Individual Title

The Prophet Ezekiel is the first example of a man in the Bible addressed as Son of Man, a title applied to him in the course of his book some eighty-seven times. As this book has the form of memoirs, being written in the first person, Ezekiel should have credit for originating the use of this quaint metonym for man as a title or personal appellation, the idiom so popular with Jesus. Yet there is a difference between the use of the phrase by Ezekiel and by Jesus. Ezekiel is addressed by the Lord or by one of the Lord's messengers as Son of Man; that is, Son of Man always stands in the second person; but Jesus ordinarily uses the title in the third person, thus giving the idiom a new variation.

Ezekiel was one of the exiles carried away from Jerusalem by Nebuchadnezzar to Babylon, along with the young king Jehoiachin, in 598 B.C. He was kept well informed about developments in Judea, and so observed the swift movement of his nation toward its catastrophic destruction in 587. The first of his oracles, according to his own system of dating, was uttered in the fifth year of his exile, that is in 592; and the last in 572. The first oracles dealt with the approaching fall of Jerusalem; subsequently the prophet was concerned with problems of the discouraged exiles in Babylonia.

So many features of Ezekiel's book have the apocalyptic style that he is properly regarded as the father of this school of writing among the Hebrews. In the first chapter Ezekiel describes the remarkable vision in which he felt himself called to be a prophet. He sees God enthroned in flaming fire upon a dome supported by four cherubim, each of which had a human body, one head with four faces—a man, an ox, a lion and an eagle—four wings, arms and legs; but the legs and feet were those of a calf, and in addition they had wheels. The creatures were therefore able to walk, run, roll on wheels or fly.

Ezekiel's description makes it clear that he saw images taking shape in whirling storm clouds on a summer day; they were full of lightning flashes, and he heard the continuous rushing of the wind and roar of thunder. He saw God riding in his flaming sky chariot as if jet-propelled across the heavens.

The first vision was by the river Chebar, possibly an irrigation canal in the Euphrates Valley. Later when Ezekiel had been miraculously transported to Jerusalem, he was permitted to witness the departure of the Lord from that doomed city just before it was destroyed by the Babylonians (10:1–11:24). This time the Lord took up the prophet Ezekiel himself into his mysterious chariot and flew away on the wings of the cherubim to join the exiles in Babylon. Nearly twenty years later, after some Hebrews were re-established in Jerusalem, Ezekiel says he saw the Lord return to the holy city in the same fashion (43:1–5).

These visions of Ezekiel, fascinated by what he saw in turbulent clouds, showing how both the Lord and the prophet were borne on supernatural wings through the sky, so stimulated the imaginations of apocalyptic writers that his imagery of traveling on the clouds was never forgotten; and the four strange synthetic creatures supporting God's throne—somewhat akin to Mesopotamian, Egyptian and Greek sphinxes—set a pattern for weird animals in later apocalypses.

The way "son of man" is applied to Ezekiel is shown in the following quotation from 1:28–2:6:

> Such was the appearance of the likeness of the Lord. And when I saw it, I fell on my face, and I heard the voice of one speaking.
> And he said to me, "Son of man, stand upon your feet, and I will speak to you." And when he spoke to me, the Spirit entered into me and set me upon my feet; and I heard him speaking to me. And he said to me, "Son of man, I send you to the people of Israel, to a nation of rebels, who have rebelled against me; they and their fathers have transgressed against me to this very day. The people also are impudent and stubborn: I send you to them; and you shall say to them, 'Thus says the Lord God.' And whether they hear or refuse to hear (for they are a rebellious house) they will know that there has been a prophet among them. And you, son of man, be not afraid of them, nor be afraid of their words, though briers and thorns are with you and you sit upon scorpions . . ."

As Ezekiel does not explain the meaning of "son of man," the title by which the Lord addresses him throughout the book, we are left to infer what it means as he uses it. The key is probably to be found in the fact that only God or another supernatural spokesman addresses the prophet in this way. As we have seen, the phrase is a metonym for man, a word which we still use as a form of address in our contemporary English idiom. We also could say, "Man, stand upon your feet." Obviously the title is intended to call attention to Ezekiel's mortal character as contrasted with God. This is supported by the prominence

Ezekiel gives to his concept of the holiness of God as compared with the profane nature of man. The choice of Son of Man as the favorite title by which God addresses Ezekiel would indicate that the prophet endeavors in this way to express his feeling of humility; at the same time, to indicate the qualitative difference between man and God, the gulf that stands between them. Whatever reason Ezekiel had for selecting the title, his use of it was the beginning of a tradition reflected throughout the school of apocalyptic literature of which he was the founder. All of the apocalypses, like Ezekiel, purport to give revelations from God to man; hence the literary name *apocalypse*, which means a *revelation*.

A Symbol for the Hebrew People

We encounter Son of Man next, together with much more of Ezekiel's symbolism, about four centuries later in the Book of Daniel, an apocalypse written at the time the rebellion of the Maccabeans against the Seleucid kingdom of Syria, about 167 B.C. This book is a collection of episodes in the form of fictional stories, in a literary sense independent of one another, but all held together by the common theme that God will give the Hebrews victory in the heroic struggle if they will keep their faith.

The episode in question is the vision related in chapter 7, which Daniel purports to have seen in the first year of Belshazzar, king of Babylon. In this notable vision, Daniel first sees four terrifying beasts emerge from the sea: a lion with an eagle's wings, a great bear, a leopard with four wings and four heads, and a fourth beast with iron teeth and at first ten, then eleven, then eight horns, one of which has the head of a man. Next thrones are placed and a judge, one Ancient of Days, in white robes and with hair like wool, takes his seat on a throne draped in fiery flames and with wheels of fire, surrounded by thousands of servants.

Record books are immediately opened and the court is in session. The first beast is condemned and executed; the three others are granted a temporary reprieve. Then the story continues in 7:13-14,

> I saw in the night visions,
> and behold, with the clouds, of heaven there came one like a son
> of man,
> and he came to the Ancient of Days and was presented before
> him.

And to him was given dominion and glory and kingdom,
that all peoples, nations, and languages should serve him;
his dominion is an everlasting dominion, which shall not pass
away,
and his kingdom one that shall not be destroyed.

When the bewildered Daniel asked the meaning of these things, an attendant at the throne explained that the four beasts represented four kingdoms, but "that the saints of the Most High shall receive the kingdom, and possess the kingdom forever." It is reasonably clear that the fourth beast against which the saints were struggling was the kingdom of Syria, at the time ruled by Antiochus Epiphanes, who was attempting to destroy Hebrew religion in order to break their rebellious spirit. The earlier beasts appear to have been the Babylonians, the Persians and the Greeks.

In this vision, as in all the other episodes of the book, the theme is the same: if the Hebrews are faithful, God will give them triumph; their kingdom will be restored, never to fall again. In contrast with the earlier kingdoms, each represented by a vicious beast, the Hebrew nation is represented by "one like a son of man." This picturesque symbol does not mean an individual man, but the people.

The marvelous scene of the vision is set in the clouds of heaven, where God has his throne and "one like a son of man" appears before him. All is clearly based on the symbolism of Ezekiel.

A Symbol of the Messiah

Not long after the author of Daniel wrote his memorable stories and visions, a nameless Hebrew poet was inspired by Daniel's vision of "one like a son of man," who appeared before "the Ancient of Days" seated on a fiery throne in the clouds. That unnamed disciple of the author of Daniel wrote most of the beautiful poems now collected in I Enoch 46–71. R. H. Charles, in his great edition of the *Apocrypha and Pseudepigrapha* (1913), calls this book the most important pseudepigraph of the first two centuries B.C., and states that a history of the theology of that period could not be written without it. This is a true estimate.

Here again we come upon the Son of Man, introduced to apocalyptic writers by Ezekiel. But this time the title has attained a new stage of growth. Obviously the author stands under Daniel's influence. Over and over (46:1 ff.) he reflects Daniel's vision of the Ancient of Days seated on a throne in the clouds, when one like a son of man appears before him. However, there is here a great difference. Son of Man has the definite article; he is *the* Son of Man, *the* Elect one, *the* Anointed One. While in Daniel the central figure is God seated on his throne judging the kingdoms of the world and awarding a kingdom to one like a son of man, the Son of Man is now the one who occupies the throne and judges the kings of the earth as they appear before him; he delivers the wicked to punishment and the righteous to salvation.

Several of these poems describe the judgment scene with the Son of Man sitting on the throne of his glory (46:1 ff.; 62:5; 69:27). He judges and punishes wicked angels and evil spirits (55:4) as well as human beings. The Son of Man is no longer merely man, a prophet, or the symbol of the nation, but beyond question the Anointed One, the Messiah; but not the Messiah in a political and military sense, as in days of old. Here he has acquired a more spiritual character. One of his primary functions is to judge the world, a right deriving from his role as king, always the ultimate judge in matters of law affecting his subjects. But another function is also new; he drives out and destroys evil spirits now holding mankind in bondage.

Jesus and the Son of Man

The Son of Man, which Jesus used as his favorite self-designation, had an ancestry going back through Enoch and Daniel to Ezekiel, and beyond to the poetic vernacular of the ancient Hebrews, where it was used as a synonym for man. In the words of Jesus, this phrase retained important overtones from all of its ancestry, and at each step of the way it had acquired new meanings. By the time Jesus adopted the phrase as a way of designating himself, it embodied the very essence of Hebrew faith; and it was probably for that very reason that Jesus found in this title his greatest sense of self-fulfillment.

Like Ezekiel, Jesus identified himself with man, especially with the exploited poor, the needy and sick of the common people. He had no aristocratic connections; he was neither Pharisee, scribe nor priest; his parents were simple people of the land. So from personal experience he knew the lot of the common people. His most caustic sayings were directed at the wealthy and other privileged classes (Matthew 23:1–36); and he spoke with sympathy to the virtually outcast groups, who were scorned by the educated, upper-class religious leaders as unclean sinners, not because they were morally degraded, but because they were unable to keep all requirements of the ceremonial law.

In the parable of the Good Samaritan (Luke 10:29–37) Jesus identifies himself even with the despised Samaritans. Perhaps the outstanding note in the Gospel Jesus preaches is the love of God for every plain person, regardless of his social position. The most convincing expression of his sense of identification with poor and needy persons is his description of the great judgment scene. The Son of Man says to those on his right hand,

Come, O blessed of my Father, inherit the kingdom prepared for you from the foundation of the world; for I was hungry and you gave me food, I was thirsty and you gave me drink, I was a stranger and you welcomed me, I was naked and you clothed me, I was sick and you visited me, I was in prison and you came to me (Matthew 25:34-36).

The close association of the Son of Man with man in the mind of Jesus is clear in the following saying:

The sabbath was made for man, not man for the sabbath; so the Son of man is Lord even of the sabbath (Mark 2:27-28).

This is a pun; it plays on two meanings of Son of Man, indicating a touch of humor evident in several of the epigrams of Jesus. The saying has a Messianic overtone; what it means is not that man—just any man—is Lord of the Sabbath; but that the Son of Man, who is himself a man, also has power and authority to reinterpret the Sabbath.

Another remark of Jesus which has baffled interpreters is that "the Son of Man has power on earth to forgive sins" (Mark 2:10), in which Jesus seems to assume the prerogative of God. But this also should be interpreted in its context as evidence of Jesus' profound interest in the sufferings of ordinary people. What he did in this case was to relieve a man's illness, which in the popular mind was believed to be the result of sin. All early Christian sources testify that both Jesus and his disciples were able to relieve many persons of their illnesses, notably in cases of the mentally ill, at the time believed to be possessed by demons. When healing occurred, it was assumed as a matter of course that the man's sin, whatever it was, had been forgiven. In this sense, both Jesus and the disciples had power to forgive sins. Matthew 18:18-19 states that Jesus gave his disciples power to bind and loose on earth; and John 20:23 gives an interpretation of this as,

If you forgive the sins of any, they are forgiven; if you retain the sins of any, they are retained.

On the Clouds of Heaven

The most difficult sayings of Jesus about himself as the Son of Man
are those which picture him seated on a throne, surrounded by a host
of angels, and coming on the clouds of heaven. It has seemed a psychological impossibility for a human being, fully man as Jesus was, to make
such extraordinary assertions about himself. These sayings have been
regarded as so fantastic as to be incredible. It has been thought, therefore, either that this element in the tradition has been inserted by disciples at a later period in the light of their belief in his resurrection;
or that Jesus was talking about a heavenly Son of Man not identified
with himself.

This difficulty over acceptance of such assertions grows out of failure
to recognize that all the apocalypses are fiction; and that in fiction,
human beings, as well as supernatural beings, are permitted to do
things impossible in the normal routine of life. We need to keep in
mind that Jesus is the heir of a long apocalyptic tradition; that his words
about the Son of Man are freighted with meanings derived from Ezekiel,
the Son of Man who, in his visions, saw not only the Lord but also
himself transported from Babylon to Jerusalem, obviously traveling
through the clouds; Daniel, who represents the Jewish people as a
son of man, presented before the Lord seated on his throne in the
clouds; and the same type of Son of Man imagery, far more developed,
in the poems of Enoch.

We should assume that when Jesus refers to the Son of Man coming
in clouds of heaven, he is using the same poetic imagery; that he is
speaking the language of fiction. Whether the spectacular symbolism
has a concrete meaning in his mind, one cannot say; but that it does not
seem to him fantastic or preposterous is evident.

Nor does such imagery seem unintelligible or abnormal to the
disciples after his time; the story of Jesus' ascension into heaven (Acts
1:9–11) is a popular illustration of the way such ideas were accepted.
More important are various passages in the Letters of Paul. In II Corinthians 12:1–4 he says that he knows a man, meaning himself, who was
caught up to the third heaven; and in I Thessalonians 4:13–18 Paul
predicts the return of Christ and that Christians alive at the time will
be caught up to meet him in the clouds. Paul takes up the symbolism
from Ezekiel to Enoch and gives it a new application to a return of the
Messiah from heaven. The author of the Revelation of John (4:1 ff.)
affirms that he actually went right up into heaven and beheld God

on his throne, surrounded not only by the heavenly court but also by four creatures evolved from the creatures seen by Ezekiel.

It is clear that people of the New Testament period were used to this type of religious fiction; it was to them a normal expression of the wonder of the divine world; it expressed God's sovereign control of history, and their participation in it.

More than any other single person, Jesus immersed himself in the religious traditions of his people and found himself in the Scriptures. He knew the apocalyptic tradition from Ezekiel through Daniel and Enoch, though, of course, he did not limit himself to apocalyptic writings. His use of the Son of Man finds a normal interpretation, if we allow him to be a man of his time.

The Messiah Comes!

Jesus had walked with his disciples all the way from Caesarea Philippi —more than a hundred miles—through Galilee, down the valley of the Jordan to Jericho, and up through the hills to the Mount of Olives. When they arrived at that historic eminence east of Jerusalem, which lay in plain view less than a mile away, he sent two disciples into the village of Bethphage to borrow a donkey. Then he mounted this animal and, in the midst of a tumultuous procession, rode down the hillside, across the Kidron, up the slope beyond and through the gate into the ancient city.

All four of the Gospels record this episode in the life of Jesus (Matthew 21:1-11; Mark 11:1-11; Luke 19:29-44; John 12:12-15). It is therefore not easy to dismiss the incident as a matter of little importance; nor can one well say that it is only a legend created at a later time by an imaginative tradition. If we allow a reasonable reliability to the Gospels, we must agree that the triumphal entry really took place; that Jesus did secure a donkey on the Mount of Olives and ride at the head of a cheering band of admirers into Jerusalem. This was the metropolis where every king of ancient Judah had lived; it was a symbol of the national hopes of the Jewish people; and regardless of where they lived, or how far away, Jerusalem was still the center of their religion.

It is inescapable that this picturesque entry into the old city had some unusual meaning for Jesus. Once we discover that meaning, we may at the same time attain a vantage point from which to understand not only what the people in these last days had come to think about Jesus, but also what he believed about himself.

A Messianic Demonstration

There are convincing indications that Jesus planned his entrance into Jerusalem as a Messianic demonstration; that in this ride into the city on a donkey, accompanied by a cheering procession, he was proclaiming not only to his sympathetic followers, but also to the hostile Pharisees, priests and other leaders of the Jews, as well as to the Roman authorities, that he believed himself to be the fulfillment of the Messianic hopes of his people.

According to the Jewish historian Josephus, writing a generation after Jesus, there was a popular belief around Jerusalem that when the Messiah came he would approach the city from the Mount of Olives. He tells of a rebel leader who gathered a multitude of followers in the wilderness east of Jerusalem and approached the city from the Mount of Olives, where he said that at his command the walls of Jerusalem would fall down and he would then lead his followers through the breach into the city; but his advance on the city was anticipated by the Roman governor Felix, and his force was annihilated.[1]

There could not be a more attractive highway for a royal procession into the city than the road from Jericho rising to the crest of the Mount of Olives, where the ancient city bursts into view. One can see how a popular belief might associate this magnificent approach with the coming of the Messiah. It may be that Jesus was reflecting that popular belief in choosing this route.

The ride on a donkey into the city leading a procession seems deliberately chosen by Jesus because he knew the words of Zechariah 9:9,

> Rejoice greatly, O daughter of Zion!
> Shout aloud, O daugther of Jerusalem!
> Lo, your king comes to you;
> triumphant and victorious is he,
> humble and riding on an ass,
> on a colt the foal of an ass.

Neither Mark nor Luke quotes the Scripture; Matthew gives it (21:5), combining it with the opening lines of Isaiah 62:11; and John 12:12–15 also cites a fragment of Zechariah's words. All the Gospels say that Jesus made his entrance riding a donkey. Matthew has misinterpreted the Scripture, thinking that the poetic repetition means two donkeys, and that Jesus rode them both; yet his misinterpretation is no indication that Jesus misunderstood. He may have selected this method of approaching the city because Zechariah's prediction portrays the ass as a symbol of the king's humility. Under the circumstances, this is a most appropriate expression of the mood of Jesus, for he anticipates only rejection and execution at the hands of his people.

There is evidence of an old custom among the Hebrews for a crown prince to ride an ass in connection with his coronation. When

---

[1] Josephus *War*, II, xiii, 5; *Antiquities*, XX, viii, 6.

King David lay dying, and was informed that his son Adonijah had formed a plot to sieze the throne, he said to his attendants,

> Take with you the servants of your lord, and cause Solomon, my son, to ride on my own mule, and bring him down to Gihon; and let Zadok the priest and Nathan the prophet there anoint him king over Israel; then blow the trumpet, and say, "Long live King Solomon!" (I Kings 1:33–34).

The followers of Jesus took the ride as a Messianic announcement; they spread their garments and branches cut from trees in nearby fields on the path over which he rode. This also had an ancient precedent, illustrated by the coronation of Jehu in 842 B.C. When a prophet sent by Elisha anointed the young Jehu to lead a rebellion against the house of Ahab, loyal men at once spread their garments over the bare steps on which Jehu stood; then they sounded a trumpet and followed him as he rode in his chariot across the Jordan to Jezreel (II Kings 9:13).

The enthusiastic persons with Jesus shouted, "Hosanna! Blessed be he who comes in the name of the Lord! Blessed be the kingdom of our father David that is coming! Hosanna in the highest!" (Mark 11:9–10). They did not specifically hail Jesus as king. But Luke correctly interprets the words of the multitude when he says, "Blessed be the king who comes in the name of the Lord!" (19:38). All the Evangelists are clear that the declaration was meant to be Messianic. If Jesus was finding himself in the Scriptures, as we think, and had Zechariah 9:9 before him, the disciples had correctly divined his thought.

Nevertheless Jesus did not approach Jerusalem leading an army. He was not like the Egyptian prophet mentioned by Josephus, whose army was destroyed by Felix before it reached its destination. Jesus had no military intentions; he did not intend to sack Jerusalem; nor did he expect to sit on a political throne. He came with an entirely different conception of the Messiah; and the Kingdom of God of which he spoke was not the Jewish nation then ruled by the descendants of Herod and the governors of Rome.

Prophetic Precedents

This view may seem to leave us with the surprising ride of Jesus on a donkey into Jerusalem as an unsolved problem; and from a modern point of view this would be true. Yet if we search Hebrew history and culture for precedents, we discover that what Jesus did fits into an ancient and well-recognized pattern of conduct. The way Jesus proclaimed his Messiahship to Jerusalem belongs to the category of conduct called "a sign," an established form of communication in Hebrew culture. It was an emphatic way of expressing a faith. Many of the old prophets used it; and Jesus chose to make his entry into Jerusalem a sign of his own Messianic faith.

The use of names to express a faith was very common. Almost all Hebrew names had a specific meaning; they often referred to a significant incident in the life of an individual, a family or the people. About 740 B.C. the prophet Hosea spoke with intense feeling of his premonition of the approaching fall of Israel at the hands of the terrible Assyrians. He felt that this destruction of Israel was a punishment God was sending on the people because of their lack of fidelity and moral integrity, not hesitating to criticize the reigning dynasty for its decadence. The founder of that dynasty was Jehu, who seized the throne in 842 B.C. after murdering the kings of Israel and Judah and many of Israel's royal family. Jehu's violence began at Jezreel. Hosea expressed his condemnation of that bloodshed by naming his son Jezreel (Hosea 1:4). Another of his children, a girl, he named "Not Pitied" (1:6), to remind Israel of his prophetic faith that the nation was doomed to destruction. Then he named a third child, a boy, "Not My People" (1:8), attempting to convey to the nation his certainty that God would disown them because they had broken the ancient covenant.

This custom of using the names of children as prophetic signs was taken over from Hosea by Isaiah, his younger contemporary of Judah, who was also preoccupied with the Assyrian menace, but to a lesser extent also with Israel and Syria. He was so certain that his land would be devastated and its people carried away that he named his first son "A Remnant Shall Return," suggesting that only a few would survive and find their way home (7:3). At another time of great danger, he pictured his people in flight by writing on a tablet "The Spoil Speeds; the Prey Hastes," and then gave this name to another son (8:3). Again, when the nation was threatened by the combined forces of Israel and Syria, Isaiah named a child Immanuel (7:14). The name means "God Is with Us," and it represented the steady faith of Isaiah; he urged Judah always to rely solely on God for defense, not on horses and chariots.

The most graphic sign that Isaiah gave was in protest against an alliance with Egypt (20:2–4). He stripped himself naked and walked barefoot through the streets of Jerusalem for three and a half years, certainly one of the most dramatic signs of a prophet's message on record.

A century later, after Assyria had been overthrown by Babylon, Jeremiah was the great prophet at Jerusalem. In league with Edom, Moab, Ammon, Tyre and Sidon, the truculent rulers of Judah prepared to defy the powerful Nebuchadnezzar. But the wise Jeremiah knew the folly of such an effort and urged his people to submit to the Babylonians. Only in this way, he believed, could they survive; and this was God's will for them (27:1–22). To reinforce his prophecy, Jeremiah made for himself an ox-yoke and wore it around his own neck in Jerusalem; thus he indicated that wisdom required Judah and her weak allies to accept the yoke of Babylon.

Only a few years later (587 B.C.), while Jerusalem was under siege by the Babylonians, Ezekiel shaved off his beard and the hair of his head (5:1–12). Carefully weighing this hair, he divided it into three parts; a third he burned in the midst of the city when the siege was finished; a third he cut into small pieces round about the city; and the other third he scattered to the wind. Thus he proclaimed not only the imminent destruction of the city, but also the way his people would either be destroyed or scattered in exile.

On another occasion, when Ezekiel's wife died, he did not go into mourning or show signs of his sorrow. Asked by the people what the strange conduct meant, Ezekiel explained that his action was a sign of how they should act when they heard that Jerusalem had fallen, and that their sons and daughters left behind there had been slain (24:15–27).

The Symbolical Action

It is well known that Jesus had a gift for colorful language; his parables are the most famous in the world, and the same is true of his shorter sayings. The expressiveness of his metaphors, metonyms, similes, hyperboles, is hardly matched in any literature; and his paradoxes and epigrams are almost unparalleled. But it has not been so clearly recognized that Jesus was equally skillful in the choice of dramatic symbolical actions, the type of communication we should recognize in his ride into Jerusalem on an ass. The ancient prophets would have called this action a sign to the disciples and the people of Jerusalem; in our modern idiom it would be a dramatized parable, the articulation of his faith by means of action rather than speech, a visual expression of his intention. Any ceremonial procession has a dramatic character; it is a way of saying things by a calculated choice of living symbols and carefully selected actions. Such a movement has something of the character of a charade or a pantomine. Without saying expressly what it means, the actor leaves it to those who observe the action to discern its allegorical meaning. Once spectators have in this way comprehended the point of the action, its meaning is impressed forever on their minds.

The meaning of the action was not difficult to perceive; nor did Jesus mean it to be. The ride on the donkey, according to the prophet's words, represented the maturity of Jesus' understanding of himself. There had been a time when he struggled over the Messianic question. At first his disciples had little intimation of what he hoped to do. A few of the mentally deranged began to hazard their conjecture that he was the Messiah. The most trusted disciples had not found courage to express their conviction until, at Caesarea Philippi, Jesus asked them pointedly who they thought he was; but their confident answer gave him the assurance he needed. With a new courage, he immediately set out for Jerusalem at the head of the fearful little band. For three days he led them toward the dangers of the holy city. All the time he must have been planning the dramatic Messianic annunciation. The strength of his conviction was evident from the courageous ride, like a crown prince, into the defiant capital; and the public character of his symbolic action made his Messianic commitment irrevocable. Defenseless as he was, and as he had intended to be, Jesus would now meet his enemies. Quickly he would be in their hands; and, as he had foreseen, their action would be swift and inexorable.

The Money-changers

The triumphal entry into Jerusalem fell on a Sunday, the day we now call Palm Sunday, late in the afternoon. With characteristic brevity, Mark records that Jesus made a preliminary visit into the temple,

> And he entered into Jerusalem, and went into the temple; and when he had looked round at everything, as it was already late, he went out to Bethany with the twelve (Mark 11:11).

Despite his brevity, Mark has said a great deal. Jesus went into the temple courts and quickly but carefully observed what was going on. Sunday was a regular work day, the Jewish Sabbath being Saturday, the day before; business was going on as usual. But the procession arrived in the city when commercial activity for the day was almost over. Twilight is short in Jerusalem, and darkness comes swiftly. At the time of Jesus there were of course no street lamps; when night came everyone went home. No doubt the shops and concessions operating within the temple courts began to close while Jesus was inspecting them. Mark says that Jesus and the twelve then returned to Bethany, another village on the Mount of Olives, where they spent the night.

Mark does not say how Jesus felt at the time about his discovery in the temple. He must have returned to his lodgings in Bethany pondering the Scriptures which he felt described the very business operations he had found: the lack of concern for the spiritual purpose of the temple; avarice motivating transactions at the tables where money was being changed and at the concessions selling animals for sacrifices. That this desecration of the holy place had a profound effect on Jesus is shown by what follows.

On the next day, Monday, Jesus and the twelve went back to Jerusalem,

> And he entered the temple and began to drive out those who sold and those who bought in the temple, and he overturned the tables of the money-changers, and the seats of those who sold pigeons; and he would not allow anyone to carry anything through

the temple. And he taught, and said to them, "Is it not written, 'My house shall be called a house of prayer for all the nations?' But you have made it a den of robbers" (Mark 11:15-17).

As often elsewhere, Matthew (21:12-17) and Luke (19:45-48), following Mark as their source, have modified his account in rewriting it. Both have dropped Mark's statement that Jesus returned to Bethany for the night, postponing to the next day his action against the money-changers. Instead they have Jesus drive out the dealers as soon as he enters the temple on Sunday afternoon. This may have been only editorial looseness on their part, feeling that Mark's report of the seemingly trivial incident of the return to Bethany was unnecessary to the story; hence they omitted it. But Mark's account is probably the correct version.

The cleansing of the temple is also recorded by John, but with variations. The most conspicuous is the time of its occurrence. Somewhat parallel to Mark, he tells of the triumphal entry in 12:12-15, but he has already recorded driving the traders and shopkeepers from the temple in 2:13-17. It is barely possible that John is correct in placing this incident at the beginning of the career of Jesus, the first time he went to Jerusalem during his ministry. He is the only one to state that Jesus made several trips to Jerusalem; the other Gospels mention only one, and that during the last week of his life. It seems probable, however, that Mark's chronology is correct and that John is reporting the same incident described by Mark. Apparently John felt that the cleansing of the temple belonged at the beginning of the ministry; that Jesus would not have tolerated such desecration of the temple as he found there, and would have driven out the money-changers as soon as he discovered them, on his first visit.

John has also added the detail that Jesus used a scourge to drive men and animals from the temple courts. His account follows,

The Passover of the Jews was at hand, and Jesus went up to Jerusalem. In the temple he found those who were selling oxen and sheep and pigeons, and money-changers at their business. And making a whip of cords, he drove them all, with the sheep and oxen, out of the temple; and he poured out the coins of the money-changers and overturned their tables. And he told those who sold pigeons, "Take these things away; you shall not make my Father's house a house of trade." His disciples remembered that it was written, "Zeal for thy house will consume me" (John 2:13-17).

Scriptures Jesus Read

Jesus left the temple that Sunday evening deeply agitated by what he found. As on so many other important occasions of his life, we think, he turned to the Scriptures for the meaning of what he had seen and in search of motivation for his own actions. He was deeply convinced that both the mission upon which he had entered and the events in which he was participating day by day were fulfilling specific sayings imbedded in the ancient writings. This sense of the constant fulfillment of Scripture in himself, right before his own eyes, was one of the most powerful elements in his experience.

Fragments of the ancient writings preserved by the Evangelists give us some idea of the passages of Scripture which came to the mind of Jesus that evening as he walked out of the temple, back across the Kidron Valley, up the Mount of Olives, and over to the village of Bethany.

Mark writes that when Jesus saw the commercial traffic carried on in the temple courts the next day—that is, on Monday morning—he was infuriated and would not allow anything to be carried through the sacred precincts; and that he taught and said, "Is it not written, 'My house shall be called a house of prayer for all the nations?' but you have made it a den of robbers." And this same quotation, slightly modified, is repeated by both Matthew and Luke (Mark 11:17; Matthew 21:13; Luke 19:46).

The first part of this Scripture, "My house shall be called a house of prayer for all the nations," is a quotation from Isaiah 56:7; the second part, "But you have made it a den of robbers," is from Jeremiah 7:11. Jesus joined the two together tellingly as he drove the terrified merchants and dealers from the temple.

Of course, Jesus knew that money-changers were necessary, probably in the temple courts, for the convenience of pilgrims who came to worship at the temple. According to Jewish law, every male Jew was required to pay an annual tax of one-half shekel to the temple, and this had to be in Jewish coin. Many of them undoubtedly made cash gifts in addition. Those coming from far away lands, even residents of Palestine, normally carried in their wallets only coins bearing the image of a ruler; most coins at the time of Jesus bore the face of Tiberius Caesar. It was unlawful to cast such coins into the temple treasury. Therefore it was necessary for worshippers to get their money changed into Jewish coins before they could pay their taxes or make their gifts.

This Jewish law made it necessary for money-changers to be available, either in the temple courts or nearby.

In a similar way, pilgrims coming from a distance found it convenient to purchase animals for sacrifice in the courts or at least in the city. It was inconvenient if not impossible to bring animals the long distances these pilgrims traveled. Many came from Egypt and farther west in North Africa; others from Mesopotamia, Asia Minor, and Greece; some from as far away as Rome. Traffic in animals in and around the temple was therefore essential.

Nevertheless Jesus saw a difference between the modest necessary operations of money-changers and merchants and the elaborate trans-actions he observed in the temple courts. It was clear that dealers were motivated by gain rather than service to the pilgrims. The exploitation Jesus saw aroused his wrath; he was provoked by the avarice evident on all sides. Hence his charge that the concessionaires had transformed the House of God into a den of robbers. Devout pilgrims coming into the temple, inspired by emotions associated with the holy place and by their meditations on the way up to the House of God, suddenly found themselves the prey of greedy merchants, such as travelers today still encounter in the marketplaces of many a Near Eastern city.

The Violent Scene

The Gospels make it clear that the scene was marked by violence. John describes it more vividly than the others. Mark said that Jesus cast out those engaged in selling and buying, overturned the tables of the money-changers, and would not permit anyone to carry vessels through the temple. Even this description is enough to indicate that Jesus' actions created a panic in the temple courts. But John gives a more realistic description of the incident; he says that Jesus made a whip of cords, and drove out the oxen and sheep, as well as the money-changers and traders.

Anyone experienced in driving animals will visualize what happened when Jesus began to strike the cattle and sheep with his whip: they lunged about to escape the lash. The bleating of the sheep and goats and the bellowing of cattle must have terrified the throng in the temple courts. This was no ordinary occurrence. It is unlikely that the people there, whether dealers or pilgrims, had ever experienced anything like it in the temple courts.

The priests of the temple and the teachers of the law who heard and witnessed the violent action were infuriated. Not yet daring to lay hands on Jesus, they began to plot his destruction. They feared the people, who were impressed by the courage Jesus displayed; so no one interrupted him as he defied the authorities of the temple, challenged its commercialization, and reaffirmed the holiness of the sacred place. Whatever they wished to do, the leaders did nothing that day, and Jesus and his disciples, unmolested, returned to Bethany for the night.

A Messianic Sign

To some extent Jesus found precedents for his action in the ancient Hebrew prophets. He must have been inspired by Amos' denunciations of the rituals of Bethel and Samaria more than seven centuries before (5:21–24):

> I hate, I despise your feasts,
>   and I take no delight in your solemn assemblies.
> Even though you offer me your burnt offerings and cereal offerings,
>   I will not accept them, and the peace offerings of your fatted beasts
>   I will not look upon.
> Take away from me the noise of your songs;
>   to the melody of your harps I will not listen.
> But let justice roll down like waters,
>   and righteousness like an ever-flowing stream.

This insight into the superficial forms of the ancient rituals must have found a warm response in Jesus, yet there was much more in his action than anything Amos found courage to do at Bethel and Samaria. The eighth-century prophet had courage to denounce, but he did not dare to disrupt the proceedings; he did not drive traders and concessionaires from the shrines.

Also more than 700 hundred years before the time of Jesus, Isaiah said to worshippers in the temple of Solomon at Jerusalem (1:10–13):

> Hear the word of the Lord,
>   you rulers of Sodom:
> Give ear to the teachings of our God,
>   you people of Gomorrah:
> "What to me is the multitude of your sacrifices?" says the Lord:
> "I have had enough of burnt offerings of rams
>   and the fat of fed beasts;
> I do not delight in the blood of bulls,
>   or of lambs, or of he-goats.

"When you come to appear before me,
   who requires of you this trampling of my courts?
Bring no more vain offerings;
   incense is an abomination to me."

Isaiah delivered that famous denunciation probably at the very place where Jesus walked that day in the temple of Herod; and Jesus must have been familiar with Isaiah's ringing words, and responded to them. Yet Isaiah by no means went as far as Jesus did. He did not drive the animals, the traders, the hypocritical priests, from their positions. There was a different feeling of authority in Jesus from anything observable in Amos or Isaiah.

Jesus' prototypes on that occasion were not the prophets but the kings of Israel. Only they had authority and power to do violent things. While it was Isaiah who delivered scathing denunciations of the empty rituals of the temple, it was his king, Hezekiah, about 700 B.C., who with acts of violence purged that holy shrine. The historian records,

> He removed the high places, and broke the pillars, and cut down the Asherah. And he broke in pieces the bronze serpent that Moses had made, for until those days the people of Israel had burned incense to it (I Kings 18:4).

Only a king could do such things.

An even more spectacular example was King Josiah in 621 B.C., who carried out the most sweeping reform in the history of Hebrew religion. When this young king came to the throne, and had been instructed in the Law of Moses, he was amazed to discover rites of Baal and Asherah, Canaanite deities, flourishing in the temple of Solomon along with the worship of Yahweh. Indeed, licentious sex rites were carried on there in the name of religion.

> And he broke down the houses of the cult prostitutes which were in the house of the Lord, where the women wove hangings for the Asherah (II Kings 23:7).

Moreover he carried out his vigorous reformation throughout all his dominions.

The action of Jesus was not so extreme as that of Hezekiah and Josiah, but he employed the same principle of authority; he did not hesitate to use violence in ridding the temple precincts of the avaricious traders and their offensive merchandise. No other deed of Jesus more clearly indicated his sense of a Messianic, a royal authority. By this act he displayed that sense of mission and destiny for all Jerusalem to see, to friend and foe alike.

Nonviolence

Jesus undoubtedly used violence in driving the money-changers from the temple. However the Gospels vary in details, they all agree that Jesus expelled the money-changers and merchants by force (Matthew 21:12-17; Mark 11:15-19; Luke 19:45-48; John 2:13-22). Mark says Jesus would not allow anyone to carry a vessel through the temple. John adds that Jesus made a whip, and drove out all the offenders, including sheep and cattle; then he poured out the money-changers' coins and overturned their tables. What guards the temple priests had on duty that day, we do not know; ordinarily the Romans kept a garrison in the Tower of Antonio overlooking the temple, to keep a watch on the streams of pilgrims, turbulent political groups and agitators of various kinds, who passed in and out of the temple courts. But neither Jewish guards nor Roman soldiers were alert enough to prevent the surprise action of Jesus.

The brief accounts in the Gospels are too fragmentary to give a realistic picture of what took place. It seems clear that Jesus' action produced such astonishment and fright among dealers, pilgrims and priests that no organized restraint was able to intervene. In our imagination we can picture the scene of confusion which quickly developed into a riot, bringing the temple activities of that remarkable day to a close.

Turn the Other Cheek

The incident of the money-changers raises an important question about a moral principle in the teachings of Jesus. It is generally supposed that Jesus was opposed to use of violence in any form whatever; that he criticized the Old Testament because of the large place it gives to violence, and in its place proclaimed the new principles of turning the other cheek and loving your enemies.

These generalities should be examined closely. His principle of turning the other cheek is set forth in the following passage:

> You have heard that it was said, "An eye for an eye and a tooth for a tooth." But I say to you, Do not resist one who is evil. But

if anyone strikes you on the right cheek, turn to him the other also; and if anyone would sue you and take your coat, let him have your cloak as well; and if anyone forces you to go one mile, go with him two miles. Give to him who begs from you, and do not refuse him who would borrow from you (Matthew 5:38-42).

Jesus' famous words about how to treat enemies are as follows:

You have heard that it was said, "You shall love your neighbor and hate your enemy." But I say to you, Love your enemies and pray for those who persecute you, so that you may be sons of your Father who is in heaven; for he makes his sun rise on the evil and the good, and sends rain on the just and on the unjust. For if you love those who love you, what reward have you? Do not even the tax-collectors do the same? And if you salute only your brethren, what more are you doing than others? Do not even the Gentiles do the same? You, therefore, must be perfect, as your heavenly Father is perfect (Matthew 5:43-48).

Hyperbole and Paradox

The starting place in interpreting a piece of writing is an examination of its literary form and style. There are many different kinds of writing, ranging all the way from history books and news dispatches to stories like *Alice in Wonderland* and *Huckleberry Finn*, from scientific treatises to lyrical poetry. Furthermore, gifted writers often make use of figures of speech, for the sake of emphasis and to add picturesqueness to what they say. That is true of Jesus, especially in the passages quoted above, which are pervaded by hyperbole and paradox.

"Hyperbole" is exaggeration for emphasis. It is common in ordinary conversation, often overdone. Properly used, it is an overstatement of such character that it arouses attention and clings in the memory. "Paradox" is not the same as hyperbole, but in some respects is similar to it. It is a saying which on the surface is a contradiction; but when given close attention and its depth penetrated, it yields a profound truth. Both of these figures are illustrated in these astounding words of Jesus:

If anyone comes to me and does not hate his own father and mother and wife and children and brothers and sisters, yes, and even his own life, he cannot be my disciple (Luke 14:26).

This is a most extreme statement. Can anyone believe Jesus meant that one of his disciples should *hate* his own family? The saying is a hyperbole in the sense that on the face of it, it is extreme; and we can understand it only when we realize that it is also a paradox. Jesus certainly never taught that we should hate anyone. So it is necessary to look more deeply into these words. Love gets its meaning from the understanding, loyalty and affection within the inner circle of the family. For Jesus to say we must hate our family, is therefore a paradox, a contradiction in terms, a sheer psychological impossibility. Jesus of course knew that. He uses the paradox and hyperbole to shock us, to cause us to listen, to drive home his point. What he really means is that one must put God first; our sense of duty, of what is right and what is wrong, must take precedence over everything else in life—even over the wishes of parents, wife, brothers, sisters and children. Thus understood, Jesus never uttered a more profound truth.

In the same way, Jesus used hyperbole when he said we must not resist an evil person; that we must give him whatever he asks for and more. In a literal sense his injunction to this effect is also unrealistic and impractical. Jesus means that we should always be men of peace and practice charity, but not that we should deliberately give what we own to every highwayman or beggar.

When Jesus tells us to love our enemies, he knows he is telling us to do something which, in the nature of the case, we cannot literally do. It is impossible for us to have the same powerful feeling of sympathy and affection for those who are seeking to destroy us, our family or our nation that we have for our own flesh and blood. Jesus uses the wonderful word "love," which gets its meaning from the intimate relationships of our families, in his effort to explain the high sense of justice a Christian should hold even toward enemies. This is probably the greatest test of Christian morality, and Jesus uses extreme language in attempting to emphasize it.

Some of the sayings of Jesus ought to put us on guard against committing him to a philosophy of absolute nonviolence. They make him seem to say just the opposite. For example,

> Do not think that I have come to bring peace on earth; I have not come to bring peace, but a sword. For I have come to set a man against his father, and a daughter against her mother, and a daughter-in-law against her mother-in-law; and a man's foes will be those of his own household (Matthew 10:34–36).

One time Jesus told a story about an unfaithful steward. It concludes as follows:

But if that wicked servant says to himself, "My master is delayed," and begins to beat his fellow servants, and eats and drinks with the drunken, the master of that servant will come on a day when he does not expect him and at an hour when he does not know, and will punish him, and put him with the hypocrites; there men will weep and gnash their teeth (Matthew 24:48–51).

The use of this story as a lesson to his own disciples shows the kind of fidelity Jesus expected of them, if they broke faith, the kind of punishment they would receive.

Equally impressive is the parable of ten maidens who went to a wedding. Five of the thoughtless girls failed to carry an extra supply of oil, so their lamps went out. While they went to purchase more, the groom arrived, the doors of the house were locked, and the wedding began. The unhappy girls returned and knocked frantically at the door, but to no avail; they were turned away. No mercy was shown (Matthew 25:1–13).

Or consider Jesus' denunciation of the Pharisees;

Woe to you, scribes and Pharisees, hypocrites! for you build the tombs of the prophets and adorn the monuments of the righteous, saying, "If we had lived in the days of our fathers, we would not have taken part with them in shedding the blood of the prophets." Thus you witness against yourselves, that you are some of those who murdered the prophets. Fill up, then, the measure of your fathers. You serpents, you brood of vipers, how are you to escape being sentenced to hell? (Matthew 23:29–33).

Sayings like these show that Jesus did not mean to suggest that evil men should be allowed to roam at large, with no just power to stop their crimes. He knew that a civilized society must have a police; that theft and rape and murder must be restrained by force.

It was not unusual for Jesus to utter a saying which combined a tender appeal with a threat of a violent end to those who refused to accept it. Note the following:

O Jerusalem, Jerusalem, killing the prophets and stoning those who are sent to you! How often would I have gathered your children together as a hen gathers her brood under her wings, and you would not! Behold, your house is forsaken and desolate (Matthew 23:37–38).

Jesus and Caesar

One reason readers of the Bible misinterpret the sayings about turning the other cheek and loving your enemies is their failure to recognize that Jesus is speaking in figures of hyperbole and paradox. But another, fully as important, is failure to keep in mind that Jesus held no position in the political government of his time. He was not an emperor, a king, a legislator or a judge. Jesus lived in the small Jewish state of Judea, a minor part of the Roman empire. True, the Romans tried to rule it by using native Jewish princes; the dynasty of the Herods was of this type; they were "collaborators," never fully trusted by either Romans or Jews; and their kingdom would now be called a satellite state. But Jesus was not even a Roman citizen. In only exceptional cases were provincials like the Jews granted citizenship, and there is no indication that Jesus enjoyed that privilege. The apostle Paul, from the Hellenistic city of Tarsus, was a Roman citizen, but that was unusual for a Jew (Acts 22:25-29).

When Jesus formulated the principles set forth in the Gospels, there is no evidence that he was thinking of repudiating either the Roman law code or that of the Jewish state. Jesus lived under the codes of civil and criminal law the Jews had built up from ancient times; and he said clearly,

> Think not that I came to abolish the law and the prophets; I have come not to abolish them but to fulfill them (Matthew 5:17).

The law Jesus mentioned here included all Hebrew regulations in regard to crimes of every sort, together with the penalties inflicted; and he fully subscribed to them all. In an ultimate sense, this applies also to the Roman code, which then in certain ways superseded Jewish law.

In our time, the position of Christians in regard to the state is far different; we are now in a position parallel to that of the Romans in the days of Jesus. The highest position in our nation is occupied by a Christian; seats in the highest courts are held by Christians; senators, representatives, governors and judges are in most cases Christians. The laws by which we live are made by Christians. It is difficult for us to grasp the restricted political liberties and responsibilities under which Jesus lived; he did not even have a right to vote. The laws were handed down by tradition or imposed by a foreign authority; nevertheless he showed no intention to scorn, to disregard or to disobey them.

What Jesus said about the treatment of enemies and criminals therefore must be viewed in this larger setting of the laws under which he lived. Both in the acts of the temporal government and of the eternal God, the great judge of all men, force and violence were given a conspicuous place; they were considered apt and necessary in the administration of justice, human and divine. Some of the parables clearly show that Jesus accepted these principles; and in driving out the money-changers, for a brief time he took the administration of justice into his own hands, also finding the use of force necessary.

The sayings about turning the other cheek and loving enemies must have referred to actions of his disciples not as government officials or soldiers but as individuals in their private civilian roles. Even then the principles had to be first extracted from the extreme forms of hyperbole and paradox Jesus gave them, and restated as injunctions to practice justice toward both the criminal and the enemy. In that light the ethical principles of Jesus apply also to Christian officials of the state in any age. And Jesus meant to say that real Christian morality, whether private or public, will always be characterized by charity and generosity which temper justice with mercy.

Poverty

The Gospels report that during the turbulent last days in Jerusalem Jesus left the ancient city every evening to find lodging for the night ouside (Mark 11:19). Luke 21:37 notes that he went to the Mount of Olives; Matthew 21:17 gives the location of the place where Jesus spent the night more exactly, the village of Bethany, located just over the Mount of Olives from Jerusalem.

These writers do not say why Jesus left the city, but the reason is not difficult to infer. The old city of Jerusalem is small; it is completely enclosed by a wall, and the space for residence within is severely limited. It must have been difficult for visitors, especially strangers from a distance, to find hospitality in the city. Moreover, as a result of his ejection of the money-changers from the temple and other conflicts with the authorities, so much hostility was engendered against Jesus that both he and his disciples might have been in danger, had they chosen to remain inside the walls overnight. We do not know whether Jesus had friends residing in the city, although it is probable that he did; in any case rising hostility would have made them hesitant to open their houses to him for fear of being brought under suspicion. It is probable, therefore, that the only possibility of finding food and shelter for the nights was outside the walls.

This does not explain why Jesus went to Bethany. No doubt there were small villages nestling about Jerusalem on all sides offering similar facilities to travelers. But the choice of Bethany stems from the fact that he had good friends there. As we have noted, when Jesus passed over the Mount of Olives coming up from Jericho on Palm Sunday, he paused long enough to send his disciples into Bethany to borrow a donkey, which he rode into the city. Jesus must have had a good friend in that village, otherwise it is difficult to understand how his messengers found the owner of the animal ready to send the donkey at once in response to this unusual request (Mark 11:1–11). However, Mark has not identified the animal's owner, nor have we any way of knowing who the generous man was.

Yet we do know the names of at least two households in Bethany

where Jesus had good friends. One of these was a leper named Simon
(Mark 14:3–9), who once entertained Jesus for dinner in his home.
He was evidently a man of some eminence, and some of his guests
were well to do. While Jesus, according to the custom, reclined on a
rug during the meal, an unnamed woman startled the other guests by
breaking a flask of expensive ointment and anointing the head of Jesus
—an act which aroused indignation on the part of some of those
present. She must have been a person of means to possess such ointment
and to express her feeling for Jesus in this extravagant way. But Jesus
spoke to her kindly, defending her manifestation of feeling on the
ground that she had an intuition of the suffering he was about to
undergo.

The other known friends of Jesus in Bethany were Lazarus and his
sisters Mary and Martha, reported in John 12:1–9. In some respects
this story is remarkably similar to that just noted in Mark. According
to John, it is Mary, one of the sisters of Lazarus, who anoints Jesus with
an expensive perfume; but she anoints his feet rather than his head, and
then wipes his feet with her hair. The stories are so similar that one
wonders whether they may not be two traditions of the same event. If
so, it would mean that Lazarus is to be identified with Simon the leper,
although there is no good reason otherwise for making that identification. The details of the two anointings are by no means identical; it is
therefore more probable that they are records of separate incidents, each
of which reflects the ancient custom of Hebrew hospitality, in which
an honored guest was anointed with a perfume. Jesus may well have
enjoyed such recognition in Bethany on two occasions.

In Bethany Jesus would find a welcome, escape from the stifling heat
of the city, safety from its growing hostility, refuge in a comfortable
home, and refreshment in the cool breezes of the Mount of Olives.
There he could recover his strength and be ready for the conflicts and
dangers he would certainly face the next day.

Peripatetic Teachers

What we see so clearly in the living arrangements for Jesus and the
disciples during this last week of his life in Jerusalem is actually an
illustration of the way they lived throughout the years of his ministry;
and the disciples continued this type of life for a number of years in
the early church. Jesus was an itinerant teacher. He went from house
to house, from village to village, from one region to another, never
staying long in the same place; and wherever he went he asked for and

usually received hospitality from persons interested in the work he was doing.

Traces of this practice appear from time to time in the Gospels. At the very beginning of his ministry, according to Mark 1:29–34, Jesus entered the house of Simon and Andrew at Capernaum, and made his headquarters there until he finished his work in that place; and he apparently returned to the same home some days later (Mark 2:1). On another occasion he was received into the home of Levi a tax collector (Mark 2:13–17). Only once he is reported to have gone back to his own home at Nazareth (Mark 6:1–6), and his stay there was brief. While in Phoenicia, he was entertained in a home near Tyre and Sidon, but the owner's name is not mentioned (Mark 7:24).

Such practices were the customs of Jesus and his disciples. His feeling on this matter is shown by the instructions given to the twelve on sending them out,

> He charged them to take nothing for their journey except a staff; no bread, no bag, no money in their belt; but to wear sandals and not to put on two tunics. And he said to them, "Where you enter a house, stay there until you leave the place. And if any place will not receive you and they refuse to hear you, when you leave, shake off the dust that is on your feet for a testimony against them" (Mark 6:8–11).

To the seventy sent out on another occasion, his words were even more specific,

> Whatever house you enter, first say, "Peace be to this house!" And if the son of peace is there, your peace shall rest upon him; but if not, it shall return to you. And remain in the same house, eating and drinking what they provide, for the laborer deserves his wages; do not go from house to house. Whenever you enter a town and they receive you, eat what is set before you; heal the sick in it, and say to them, "The kingdom of God has come near you" (Luke 10:5–9).

Jesus felt that he had a right to hospitality, and there is no indication that he followed any other practice. This was the way he obtained lodging and food. It is true that occasionally the itinerant disciples were refused hospitality. In such cases they kicked off the very dust from their feet in a gesture of protest.

A century later wandering teachers had become a problem, and the churches had to regulate their enjoyment of hospitality.

Let every Apostle who comes to you be received as the Lord, but let him not stay more than one day, or if need be a second as well; but if he stay three days he is a false phophet.[1]

No Place to Lay His Head

Jesus was known to his old neighbors in Nazareth as a carpenter (Mark 6:3); during his youth he probably worked at this trade, but there is no indication that he continued to follow it during the mature years of his active teaching. Several things Jesus said indicate that he had divested himself of whatever property he possessed and donated the proceeds to the poor. In effect he had taken a vow of poverty. He lived entirely from the generosity of his friends day by day, feeling at the same time that his labor and that of his disciples merited the support they received.

To an enthusiastic but probably unrealistic man who impetuously declared himself ready to follow Jesus one day, he said,

"Foxes have holes, and birds of the air have nests; but the Son of man has nowhere to lay his head" (Matthew 8:20).

Jesus shocked another young man—cultured and well to do—with the sober declaration embedded in this striking episode,

And Jesus looking upon him loved him, and said to him, "You lack one thing; go, sell what you have, and give to the poor, and you will have treasure in heaven; and come, follow me." At that saying his countenance fell, and he went away sorrowful; for he had great possessions (Mark 10:21–22).

That Jesus thought long and profoundly about the principles involved in this policy and the implications it had for the spiritual life is shown by some of his most beautiful words.

Do not lay up for yourselves treasures on earth, where moth and rust consume and where thieves break in and steal, but lay up for yourselves treasures in heaven, where neither moth nor rust consumes and where thieves do not break in and steal. For where your treasure is, there will your heart be also (Matthew 6:19–21).

Again,

No one can serve two masters; for either he will hate the one and love the other, or he will be devoted to the one and despise the other. You cannot serve God and mammon (Matthew 6:24).

[1] *The Didache*, xi, 4–5. Kirsopp Lake, *The Apostolic Fathers*, vol. 1, p. 327.

Few persons would be inclined to deny that these sayings are true; that they have real validity; that they reflect a deep wisdom about the things men live for. Their principles penetrate into all human activities, challenging some of the basic things most persons are concerned about. Yet, taken in literal fashion, they are too severe for most men to attain; indeed they are impractical for the complicated industrial and economic life of the world. This may be admitted. But they forever stand as an unambiguous challenge to share one's goods with the hungry, the weak, the sick, the oppressed of this world, as a call to spirituality free from all avarice.

All through the centuries Jesus pioneers the hard and high road; the highway markers he leaves behind are his acts of generosity. He shares without limit because he identifies himself with the needy. To those whose motivation has been the accumulation of wealth, in his great parable of the Last Judgment, he says,

> I was hungry and you gave me no food, I was thirsty and you gave me no drink, I was a stranger and you did not welcome me, naked and you did not clothe me, sick and in prison and you did not visit me (Matthew 25:42–43).

Every disciple who refuses the call of a needy person turns away from his Lord.

The Underlying Philosophy

But what can be said about a deliberate choice of poverty as a way of life? Is this the right approach to religious ideals? Is it possible for a rational person to be unconcerned about house, clothing, food, drink, medicines and other such practical things of our world? How can one take these words of Jesus seriously? That Jesus had pondered these questions is evident from his analysis of the anxiety of men which he beheld on all sides.

Such words as Jesus speaks in the famous paragraph of Matthew 6:25–34 sound as if he were looking on the world through the eyes of an existentialist philosopher. He beholds all about him the lives of persons filled with worry, frustration, loneliness, dread, even terror, growing out of their uncertainty; obsessed by fears rising from the unpredictable things all men have to face; characterized by the sense of isolation and a yearning for acceptance, friendship and love, of which no person ever finds enough. Jesus sees men so filled with anxiety that they are unable to enjoy the goodness and beauty of the natural world about them, or the human companionship waiting to be entered into on all sides. Jesus is aware of these things. He sees that men feel themselves caught in a human predicament from which they are unable to escape, and the words he speaks are assurance that the one certain escape is to take seriously the providence of God—the belief that God is the sovereign of all life, that he provides for all necessary things. Jesus says:

> Look at the birds of the air, they neither sow nor reap nor gather into barns, and yet your heavenly father feeds them. Are you not of more value than they? Consider the lilies of the field, how they grow; they neither toil nor spin; yet I tell you, even Solomon in all his glory was not arrayed like one of these. Therefore do not be anxious, saying, "What shall we eat?" or "What shall we drink?" or "What shall we wear?" But seek first his kingdom and his righteousness, and all these shall be yours as well (Matthew 6:26, 28–29, 31, 33).

Other Examples of This Faith

That the teaching of Jesus about poverty as a way of life was taken seriously is shown by the practice of the first generation of Palestinian Christians after his time. The sharing of goods, so that all members of their congregations were cared for, is reflected in these words:

> And fear came upon every soul; and many wonders and signs were done through the apostles. And all who believed were together and had all things in common; and they sold their possessions and goods and distributed them to all, as any had need. And day by day, attending the temple together and breaking bread in their homes, they partook of food with glad and generous hearts, praising God and having favor with all the people (Acts 2:43–47).

The same practice is recorded also in Acts 4:32–37.

These references to the practice of poverty in the first of the early churches not only reflect a remarkable generosity; they also indicate the happiness this enthusiastic young congregation experienced. These early Christians escaped from the sort of worry of which Jesus spoke with such feeling. They found effective his recipe for loneliness and anxiety.

An earlier example of this practice of poverty was the community of Essenes at Qumran in the wilderness near the Dead Sea. Every one who became a member of that brotherhood was required to divest himself of all his possessions and present them to the Essene community. They held all things in common; the well-to-do and the poor lived

from the same simple fare. It is probable that the influence of that
community, or of others similar to it, were felt in the early Christian
movement. The Essenes had concluded that the ideal of poverty was
the best approach to the spiritual life.

Other great teachers of the ancient past who, long before the time
of Jesus, taught that poverty was a key to spirituality were found especially in India. All of the early Buddhists gave up their property when
they entered the order. The same was true of the Jains, and followers
of many other forms of Indian religion. The best known were the holy
men known as Sannyasis, each of whom had given up all possessions
and embarked on a career as a wandering beggar, to live this way
until he died. They were said to radiate a happiness from their faces
not experienced by other men. They had learned the secret which
Jesus was also to discover. They were in agreement with him that the
greatest freedom, the deepest peace, is found through generosity; that
the best way to rise above anxieties is to cease to follow worldly ideals,
to replace all such interests and activities with the pursuit of things
eternal, and to substitute for the worship of mammon the love of God.

Celibacy

Most readers of the Bible are aware that Jesus had no wife. Yet little attention has been paid to this fact, as if it were not unusual or of little importance for understanding him. But viewed against the background of ancient Hebrew life, it was most unusual for him to remain unmarried. The Hebrew people emphasized the importance of marriage. They believed that it was a divinely ordained relationship; that it provided for the family, the basic unit of society; that it was the means by which God arranged for the perpetuation of the race. Marriage was therefore a religious duty of every man and woman, and was of tremendous importance.

The Hebrew view of the origin and importance of marriage is set forth in the ancient story of Adam and Eve in the Garden of Eden (Genesis 2:1–24). Adam was created as the keeper of the Lord's garden, but he was lonely. In an effort to dispel that loneliness, the Lord formed the animals one after another in an effort to give man an interesting diversion and provide him with a suitable companion. Yet after all the animals had been made Adam was still unhappy. So God finally put him to sleep, removed one of his ribs, and made him a wife. With this new companion Adam was pleased. According to the Scripture, Adam and Eve were the first human pair. So the author explains that a man leaves his father and mother and cleaves to his wife, and they become one.

This story presents the ideal adult existence which every Hebrew man and woman was expected to adopt. There were few, if any, exceptions in the Old Testament. A Hebrew bachelor or spinster would have been an anomaly—certainly a rarity, almost an impossibility. In any case, it would have been regarded as disloyal to the Hebrew people for a man or woman of sound health to live a single unprocreative life. Such a person would have repudiated his obligation to do his part toward perpetuation of the race.

It is indeed worthy of note, therefore, when we find Jesus an exception to the general rule. It is also appropriate for us to ask why he refrained from marriage, thereby setting himself apart from one of the fundamental Hebrew customs and from the concept of the religious duty of man as understood by his people.

His Appreciation of Marriage

It cannot be that Jesus disapproved of marriage as such. The Gospel of John (2:1–11) relates that on one occasion, along with his mother and disciples, Jesus was a guest at a wedding in Cana of Galilee. He evidently entered fully into the spirit of the celebration, even providing the best of the wine. After the supply of wine provided by the groom was exhausted, in desperation he cast about for more. When Jesus was informed of the groom's embarrassment, after pretending for a time to be uninterested, he told the servants to fill water jars there, used by the Jews for purification; then to draw their decanters full and carry the sparkling beverage to the steward of the festivities. The steward was astonished to taste a more delicious wine than that first served when the party began. He even chided the groom for holding back the best wine until everybody had drunk his fill! The story is a humorous tale, and Jesus must have enjoyed it more than anyone else. Indeed it is an allegory setting forth the superiority of the Christian faith over Judaism; the Jewish faith is represented by the water, the Christian by the wonderful wine. As it now stands, the story may be a modified version of a parable Jesus had once related, not intended to be taken as an historical episode. In any case, the joy with which he entered into the celebration has not been obscured.

Another of his best parables was a story Jesus told about ten girls going to a wedding (Matthew 25:1–13). No man opposed to the institution of marriage would have used such a story to set forth his teaching. On the contrary, Jesus must have derived much satisfaction from using this picturesque setting for his urgent message that God's Kingdom was imminent.

Concerning Divorce

The high estimate Jesus had of marriage is shown nowhere more clearly than by his sayings about divorce. One of them is as follows:

> And Pharisees came up and in order to test him asked, "Is it lawful for a man to divorce his wife?" He answered them, "What did Moses command you?" They said, "Moses allowed a man to write a certificate of divorce, and to put her away." But Jesus said to them, "For your hardness of heart he wrote you this command-

ment. But from the beginning of creation, 'God made them male and female.' 'For this reason a man shall leave his father and mother and be joined to his wife, and the two shall become one.' So they are no longer two but one. What therefore God has joined together, let not man put asunder" (Mark 10:2–9).

Jesus not only recognizes marriage; he considers it, ideally at any rate, indissoluble, and traces it back to God's own arrangement for man and woman from the very beginning.

Jesus' Love for Children

Nor can it be said that Jesus refrained from marriage because of an aversion for children, for whom in various ways he showed a deep love. Young mothers liked to bring their children to receive his blessing; and when the disciples sought to restrain them, Jesus was indignant. He said,

> "Let the children come to me, do not hinder them; for to such belongs the kingdom of God. Truly, I say to you, whoever does not receive the kingdom of God like a child shall not enter it." And he took them in his arms and blessed them, laying his hands upon them (Mark 10:14-16).

This is not merely a formal display of affection to impress others, as with politicians during election campaigns. The disciples probably realized that Jesus was exhausted and had little strength to carry on his work; hence they discouraged the mothers who sought to bring their children to him. But Jesus would have none of it; he went out of his way to show his feeling for the children and understanding for their mothers. Taking the babies into his arms, he pronounced benedictions over them; he was never too occupied nor too tired for such manifestations of his love. One would probably not go wrong in inferring that such expressions of sentiment for the children of others was due in part to the fact that he had none of his own.

Friendship with Women

There is no evidence that Jesus was ever involved in a romance with a woman, no indication that he at any time contemplated marriage. Yet it is perfectly clear that he had no hostility toward women as such. On the contrary, throughout the story of Jesus one comes upon evidences that he understood women, that he got along well with them, that he had many good friends among them.

Some of the finest traditions about Jesus reflect his understanding of women. He often used the plight of some poor woman to teach a lesson. The story about a woman who lost a tiny coin in the dust of her dirt floor (Luke 15:8-10) makes her a parable of God's love for lost human beings: she lights a lamp and sweeps the floor, searching for the lost piece of money. Again, standing with his disciples in the temple, watching the people casting gifts into the treasury (Mark 12:41-44), Jesus saw a widow drop in two copper coins, the last money she had. This woman, he said, has given more than anyone else; she has been more generous than the wealthy with their huge contributions. The widow was an example of a deliberate acceptance of poverty as an act of faith; she did what Jesus himself practiced. Still another example: Jesus told the quaint story (Luke 18:1-8) of a widow scorned by an arrogant judge to whom she went for justice, but her determined importunity at last moved the heartless man to hear her case. Jesus called the woman's determination an illustration of the principle of steadfastness in prayer, the kind that brings results.

Some of the healings Jesus performed show his compassion for women. Luke 8:43-48 tells of a woman who had suffered from an issue of blood for twelve years. She forced her way through a crowd to touch Jesus, and was immediately healed. When Jesus discovered who had touched him, he spoke to her with reassurance, "Daughter, your faith has made you well: go in peace." Later, according to Luke 13:10-17, Jesus defied the Jewish legal authorities by breaking the Sabbath law in order to heal a woman afflicted eighteen years with curvature of the spine. He said to her gently, "Woman, you are freed from your infirmity." When he laid his hands upon her, she stood up and was well. The raising of the only son of the widow of Nain, as the body was being carried on a bier to the cemetery, is yet another example of efforts he made to do something for helpless women (Luke 7:11-17).

While on an excursion in the region of Tyre and Sidon, Jesus went out of his way—again going beyond the Jewish law—to cure the daughter of a Greek woman. First he demurred, saying,

> "Let the children first be fed, for it is not right to take the children's bread and throw it to the dogs." But she answered him, "Yes, Lord, yet even the dogs under the table eat the children's crumbs." And he said to her, "For this saying, you may go on your way; the demon has left your daughter." And she went home, and found the child lying in bed and the demon gone.

The apparent harshness between Jesus and this woman is more likely to have been originally a humorous exchange; he probably intended to heal the child all along. The reluctance was a test of the woman's faith. She not only believed Jesus could do it, she also had a keen wit, and her clever reply instantly brought a sympathetic response.

One of the most spectacular healings performed by Jesus was to cast out seven demons from Mary Magdalene (Luke 8:2), although there is no full account of it. The tradition that Mary Magdalene was a prostitute is without foundation in the Scriptures; it is only a legend which inferred that her demon possession was manifested by sexual immorality. But we are now in a position to form a more charitable judgment. Demon possession refers to mental illness. This woman was relieved of a serious psychosis, the nature of which cannot now be determined because of the lack of a description of her symptoms. She was so grateful to Jesus that she became one of his most faithful followers, even at the cross and the grave (Mark 15:47; 16:1; John 20:1-18).

Furthermore, it cannot reasonably be concluded that Jesus was personally unattractive to women; all evidence is to the contrary. One of the characteristic things about his ministry is the prominence of women: several times women were in the group of disciples that journeyed with him. Women from Galilee were among the disciples who followed Jesus to Jerusalem on that last journey. They traveled close to a hundred miles, perhaps on foot, from Galilee down the Jordan Valley, then up through the hills from Jericho to Jerusalem, an exceedingly difficult trip (Mark 15:40-41).

Moreover, there are indications that certain women held a real, personal affection for Jesus. One of these was Mary, the sister of Lazarus (John 12:1-8), in whose home Jesus once found entertainment. She showed her feeling for Jesus by anointing his feet with a rich perfume as he reclined for dinner. Then she expressed her devotion even more by wiping his feet with her hair. On another occasion she sat at his feet to hear his teaching while Martha complained about being left alone to do the chores (Luke 10:38-42). A similar case was that of a woman who anointed the head of Jesus when he was in the home of Simon the leper (Mark 14:3-9). Still another is recorded in Luke 7:37-38, although the setting is not stated.

While we do not know the ages of these women, in any case their reactions and responses are strong evidence that women in general were attracted to Jesus. There are no grounds for assuming that Jesus could not have found a wife had he chosen to do so. He must, rather, have held some strong conviction that caused him by deliberate choice to deny himself the satisfaction of marriage, but also to refrain from the attendant responsibilities. He chose the lonely life of the single man. In effect, he took a vow of celibacy.

For the Kingdom of Heaven

In our quest for understanding we should ask, What was the most powerful preoccupation of Jesus? What was the great concern of his life? If not to marriage and family, to what more profound expression of his energy and personality did Jesus devote himself? In what enterprise did his mind and heart find real fulfillment? How was the destiny God had in mind for him to be realized?

The answer to these questions is not far to seek. Everyone who reads the Gospels perceives that the all-consuming passion of Jesus was the Kingdom of God. His own personal relation to that kingdom was no ordinary role. As he read the prophets, he discovered himself as the Anointed One, the Messiah, the Christ. Not as a rebel against Rome, not as a political leader nor as a military commander, not as a temporal king reigning in oriental splendor; but the gentle servant whose heart was identified with all the needy of the world, willing to die as he believed the Scriptures foretold, to bring all mankind to comprehend the breadth, the height, the depth of God's love.

Strange philosophy to our contemporary mind? Perhaps, but not to the intuitive thought of the ancient East. One finds similar ideas, along with celibacy too, among the Jewish Essenes, as Josephus reports[1]; also in the old religions of Hindus and Buddhists; and there might still be wisdom in this faith of Jesus for western man to rediscover.

We need not base our answer as to why Jesus chose celibacy solely on conjecture. One of his most startling sayings probably gives us the answer. Always fond of cryptic words, Jesus once remarked, in connection with a discussion of divorce,

> For there are eunuchs who have been so from birth, and there are eunuchs who have been made eunuchs by men, and there are eunuchs who have made themselves eunuchs for the sake of the kingdom of heaven (Matthew 19:12).

The first part of this strange proverb refers to a male child born without the capacity to develop sexual virility; the second part alludes to the

[1] *War*, II, viii, 2–14.

oriental practice of castration; but the third refers to Jesus, or any person like him who refrains from marriage, who denies himself the delights of sex, who sacrifices the joys of conjugal companionship and parenthood for the sake of God's Kingdom.

This interpretation of the celibacy of Jesus is supported by Paul's advice to young people a generation later. He thought it was wise for them, if they could keep their sexual desires under control, to refrain from marriage. He said,

> I want you to be free from anxieties. The unmarried man is anxious about the affairs of the Lord, how to please the Lord; but the married man is anxious about wordly affairs, how to please his wife, and his interests are divided. And the unmarried woman or girl is anxious about the affairs of the Lord, how to be holy in body and spirit; but the married woman is anxious about worldly affairs, how to please her husband. I say this for your own benefit, not to lay any restraint upon you, but to promote good order and to secure your undivided devotion to the Lord (I Corinthians 7:32–34).

Jesus put his devotion to God's Kingdom before all other attractions; in this commitment he found fulfillment. The daring role he assumed for himself had no place in it for a woman at his side. The uncertainty, the poverty, the danger, the implied final agony, were not the basis on which to found a marriage, to rear a family. The terrifying responsibility of the Messianic destiny he chose to assume alone; he knew he had no right to ask another to share the fearful isolation of soul into which he must go.

"Not One Stone upon Another"

According to Mark's arrangement of events in the last week of the life of Jesus—the period we call Holy Week—the triumphal procession into Jerusalem took place on Palm Sunday and the driving of the money-changers from the temple on Monday. It was on Tuesday that Jesus made a striking observation as he and the disciples left the holy place.

> And as they came out of the temple, one of his disciples said to him, "Look, Teacher, what wonderful stones and what wonderful buildings!" And Jesus said to him, "Do you see these great buildings? There will not be left here one stone upon another, that will not be thrown down!" (Mark 13:1–2).

This explicit prediction of the destruction of the temple conforms so exactly with what the Romans did to it when they destroyed Jerusalem in A.D. 70 that many scholars have found it impossible to believe that Jesus could have uttered such a prediction forty years earlier. This accuracy of prediction is held to be humanly impossible—and our interpretation has to assume the full humanity of Jesus. So it has been concluded that these words were formulated by some Christian writer —whether Mark or another—after A.D. 70, and ascribed to Jesus; at any rate, that this passage was written after the temple was destroyed.

One must admit that this interpretation which denies to Jesus this specific prediction is a rational, an apparently convincing, conclusion. Yet when we give it further consideration, recalling that Jesus was profoundly influenced at this time, not only in his thinking and actions but also in what he said to the people, by what he read in the Scriptures, another possibility opens: these words of Jesus may be one of his authentic sayings.

It is appropriate for us to give attention to the Scriptures Jesus was reading in connection with these events; and we are not left in the dark on this point. Jesus' words at the time he drove out the traders and money-changers lead us at once to the Scripture which filled his mind, a Scripture he no doubt believed referred to the temple of Herod, whose demolition he foretold.

At the climax of his passionate denunciation of the temple concessionaires, Jesus justified his violence with the words, "Is it not written,
'My house shall be called a house of prayer for all the nations?' But
you have made it a den of robbers (Mark 11:17)." The first part of this
statement, suggesting the universality of religion so characteristic of
Jesus, is a quotation from Isaiah 56:7, but the scathing conclusion is
based on Jeremiah 7:11, "Has this house, which is called by my name,
become a den of robbers in your eyes?"

Before reaching a conclusion about the authenticity of the words of
Jesus, one ought to read carefully Jeremiah 7:1–34 and 26:1–24. Jeremiah uttered these vivid predictions of the destruction of the temple
of Solomon a short time before the Babylonians captured Jerusalem
in 587 B.C., and destroyed not only the city but also the famous temple.
Jeremiah stood in the gate of the Lord's house and said,

> Has this house, which is called by my name, become a den of
> robbers in your eyes? Behold, I myself, have seen it, says the Lord.
> Go now to my place that was in Shiloh, where I made my name
> dwell at first, and see what I did to it for the wickedness of my
> own people Israel. And now, because you have done all these
> things, says the Lord, and when I spoke to you persistently you did
> not listen, and when I called you, you did not answer, therefore
> I will do to the house which is called by my name, and in which
> you trust, and to the place which I gave to you and to your fathers,
> as I did to Shiloh. And I will cast you out of my sight, as I cast
> out all your kinsmen, all the off-spring of Ephraim (7:11–15).

The allusion to Ephraim refers to the destruction of Samaria in 721
B.C. by Assyria. What the Assyrians did to Samaria and what the
Babylonians did to Jerusalem in 587 is of course well known; both had
been utterly destroyed by ruthless conquerors.

But the prediction of the destruction of the temple by Jeremiah was
not a superhuman prophecy of what the future would bring. His reference to the destruction of Shiloh shows what he thought would surely
befall Jerusalem with its holy place. Jeremiah knew, and the people
he addressed knew, that this ancient shrine at Shiloh had been con-
verted into a ruins by some hostile power. Shiloh was apparently the
first shrine of major importance for the religious life of the Hebrews
after their penetration into the land of Canaan. They still patronized
other shrines, notably Shechem; but Shiloh was their own first great
holy place, and there the ark of the covenant had been located after
the time of Moses.

The first indication of Shiloh's importance appears in Judges 21:1–25.

There two hundred young Benjaminites secured wives from among the maidens as they came dancing through the vineyards. But the fullest account of this shrine is found in I Samuel 1:1—7:2. The story centers around the priesthood of Eli and Samuel, his successor. The Hebrews were dominated by the Philistines. First Eli, then Samuel after him, and finally Saul led the Hebrews in a desperate effort to throw off the Philistine yoke. The effort of Eli obviously ended in disaster; the Hebrews were routed by the Philistines at Aphek even though the ark of the covenant had been carried onto the battlefield. The Philistines bore off the holy object as a trophy; and, although it is not so stated in the passage, it is reasonably clear from allusions in other Scriptures that the victors pressed on to Shiloh and celebrated their triumph by demolishing that great shrine, which had been the center of the Hebrew rebellion.

This catastrophe may also be inferred from the account in I Samuel itself. When the superstitious Philistines found themselves decimated by a plague, they concluded that the cause was the presence in their midst of the Hebrew fetish. In an effort to rid themselves of the plague, they returned the dreaded object. But the Hebrews surprisingly took the ark not to Shiloh but to Kiriath-jearim, where it remained for twenty years (I Samuel 7:1-2), indicating that Shiloh no longer served as a shrine.

Common knowledge of the ruin of Shiloh is reflected in Psalm 78:60–62:

> He forsook his dwelling at Shiloh,
> the tent where he dwelt among men,
> and delivered his power to captivity,
> his glory to the hand of the foe.
> He gave his people over to the sword,
> and vented his wrath on his heritage.

It was this memory among Hebrews of what happened to the ancient shrine that filled the mind of Jeremiah when he stood in the temple of Solomon at Jerusalem and charged that the people had made the place a den of robbers. Jeremiah said,

> Go now to my place that was in Shiloh, where I made my name dwell first, and see what I did to it for the wickedness of my people Israel (Jeremiah 7:12).

Shiloh's fate was a well known fact. The people in the temple that day certainly knew what Jeremiah meant when he warned them that without repentance a similar catastrophe was bound to strike the holy place in which they were standing. The prophet was drawing a clear and logical lesson from history.

Religious belief of the time held that God's control over the prosperity and adversity of the Hebrew nation reflected the degree of its loyalty to his covenant. In theory at any rate, every Hebrew accepted this belief; yet in a practical sense they were ignoring it. Jeremiah's perceptivity made it clear to him that God's justice required that, without an immediate repentance, the temple at Jerusalem was bound to be destroyed just as Shiloh had been. And it was, in 587 B.C.

The words Jesus used when he drove out the money-changers were based in part on Jeremiah 7:11, and it is obvious that his action was inspired by that very seventh chapter of Jeremiah. Undoubtedly he had pondered this passage, and reread it, perhaps again and again, that Sunday night in Bethany after he made his first visit to the temple. When he returned to the temple courts on Monday morning, the ominous words of Jeremiah must have been ringing in his ears. Moreover, when his disciples pointed to the magnificent stones as the little party was leaving the temple, Jesus must have recalled the foreboding prophecy of Jeremiah and how it was fulfilled when Nebuchadnezzar battered down the walls of Jerusalem—a repetition of the Philistine destruction of Shiloh 500 years earlier.

When Jesus uttered the startling prophecy, "Not one stone shall be left upon another," he had freshly in mind the demolition of two great Hebrew sacred places—the shrine at Shiloh and the temple of Solomon. If we recognize the authenticity of Jeremiah's prediction that the temple of his day would be destroyed, then we ought to grant the authenticity of these words of Jesus. It is unnecessary to suppose that they were formulated by some Christian writer after the fall of Jerusalem in A.D. 70. We need instead only to keep in mind that Jesus was reading the Scriptures and basing his interpretation of history upon them. He found the same superficiality of religion and the same desecration of the temple of Herod that the earlier prophets had witnessed at Shiloh in Eli's day and at Solomon's temple in Jeremiah's time. His conclusion that a similar fate would befall Herod's temple appears to have been both logical and inevitable.

The New Covenant

All of the Gospels, and Paul too, agree that the last significant act of Jesus before he was arrested in Gethsemane by the Jewish authorities was to eat a final meal with his disciples; and that this meal was of great importance as the culmination of his ministry. Its influence on the theology and the rituals of the church has also been profound. Yet the early records of that meal vary considerably both as to the time it occurred, the meaning Jesus gave to it then and the ultimate significance he expected it to have for his followers. Is it possible at this date to answer all these questions? Probably not, but a study of the incident on the basis of the early records throws light on Jesus as well as on the church he left behind.

Mark's Record

Mark records that historic meal as follows,

> And as they were eating, he took bread, and blessed, and broke it, and gave it to them, and said, "Take; this is my body." And he took a cup, and when he had given thanks, he gave it to them, and they all drank of it. And he said to them, "This is my blood of the covenant, which is poured out for many. Truly I say to you, I shall not drink again of the fruit of the vine until that day when I drink it new in the kingdom of God" (Mark 14:22–25).

Mark makes it clear that this ceremonial eating of bread and drinking of wine took place at the *seder,* the Passover meal, and both Matthew and Luke agree with him. They relate that Jesus and his disciples went down from Galilee to Jerusalem, presumably with many other pilgrims, to celebrate the Passover, which could be observed only there. Paul (I Corinthians 11:23–26) does not say the meal was Passover; nor does he say anything to the contrary. But John (13:1, 18:28) explicitly states that the last meal was eaten the day before Passover; and that Jesus was crucified at the time the lambs were slaughtered for the Passover meal. Moreover, John does not mention a ceremonial eating of bread and drinking of wine at that meal. Instead he relates that Jesus washed the disciples' feet. Whereas, according to the Synoptic Gospels, Jesus seems to institute the rite of Holy Communion, in John he institutes the rite of foot-washing.

Scholars have long debated the issue between John and the Synoptics as to the chronology of the Last Supper and the death of Jesus. Of late the tendency appears to have swung toward John's view, largely on the ground that according to Jewish law it was illegal for the arrest, trial and execution of a person to occur during the night before and on the day Passover was to begin; hence that John is correct. Nevertheless the Synoptics, it seems to me, are to be preferred. First, it was the celebration of the Passover that brought Jesus and the disciples to Jerusalem at this time; second, the author of John shifted the time of the meal in order to allow Jesus to be crucified at the hour the Passover lambs were slain. This was in line with the elaborate symbolism in which he has enveloped his Gospel throughout; Jesus is the Passover lamb, a view derived from Paul (I Corinthians 5:7). It suited John's plan to drop the reference to the bread and wine at the last meal, for he preferred to transfer his treatment of the Lord's Supper back to chapter six, where he develops it as his interpretation of the miracle of the loaves and fishes. There he records that Jesus said,

> Truly, truly, I say to you, unless you eat the flesh of the Son of man and drink his blood, you have no life in you; he who eats my flesh and drinks my blood has eternal life, and I will raise him up at the last day. For my flesh is food indeed, and my blood is drink indeed. He who eats my flesh and drinks my blood abides in me, and I in him. As the living Father sent me, and I live because of the Father, so he who eats me will live because of me. This is the bread which came down from heaven, not such as the fathers ate and died; he who eats this bread will live forever (John 6:53–58).

John has completely revised the presentation of the Lord's Supper and recasts the sayings of Jesus into his own words, as he has done throughout his Gospel. His account is the most highly developed and, therefore, the latest New Testament version of the last meal Jesus ate with the disciples.

The argument against the accuracy of the Synoptic dating of the Last Supper, on the ground that the Jews would have violated their law to try Jesus by night and to execute him on the holy day of Passover, it seems to me, has little weight. When men in power have already determined to destroy a man, and have hired an informer to betray him, as was the case here, their scruples about strict obedience of the law recede; with law or without it, they accomplish their purpose. According to the Synoptic Gospels, that is just what the authorities did in putting Jesus to death.

Blood of the Covenant

What now seems to have been the institution of the Lord's Supper was at the time a regular part of the Passover meal. Bread and wine were the staple items in any Jewish meal, and it was customary to give thanks for them. In addition, Jesus and the disciples must have eaten a lamb with certain vegetables prepared in the traditional manner. So the Lord's Supper was in many ways a continuation of old Jewish practices. In the early days of the church, breaking bread and drinking wine in this religious sense accompanied every meal (Acts 2:46), as was the case in other Jewish homes, whereas Passover occurred only once a year; frequent rather than annual observance of the Lord's Supper has continued through the centuries. So Passover was by no means the only influence which entered into this picturesque rite.

When Jesus broke a loaf of bread and asked the disciples to eat it, saying, "This is my body," and likewise gave them wine, with the words, "This is my blood of the covenant, which is poured out for many" (Mark 14:22–24), he was investing this part of the Passover meal with the symbolism of an ancient Hebrew covenant ceremony. A familiarity with that important ritual helps one to understand the words of Jesus.

Hebrews had various ways of making covenants, contracts, and agreements, but the most important was by sacrificing one or more animals; their bodies were cut in two, and the blood poured out. The simplest form of this ceremony, one commonly observed in making contracts of many types, is referred to in Jeremiah 34:18–19. A calf was cut in two, and two persons forming a contract passed between the parts. Jesus meant that the bread represented his body, which would be cut in half; the wine represented his blood, which would be shed.

This form of the ceremony is represented in Genesis 15:7–17, where Abraham and God enter into a covenant with one another. By symbols of a torch and a smoking pot they are represented as passing between the parts of the sacrifice. An illustration of the way a multitude of people made a contract with God is given in Exodus 24:8. Moses threw half of the blood against the altar representing God, and the other half on the people. A third form of the covenant ceremony was the rite of circumcision, in which every male child was brought into the covenant with God on the eighth day of its life. Drops of the infant's own blood were in this case the blood of the covenant (Genesis 17:9–14).

In all these instances the essential element in the creation of a covenant was the blood. Ordinarily the rite involved both the body and the blood of the animal. This explains the reference of Jesus to bread and wine as his body and blood. According to Hebrew religion, blood was sacred; it belonged to God; in a sacrifice it was always returned to God. When two persons passed through the same blood in such a ritual, or had the same blood sprinkled on them, in a mystical sense they became of the same blood; that is, they became brothers—the closest relationship known to man. As blood was sacred, the covenant bond at the same time involved God, making him a third party to the agreement. Every contract, therefore, was religious in a high sense.

How extraordinary that Jesus would ask a company of Jewish persons, even in a symbolical sense, to drink blood, an act so foreign to the faith of Hebrews! No Jew under any circumstances would drink blood.

The saying of Jesus is a metaphor. It means that in the picturesque rite of the Lord's Supper worshippers feel themselves entering into life, eternal life. To state the matter in this way is to bring out the sense of participation in the divine life here and now experienced by the first Christians; their realization of salvation as an existential fact in the present life. It was their victory over the world; their experience of identity with Christ; their mystic union with the divine; their feeling that they, like Paul, had died with Christ. It was no longer they that lived, but Christ that lived in them (Galatians 2:20).

The author of John has shown a more profound apprehension of the early Christian experience of salvation than the earlier Evangelists. At this time the Lord's Supper was beginning to have a genuinely sacramental character; and through the centuries the experience he grasped and expressed with such penetration has been a profound influence in the worshipping church.

For modern persons the difficulty of the symbolism is relieved when one realizes that Hebrews regarded blood as life. Let us then speak of life rather than blood. The identification of one's own life with that of Christ, such as one finds in Paul, indicates the true nature of the

Christian experience. It is not a realistic drinking of blood, but a mystical realization of life. More than any other New Testament writer after Paul, John grasped the dimensions of height and depth in the new faith.

What Covenant?

A considerable development is apparent in the various accounts of the Last Supper. In their oldest surviving texts, the Synoptic Gospels are agreed in omitting the word "new" from the statement, "This is my blood of the covenant." In later manuscripts "new" has been inserted, but the evidence is conclusive that the earliest form of the Synoptic tradition did not contain this word. Nor did the oldest tradition say, "Do this in remembrance of me." Jesus did not instruct the disciples to celebrate this Supper in memory of him after he was gone. It is easy to see, however, that after the death of Jesus, this was the natural thing to do, as is clearly indicated in Paul's version, which in a purely literary sense is the oldest of them all, for I Corinthians was probably written fifteen years earlier than Mark. Nevertheless, the form of the tradition Mark preserves is older than that of Paul.

The idea of the New Covenant was widely used in the New Testament as a designation of the new relationship with God established by the death of Jesus. The author of Hebrews gives special prominence to the belief that a new covenant had been established by Christ (8:8–13; 9:15). Early Christians shared with the Essenes of Qumran the belief that they had entered into a new covenant with God. The first part of the Essene Manual of Discipline gives the ritual for entering the covenant.[1] And the Habakkuk Commentary 1:5 refers to it as the "new covenant."[2] This agrees with the Christian usage. The people of Qumran usually simply said "the covenant"; but occasionally they said, "the new covenant." The Christian idea of the new covenant is indicated in Hebrews 8:8–13, where the famous passage about the new covenant from Jeremiah 31:31–34 is quoted as fulfilled in Christ.

The Essenes of Qumran were devout Jews, and their covenant was new only in the sense that it was a renewal of the ancient covenant Abraham made with God. The Qumran community was organized for the purpose of bringing about a new commitment to the old covenant. Moreover, the covenant Jesus made with his disciples was very similar.

---

[1] Millar Burrows, *The Dead Sea Scrolls*, p. 371–374.
[2] *Ibid.*, p. 365.

When he said, "This is my blood of the covenant," he meant to establish a covenant binding himself and his disciples together in a deep loyalty to one another, but no doubt also as a reaffirmation of the bond that existed between Hebrews and God from time immemorial. The newness of the Christian covenant was that it gathered into a fellowship Jesus and the company of disciples who had made their commitment to him. This covenant was based on the new realization of God's will Jesus had brought to the disciples.

It is probable also that at the time Jesus anticipated his death. "This is my blood of the covenant," was a solemn announcement. Only a bare fragment of the conversation of Jesus and his disciples on that occasion has been preserved. The excitement of the little group must have been intense; wonder, foreboding, a beginning fear gripped them. Jesus felt that his own death would ensue. The words he spoke and the dramatic ritual he observed were intended to prepare the disciples for what was to follow. Yet even in this grim situation, as his custom was, Jesus turned everything into a symbol, a metaphor, an allegory, creating memories to remain vivid in the minds of the little band as long as they lived, and then to pass on through tradition and find their place in the new Scripture to emerge.

As noted before, during these ominous last days, Jesus must have been reading the fifty-third chapter of Isaiah, convinced that he found himself there. He read (53:7):

Like a lamb that is led to the slaughter,
    and like a sheep that before its shearers is dumb, so he opened
    not his mouth.

From these very words, the symbolical identification of Jesus with the Paschal lamb was probably derived; and in the words of Isaiah 53:12, "He bore the sin of many," Jesus may have found the idea that his blood would become the seal of a new covenant.

Judas Iscariot

The one thing for which Judas would be remembered was that he betrayed the Christ, and that deed has made him a subject of inexhaustible interest. Readers of the Gospels wonder what kind of man could do such a thing. But Judas offers a problem of another sort in our effort to understand Jesus. What caused Jesus to select this man to belong to the twelve, the special group he chose to carry on his work? Did Jesus from the beginning understand the kind of man Judas was? Did he know that in the end Judas would reveal his character by an act of treachery? And Judas is also a theological problem. How does he fit into the Christian belief that according to God's plan it was necessary for the Christ to die, therefore for someone to betray him and also for someone to execute him? If Judas carried out what was divinely ordained, was he responsible?

The Name

The name Iscariot has been taken by most scholars to indicate the native village of Kerioth of southern Judah. The supposition that Judas came from that town was based solely on the name he bore, which was thought to mean "man from Kerioth." But according to John 6:71 and 13:26, Judas' father was named Simon Iscariot, which makes it appear that Judas bore his father's name. This tends to discredit the view that Judas got the name Iscariot from a village.

Others think the name Iscariot was derived from *sicarius*, the Latin word for a short sword worn concealed under their garments by the *sicarii*, a fanatical fringe of the Zealots operating as an underground movement against the Romans. They were violent men who assassinated Roman officials and Jewish collaborators; hence they were regarded by the Romans as bandits. We know from Mark 3:18 (Luke 6:15; Matthew 10:4) that Jesus chose a Zealot named Simon as one of the twelve. It may be, therefore, that Judas was a second member of the Zealot underground selected by Jesus to belong to his inner group.[1]

[1] On the meaning of Iscariot, cf. Arndt and Gingrich, *A Greek-English Lexicon of the New Testament*. The University of Chicago Press, Chicago, 1957, p. 381.

Historical Fact

The character of Judas is based on historical fact, although relatively little is known about him. However, the early church was not slow in supplementing its information about Judas with legendary details. Mark, the earliest Gospel, provides the few known facts. The other Gospels have taken Mark's statements, and each in its own way has contributed to the Iscariot legend. The first time Mark mentions Judas Iscariot is in his catalog of the twelve (3:14–19). At the head of the list Mark puts Simon Peter, undoubtedly the one he considers the most highly honored. At the end is Judas Iscariot, characterized by the epithet of his ignominy, "who betrayed him." Mark could introduce Judas thus briefly because what he had done was so well known that Christian readers knew who was meant without further explanation.

Mark does not refer to Judas again until the story arrives at Wednesday of Passion Week, the day before Jesus was to eat the Passover with his disciples (14:10–11). He records there that Judas went to the chief priests and, in return for a promise of money—the amount not specified—agreed to deliver Jesus over to them; and that then he began to seek for an opportunity to do it.

Jesus evidently learned of this bargain. During the Passover meal, without mentioning anyone by name, he said, "One of you will betray me, one who is eating with me" (14:18), implying that the traitor was present and participating in the meal. The announcement filled the little band with consternation, and they began to search for the criminal, but without success. As Jesus adjourned the party, to assemble again in Gethsemane, Judas slipped away and carried word to the priests.

The third time Mark mentions Judas is in 14:43, when the defector suddenly enters the garden at the head of a police detail sent out by the priests to take Jesus. As at least a dozen men were in the party with Jesus, and the police did not know him personally, Judas ran forward and kissed him, thus giving the sign of identification they had agreed on. So the police seized Jesus and led him away.

Mark gives nothing more about Judas, evidently feeling that it is enough to recite the facts without comment, allowing Judas' act to make its own impression. He shows Judas as a hard, cynical man, moved by avarice, unrepentant, with no redeeming trait. Yet the picture Mark gives is obviously incomplete, presenting only fleeting glimpses of the callous man who took the role of villain in the world's greatest tragedy.

The few things Mark does record are only fragments of a colorful human story, if we only knew the details. The tantalizing bits of information were an invitation to the legend-makers.

Matthew Begins the Legend

The first legendary touch Matthew contributes is the amount of money the priests gave Judas. He says it was thirty pieces of silver (26:15); Mark had only said they promised to give him money, presumably after the deed was done (14:11); and Luke repeated this (22:5). Matthew not only specifies the amount of the bribe, but, contrary to Mark and Luke, says the priests paid Judas in advance.

The second legend Matthew introduces is an addition to the statement Jesus made during the supper about the betrayer. Mark had left this statement indefinite (14:18–21). According to his version, only Jesus (and of course Judas) knew who was guilty; but Matthew has added (26:25),

> Judas, who betrayed him, said, "Is it I, Master?" He said to him, "You have said so."

Thus the mystery is removed; all present know that Judas is to become a traitor.

Matthew greatly enlarges the legend in 27:3–10, a passage inserted into Mark's story, and without parallel in either Mark or Luke. It follows:

> When Judas, his betrayer, saw that he was condemned, he repented and brought back the thirty pieces of silver to the chief priests and the elders, saying, "I have sinned in betraying innocent blood." They said, "What is that to us? See to it yourself." And throwing down the pieces of silver in the temple, he departed; and he went and hanged himself. But the chief priests, taking the pieces of silver, said, "It is not lawful to put them into the treasury, since they are blood money." So they took counsel, and bought with them the potter's field, to bury strangers in. Therefore that field has been called the Field of Blood to this day. Then was fulfilled what had been spoken by the prophet Jeremiah, saying, "And they took the thirty pieces of silver, the price of him on whom a price had been set by some of the sons of Israel, and they gave them for the potter's field, as the Lord directed me."

All of this passage is legendary, the main legend being that Judas was at heart a good man, who committed suicide as soon as he realized the enormity of his crime. The details about returning the money and the purchase of the potter's field with the price of blood are legends of an incidental character. It is not difficult to see where Matthew got part of this particular cluster of legends. His statement that the incidents took place in fulfillment of a prophecy of Jeremiah is an error; the Scripture in question is obviously Zechariah 11:12–14, which goes,

> Then I said to them, "If it seems right to you, give me any wages; but if not, keep them." And they weighed out as my wages thirty shekels of silver. Then the Lord said to me, "Cast it into the treasury"—the lordly price at which I was paid off by them. So I took the thirty shekels of silver and cast them into the treasury in the house of the Lord. Then I broke my second staff Union, annulling the brotherhood between Judah and Israel.

This passage in Zechariah relates an experience of the prophet in his own time, as shown by the concluding statement. Yet it answers the question where Matthew got the thirty pieces of silver; it gives the background for his legend that Judas returned the money to the priests and threw it down in the sanctuary; but it does not indicate his source for the idea that the remorseful Judas committed suicide.

The legend about the purchase of the potter's field appears to be derived from a misinterpretation of the Hebrew term for treasury (Zechariah 11:13), which was mistaken for the closely related word for potter. The only passages in Jeremiah which could be remotely associated with this episode are 18:2–4, where the prophet visits a potter to observe his work; and 32:6–15, where he buys a field for himself.

Matthew's erratic interpretation of Zechariah 11:12–14 is typical of his procedure in other places. More than any other Evangelist, he has a penchant for supplying details of the story of Jesus from fancied Old Testament predictions which turn out to be relevant not to the time of Jesus, but to the times when they were written.[1]

Nevertheless, it may be true, as Matthew indicates, that Judas did come to a violent end. A supporting legend in Acts 1:18–19 allows one to draw the same conclusion. It goes,

> Now this man (Judas) bought a field with the reward of his wickedness; and falling headlong he burst open in the middle and all his bowels gushed out. And it became known to all the residents

[1] Cf. S. V. McCasland, "Matthew Twists the Scriptures," *Journal of Biblical Literature*, vol. LXXX, part, II, 1961, pp. 143–148.

of Jerusalem, so that the field was called in their language *Akeldama,* that is, Field of Blood.

This legend does not say that Judas was a suicide, or that he repudiated his perfidy by returning the bribe, but that he purchased a field with the money; and that then, for some unstated reason, he met a violent death. The description does not sound like a death by hanging, as stated in Matthew. This passage also gives a different explanation for the Field of Blood; it is the blood of Judas, not of Jesus.

Luke Adds Satan to the Legend

Luke knows nothing of the legends Matthew adds, but he makes an interesting addition of his own. On the whole, he closely follows Mark, although his own record has more depth than Mark's. He makes an effort to show why Judas committed the villainous act. Luke does this by introducing Satan into the story (22:1-6). As the Passover approached, the priests and scribes formed a plot to put Jesus to death, no doubt letting it be known that they were willing to pay a reward for information about the movements of Jesus. So Luke says,

> Then Satan entered into Judas called Iscariot, who was of the number of the twelve; and he went away and conferred with the chief priests and captains how he might betray him to them. And they were glad, and engaged to give him money. So he agreed, and sought an opportunity to betray him (22:3-6).

Luke believes that Satan took possession of Judas, entering into him, controlling his actions, causing him to disclose information the priests needed; to betray his master and his old associates for a sum of money. Among both Jews and Christians of the time the concept of demon possession was a standard interpretation of mental aberrations.[1]

John's Elaborations

Although the author of the Gospel of John takes over some of the earlier legends, he discards others and goes his own way. He drops the idea that Judas was bribed; also Matthew's story that Judas committed suicide, or, as Acts indicates, that he met a violent death in some other way; and he makes no reference to the Field of Blood. However, instead of the idea that Judas received money for becoming an informer, John says he was a thief. According to 12:6 and 13:29, Judas served as treasurer for

[1] Cf. S. V. McCasland, *By the Finger of God,* New York: The Macmillan Company, 1951.

Jesus and his disciples; so ". . . because he was a thief, and as he had the money box, he used to take what was put into it" (12:6). No other Evangelist accused Judas of being a thief.

John adopts Luke's view that Judas was controlled by Satan and gives it a considerable expansion. The first time Judas is mentioned in John, Jesus says to the disciples,

> Did I not choose you, the twelve, and one of you is a devil? (6:70).

Then John explains that Jesus meant Judas who was to betray him, creating the problem—not for John, but for us—why Jesus chose such a person as one of his apostles. At the last supper, John relates, when the devil had already put it into the heart of Judas to betray him (13:2), Jesus washed the disciples' feet, no doubt including those of Judas. At the end of that meal Jesus told the disciples one of their group would betray him, and then revealed who it was by handing a morsel of food to Judas. This evidently angered Judas, for after that Satan entered into him (13:27), and immediately he went out into the night (13:30).

What Kind of Man Was Judas?

Mark's view that at the end Judas turned out to be an informer, the willing agent of those who brought about the execution of Jesus, is probably correct. He was like Delilah, whose deception led to the death of Samson; Absalom, who drove David, his own father, from the throne; Benedict Arnold, who betrayed the American colonies; and persons in confidential government positions who sell security materials to the enemy.

At the same time we may draw certain inferences as to why Jesus chose him in the first place. We may reject as unwarranted John's view that Judas was a devil from the beginning, and that Jesus knew it; that view casts a shadow on the integrity of Jesus. It is better to recognize that Judas was an attractive person, as were all the infamous characters noted above; they had ability and charm. Jesus saw admirable qualities in this man which he wished to use in his program for the Kingdom of God. But when Jesus chose a disciple, he could never be certain in advance of the man's loyalty and development into the kind of man he hoped all the disciples would be. Many of the disciples turned their backs on Jesus; even Peter denied him; and at the end all of them fled and sought security in anonymity. Judas was not entirely different from the other disciples, or from their successors through the centuries.

As Jesus was leading a Messianic movement, we ought to interpret Judas in that light. He was probably one of those who anticipated spectacular developments, a kingdom which would restore political independence to the Jews and bring rewards to the followers of Jesus. It is clear that several of the disciples had such ideas. Jesus did not make his own intentions plain before the turning point of his ministry at Caesarea Philippi, when the disciples admitted they believed he was the Messiah and he thereupon headed for Jerusalem.

It is probable that Judas was disturbed by this decision; and that as with dismay he watched Jesus challenge the intrenched authorities at Jerusalem, he decided that the movement would fail, and that the actions of Jesus had compromised his followers, putting their lives in jeopardy. So Judas must have concluded that Jesus was a false messiah.

It is an error to overemphasize the theological problem of Judas Iscariot. There is really no more of a problem in Judas than in all other men. To see more is a result of extreme views of foreordination and predestination. It is true that Christianity has held these ideas, but it also holds to the freedom of man's will, and this belief keeps those doctrines in balance. Forces of heredity and environment do exercise decisive influences on a man's life, and these may be regarded as deterministic or mechanistic. Yet there remains in every normal person's life an area of freedom, so that he alone makes the moral decisions by which he lives. This was true of Judas just as it is of all other men. No man who violates covenants, betrays friends, abandons moral integrity, can escape responsibility. When the Bible states that man is created in the image of God, it means that he possesses moral autonomy, that he is responsible for his actions. The only problem in Iscariot, as in all other men, is the impenetrable mystery of freedom of the will.

The Crucifixion

The execution of Jesus was instigated by the Jewish leaders, but it was the Romans who put him to death. The teachings and actions of Jesus had antagonized the teachers in the synagogues, the priests of the temple, and the political revolutionaries agitating rebellion against Rome. The only professional Jewish group not antagonized by Jesus was the Essenes, who are not once mentioned in the Gospels, making it clear that he had no clashes with them. Their headquarters at the time appears to have been the settlement at Qumran near the Dead Sea, where they were isolated from most of the turmoil which disturbed the Jewish population as a whole. The common people—the people of the land—who comprised probably ninety per cent of the Jewish populace were friendly and receptive to the Gospel Jesus preached; but they were without leadership of their own, and were easily aroused or cowed by leaders from the professional and aristocratic classes. One day they might be found among the ardent followers of Jesus, the next in a hysterical mob shouting for his blood, on still a third day running for cover. The Romans were not concerned about Jesus except insofar as they thought his religious teachings had political, and possibly military, implications. The empire and its legates and procurators wanted no trouble-making.

Pharisees

Jesus encountered some of his most bitter opposition from the Pharisees, yet he held many beliefs in common with them. The Pharisees were the most liberal and progressive party among the Jews at the time, their origin going back at least to the early Maccabean period. Most of the scribes and rabbis were Pharisees; their main interest was centered in the law, which they believed covered every aspect of life. Observance of the law in all of life, from their point of view, was as important, if not more important, than the rituals of the temple. At the same time, in addition to the written law, they held to the oral tradition, which included belief in resurrecion of the dead, immortality of the soul, and several other important items not accepted by the Sadducees.

It is true that Pharisees exaggerated the importance of ceremonial purity, trivial things having to do with the Sabbath, and separation from common people they thought were unclean because they did not keep all the rituals. So much did the Pharisees emphasize legal matters that Jesus criticized their failure to go beyond the letter of the law to its spirit, and some of his most scathing denunciations were delivered against them.

Matthew has brought together a collection of these denunciations in chapter twenty-three. Here Jesus condemns the scribes and Pharisees together, and in the course of his diatribe he includes the rabbis, showing that scribes and rabbis were the professional leaders of the Pharisees. In fact the scribes and rabbis at the time were probably identical or alternate names for the same individuals. Some of them may have had a priestly background, but essentially they were Pharisees. Jesus summons the most vitriolic language in his colorful vocabulary to denounce them as hypocrites worthy of the judgment of hell. In a general sense these criticisms are valid; at the same time, they are an overstatement. Exaggeration for emphasis is one of the most common elements in the language of Jesus; when he encounters those who set themselves in opposition to his simple and humane interpretations of the law, he reacts with strong, violent language.

We know that these denunciations of the Pharisees are exaggerated because many excellent sayings of rabbis of the time are preserved in a chapter of the Mishnah called "Sayings of the Fathers." Here one can read sayings by Shammai and Hillel, teachers during the reign of Herod the Great, and of Gamaliel, under whom Paul was a student about A.D. 30. The quality and spirit of their teachings remind one of the words of Jesus. Even Paul, certainly one of the most devout early Christians, had been trained as a Pharisee. Throughout his career as a Christian apostle, he never forgot that training and referred to it with pride (Philippians 3:4–6).

Not all of the Pharisees were of this generous type. They saw the teachings and popularity of Jesus as a threat to their own position and power. As the story of Jesus develops, it is clear that they did what they could to bring about his death. They were ready to join with priests of the temple in arousing the people and carrying through a carefully laid plot to get him executed by the Romans.

Sadducees

The Sadducees were a wealthy Jewish aristocracy consisting largely of the priesthood, who were responsible for the magnificent rituals of the temple at Jerusalem and derived most of their income from sacrifices they performed and concessions they operated there. They were the wealthiest class of the Jews, and the most conservative, rejecting the oral tradition, together with all beliefs not found in the written law. They had little enthusiasm for the synagogues, which are not mentioned in the law, along with new beliefs drawn not only from the oral tradition but also from uncanonical books, such as the apocalypses. All of these, the priests felt, endangered their professional and economic life.

Jesus was not opposed to the temple as such; the Gospels show that he often worshipped there. At the same time, as we have seen, Jesus was profoundly disturbed by the commercialization of the temple and drove out the money-changers. The teachings of Jesus did not disturb the Sadducees so long as he did not interfere with the temple; but when he boldly went into the temple courts and cast out the merchants, the priests became furious. Such action they would not tolerate. No doubt this is what caused them to lay the plot which brought about the execution of Jesus.

Zealots

Josephus[1] traces the Zealot movement back to Judas of Gamala, who led a rebellion against the Romans about A.D. 10 because of his opposition to payment of taxes to Rome. That occurred during the childhood of Jesus, and apparently the action was based in Galilee where Jesus lived, a region well known for its love of independence. Yet Zealots of the time of Jesus carried on the nationalistic tradition shown by the Maccabeans a century and a half before, and by Hebrew patriots still earlier. They resented foreign oppressors, who at the time of Jesus were Romans.

The Zealots had no argument with Jesus over his theological teachings; their ranks were drawn in part from the common people Jesus himself came from. When he talked about the Kingdom of God, these revolutionaries were interested; they sympathized with anyone who made an effort to recover Jewish independence, but they were puzzled by the nature of the kingdom Jesus talked about. As we have already seen, Jesus selected Simon the Zealot as one of the apostles, and it is probable that Iscariot was also a Zealot. They would have been interested in the political overtones of what Jesus said; but they were disillusioned when he urged them to love their enemies and pronounced benedictions on peacemakers. It is doubtful that the movement as a whole aroused more than a casual interest among the Zealots. Except for the avarice of

[1] *Antiquities of the Jews*, XVIII, i, 1.

the disillusioned Judas Iscariot, there is no evidence that these violent men had anything to do with the execution of Jesus. Indeed it is probable that Barabbas, released by Pilate at the same time, was himself a popular Zealot leader; and that the two robbers crucified with Jesus were two comrades of Barabbas, taken together with him by Roman soldiers in some recent action. The policy of nonviolence Jesus advocated would not have attracted the typical member of this group.

The Arrest

Here again Mark relates the essential facts in a straightforward way. Once Judas had identified Jesus, the police seized him, and this was accompanied with some violence. Anticipating danger, the police no doubt rushed in with weapons drawn, and one of the disciples drew his sword and cut off a policeman's ear, evidently fully intending to kill him. It hardly seems likely that only one of the followers of Jesus wore a sword. It was characteristic of the life of the time for all Palestinians to go armed. Almost certainly all of the disciples carried daggers at least. The police expected this and took no chances. The struggle was brief; the disciples forsook Jesus and fled away into the darkness. One of the followers of Jesus was a young man, probably unarmed, dressed only with a linen cloth. When the police, attempting to capture him, seized the garment, he slipped out of it and fled naked—a touch one could hardly invent. Calm through it all, Jesus addressed the police politely and surrendered (Mark 14:43–51).

These few details are all we know with reasonable certainty about the arrest, but supplementary legends quickly developed. With some probability tradition has identified the youth who fled away naked as Mark, author of the Gospel, whose home was in Jerusalem (Acts 12:12). In this subtle way, as it were, he may have attached his autograph to the Gospel.

Luke (22:50) notes that it was the policeman's *right* ear, and that Jesus touched the ear and healed it. When John tells the story (18:10), he identifies the pugnacious disciple as Simon Peter and also informs us that the wounded policeman was a man named Malchus.

Matthew, one of the most prolific of the legend-makers, (26:52–54) has Jesus pause in the midst of the struggle and rebuke the angry disciple, saying,

> Put your sword back into its place; for all who take the sword will perish by the sword. Do you think that I cannot appeal to my

Father, and he will at once send me more than twelve legions of angels? But how then should the scriptures be fulfilled, that it must be so?

The Jewish Trial

Mark's account of the Jewish trial of Jesus (14:53–72), as has often been pointed out, abounds in legal difficulties from the point of view of Jewish law, as reflected in Sanhedrin,[1] the chapter of the Mishnah covering such matters. It was against Jewish law to hold a trial involving a capital crime at night or during a festival. As Mark records the trial, the Pharisaic law concerning witnesses was not observed. All of this may be granted. Yet, although Mark was not written before A.D. 70, it incorporates tradition going back to the time of Jesus, which cannot be completely discounted. That Jesus was executed during the festival is a fact; and the processes leading to the execution were initiated by his Jewish enemies. Whether legal or not, some kind of examination of Jesus before Jewish authorities took place that Thursday night; and there are ways in which records of such closed sessions become known.

It was only when the high priest took over the examination in person that evidence was produced leading to the condemnation of Jesus. The high priest asked him,

"Are you the Christ, the Son of the Blessed?" And Jesus said, "I am; and you will see the Son of man sitting at the right hand of power and coming with the clouds of heaven." And the high priest tore his mantle, and said "Why do we still need witnesses? You have heard his blasphemy. What is your decision?" And they all condemned him as deserving death (Mark 14:61–64).

The episode of Peter warming himself in the court and identified by a maid as one of the Nazarenes is a minor diversion which provides temporary relief of the mounting tension of the powerful story.

"Son of the Blessed" means Son of God. "the Blessed" being a metonym for God. Jesus categorically affirms that he is the Messiah, and elaborates in the apocalyptic imagery of the Son of Man sitting at God's right hand. This is Mark's version of what Jesus said, but it is essentially an accurate statement of what Jesus believed about himself. "Power" is another metonym for God.

That this testimony of Jesus was blasphemy has been challenged.

[1] Cf. Sanhedrin 4:1; 4:5; 5:1–5. Herbert Danby, *The Mishnah*, The Clarendon Press, Oxford, 1933, pp. 387, 388–389.

According to Hebrew law (Leviticus 24:16) blasphemy meant to speak evil of the name of the Lord, which Jesus did not do. Yet numerous statements show that blasphemy was used in a more general sense. One could blaspheme against the Holy Spirit (Matthew 12:31). James 2:7 says the rich blaspheme; and Paul (I Timothy 1:13) says he was a blasphemer when he was persecuting early Christians. The original meaning of "Son of God" in a Messianic sense, as Jesus uses it here, is the ancient Hebrew view that every king from the time of his coronation becomes God's son by adoption (II Samuel 7:14; Psalm 2:7). The high priest and the council appear to have taken the phrase in the sense of Greek religion, where it was held that numerous persons were sons of God in a biological sense. Such a view was not in the old Hebrew theology, nor was it in the mind of Jesus. The precise sense in which the Sanhedrin regarded the words of Jesus as blasphemy cannot now be discerned. What the high priest was really interested in was the political implication he could draw from the Messianic claim. He knew that this gave him a basis for taking Jesus before the Roman governor, before whom nothing would be said about the charge of blasphemy; and a Messianic claim was certainly no crime before a Jewish court. Testimony which could be regarded as blasphemy by the Jews and treason by the Romans was just what the high priest wanted.

The Roman Trial

As soon as it was morning the next day, Friday, the chief priests consulted with their council and then led Jesus away and delivered him to Pilate (Mark 15:1), the Roman governor of Palestine A.D. 26–36. This was not far from A.D. 29, but no one knows the date beyond question. The priests must have made their move that morning by daybreak, for it was only nine o'clock when Jesus was crucified (Mark 15:25).

The Roman trial was brief, Pilate showing little concern for justice. The governor's duty in Palestine, as he understood it, was to keep the Jews at peace and collect taxes for Rome. All else was incidental. Had he desired to do it, he could have set Jesus free. But the charge he put over the head of Jesus on the cross shows the issue on which he was condemned. The inscription read "The King of the Jews." The governor made no serious effort to investigate the validity of the charge. Pilate asked Jesus,

"Are you the king of the Jews," and he answered him, "You have said so." And the chief priests accused him of many things.

And Pilate again asked him, "Have you no answer to make? See how many charges they bring against you." But Jesus made no further answer, so that Pilate wondered (Mark 15:2–5).

The answer of Jesus to Pilate is not as clear cut as it was to the Sanhedrin—at least, not as Mark reports it; but no doubt the prosecutors filled in the details with their own interpretations so that Pilate was not left uncertain as to the issue for which the action was brought. Jesus was presented to him as leader of a revolutionary movement against Rome, as one who intended to overthrow the Roman government of Palestine and re-establish Jewish independence. It is doubtful that Pilate was convinced of the truth of the accusation. Yet it was obvious to him that the Sanhedrin, supported by a shouting mob in the streets, demanded the death of Jesus. His only concern was to pacify the people.

Moreover, Jesus made no effort to defend himself. This also gave Pilate an excuse for what he did. He wondered why Jesus was silent. Perhaps he suspected there might be more to the charge than appeared on the surface. At any rate, without concerning himself further, he delivered Jesus to be crucified. From the point of view of the empire and his duty as governor, the charge as formulated, and not denied by the prisoner, gave the execution the technical appearance of an act of justice.

The silence of Jesus was no doubt intentional from the beginning. He knew that defense against the fanatical charge of the envious priests would be futile; also the course events were taking fitted into the pattern he had discovered by reading the Scriptures. Perhaps he had in mind,

> He was oppressed, and he was afflicted,
> yet he opened not his mouth;
> like a lamb that is led to the slaughter,
> and like a sheep that before its shearers is dumb,
> so he opened not his mouth (Isaiah 53:7).

Crucifixion

Crucifixion is one of the most horrible modes of execution ever devised. There were different forms of crosses. The one on which Jesus died was probably the Latin cross, *crux immissa,* of which the upright shaft projects above the crossbar, the *patibulum.* The upright shaft was equipped with a *sedile,* a support attached at right angles like a saddle, on which the body rested. The upright was permanently set in the ground and used over and over. It was only the crossbar which the prisoner was required to carry. The condemned was first tied to the crossbar; then both were raised on ladders until the bar dropped into a notch prepared for it. The victim's hands were tied or nailed to the ends of the crossbar, and his feet to the upright.[1]

Josephus[2] relates that during the siege of Jerusalem by Titus in A.D. 70 about 500 Jews were crucified outside the walls daily. First they were scourged, then brutally tormented, and finally nailed to crosses. He[3] also records that the Jewish king Alexander Jannaeus, about 80 B.C., crucified 800 rebels in Jerusalem. He had the throats of their wives and children cut before their eyes, and watched these things himself as he celebrated the triumph eating and drinking with his concubines.

Romans ordinarily used crucifixion to execute slaves, but they applied it also to provincials; in a few cases they crucified Roman citizens. In any case, Jesus died as thousands of others before and since have died.

Death came to Jesus after he had hung on the cross about six hours, while a sadistic crowd loitered about the three dying men with taunts and jeers (Mark 15:25-41). About three in the afternoon Jesus was heard to utter the prayer, "My God, my God, why hast thou forsaken me?" manifesting the same uncertainty he showed in Gethsemane, when he prayed,

". . . remove this cup from me; yet not what I will, but what thou wilt" (Mark 14:36).

Jesus asked the same question Job raised centuries before when he faced this mystery—a question for which suffering innocent persons in all ages have sought an answer. The later Gospels have removed most of the hard realism of Mark's description of the uncertainty of Jesus; they have painted out the reflections of doubt in the revealing portrait; but it is better for us to ponder the original as it comes from Mark. That is the way life is. Mark lays bare for every one to read the struggle of Jesus for faith as his life ebbed away.

The only sympathetic persons present there that day were the Roman centurion in charge of the crucifixion and some friendly women from Galilee who watched from a distance (Mark 15:39-41).

[1] W. Adams Brown, "Cross," *Hastings Dictionary of the Bible*, T. & T. Clark, Edinburgh, 1898, vol. 1, p. 528.
[2] *War*, V, xi, 1.
[3] *War*, I, iii, 6.

The Resurrection

Both Jewish and Roman officials assumed when Jesus died that they were through with this man from Galilee, but before many days they were amazed to hear his disciples proclaiming that he had risen from the dead. The officials were shocked because what the disciples were affirming sounded so irrational, so absurd; it was such nonsense. They were troubled also because the report seemed to question the justice of what they had done in putting Jesus to death. At best, the report sounded in their ears as irony, if not ridicule; at worst, it struck them as sarcasm or derision. The disciples seemed to be laughing the rulers to scorn, and indeed they were. For the story they were now telling made their Lord a triumphant victor over enemies who believed they had so easily got rid of him forever. The Jewish authorities were especially chagrined to hear the disciples declare that all the brutality inflicted upon Jesus was in fulfillment of the Hebrew Scriptures, contending that those who condemned and executed Jesus had only aided him in attaining the very goal for which he had come into the world.

This extraordinary turn of events embarrassed the Jewish leaders, on the one hand because they found themselves involved in arguments with the disciples about the meaning of their own Scriptures; on the other hand they were disconcerted because they were now powerless to lay their hands on this man they thought they had destroyed. For, according to what the followers of Jesus were asserting, the crucified victim had not only escaped from the tomb, but was going about from place to place in an invisible spiritual form.

This astonishing report about Jesus was certainly no ordinary story, and it had a powerful impact. Belief that Jesus arose from the dead was what revived the faith of his terrified and scattered followers and caused them to reassemble in Jerusalem, and then to organize the first Christian churches. This same faith continued to be at the very heart of Christian churches through the centuries. It is the foundation of Christianity.

But it is hard for many people of our own time to believe in the resurrection of Jesus, just as it was hard for many of his own generation long ago. The question is important for us even as it was for them. What answer can scholars give to those who come today with honest doubts?

There is much evidence in support of this claim of the early disciples, but it is of diverse types and needs to be carefully sifted. The trustworthy evidence has been covered over by popular traditions of later origin, which must be dealt with before we can get back to the real beginning of the Christian faith. It is not my intention to analyze all of the biblical records fully,[1] but only to comment on them sufficiently to enable readers to find their own way through these fascinating ancient documents.

Paul's Testimony

It is necessary to keep the historical perspective before us. Mark is the oldest Gospel; Matthew and Luke are revised editions of Mark; and John is considerably later. As we are most familiar with the records of the resurrection of Jesus in the four Gospels, we would normally turn to them first. But as Paul's Letters were written some fifteen or twenty years before Mark, the oldest Gospel, we must first turn to them. For Paul presents the oldest records of the resurrection of Jesus. His fullest account is I Corinthians 15:1-8:

> Now I would remind you, brethren, in what terms I preached to you the gospel, which you received, in which you stand, by which you are saved if you hold fast—unless you believed in vain.
>
> For I delivered to you as of first importance what I also received, that Christ died for our sins in accordance with the scriptures, that he was buried, that he was raised on the third day in accordance with the scriptures, and that he appeared to Cephas, then to the twelve. Then he appeared to more than five hundred at one time, most of whom are still alive, though some have fallen asleep. Then he appeared to James, then to all the apostles. Last of all, as to one untimely born, he appeared also to me.

This summary of evidence for the resurrection of Jesus from the dead appears in a letter Paul wrote to the church at Corinth from Ephesus about A.D. 54. It presents the strongest proof he could bring together in his effort to convince some of the Christians at Corinth that Jesus had risen. Native Greeks as they were, these Christians refused to accept the doctrine of resurrection. So we may be certain that Paul did his best.

It is important therefore to analyze Paul's evidence. One of its most notable features is what it does not contain. Nothing is said here about the empty grave; nor anything about women who visited the tomb and

[1] I did this in an earlier book, *The Resurrection of Jesus*, Thomas Nelson and Sons, New York, 1932.

saw the risen Christ. What Paul does is to list a series of persons who believed that Jesus appeared to them alive after his crucifixion. The last was Paul himself.

For our purpose, this last appearance is the most significant. It shows that Paul believed that all the earlier appearances, beginning with that to Peter, were like his own vision of the risen Christ. In other words, what Paul considers decisive evidence of the resurrection is not material appearances that historians could record, but spiritual apprehensions discernible only in the hearts of believers. Paul refers to his experience again in Galatians 1:12, where he calls it "a revelation of Jesus Christ"; also in Galatians 1:16, where he remarks that "God was pleased to reveal his son to me, in order that I might preach him among the Gentiles."

These statements of Paul are exceedingly important for believers even to this day. They show that Paul based his faith in the resurrection on the same kind of evidence still accessible to every believer. In other words, the resurrection is historical in the sense that it is an affirmation of the faith of believing persons who in their hearts have apprehended the presence of the living Christ; but it is not historical in the sense that it can be demonstrated by any kind of research, whether historical, scientific, or philosophical.

Faith in the resurrection always retains elements of both certainty and uncertainty. Its inner certitude, based on intuitive spiritual apprehension, will at times be accompanied by doubts raised by efforts of one's own reason to turn this inner certainty into historical information. But faith is never to be equated simply with historical facts; it has to do with historical information but is not the same as historical knowledge.

The Empty Tomb

Many persons through the centuries have sought to prove that Jesus arose from the dead by the story of the empty tomb. All the Gospels, with variation in details, contain accounts of the discovery after Jesus died that his tomb was empty, that the body was gone; and this has been taken as evidence of the resurrection. We have seen that Paul did not explain belief in the resurrection in this way; and the same is true of Mark, who wrote his Gospel later than Paul. His account of the visit of three women to the grave early on the first day of the week relates how they found the tomb open and a young man in it who explained that Jesus had risen. This young man said to the women,

"But go, tell his disciples and Peter that he is going before you to Galilee; there you will see him, as he told you." And they went out and fled from the tomb; for trembling and astonishment had come upon them; and they said nothing to any one, for they were afraid (16:7–8).

All scholars know that the Gospel of Mark ends at that point. What follows (16:9–20) in most editions of the Bible has been added by a later hand. Apparently in its original form Mark had continued to record an appearance to Peter and others in Galilee, but the original ending was lost. This Galilean appearance, according to Mark, was the basis of the belief that Jesus had risen. That was probably the appearance to Peter of which Paul speaks. In Mark's story, however, the women fled from the tomb, and did not report what they had seen and heard; they were afraid to do it.

But, as in so many other cases, Mark's account has been changed by the later Gospels. Matthew, following Mark, says the women "departed quickly from the tomb with fear and great joy, and ran to tell his disciples" (28:8). Thus he changes Mark, obviously thinking it was the open tomb which produced belief that Jesus had risen. But on the basis of Paul and Mark we have a right to conclude that it was not an empty grave which caused the first disciples to believe Jesus had risen. That being the case, there is no reason why we need to base our faith today on that story.

These accounts of the open grave are wonderful stories. Behind them all, at first, there were visions of Jesus on the order of those related by Paul. But there were many persons then, just as now, eager to remove every possibility of doubt by basing faith on historical information. So as these stories took shape during the period of some forty years, when they were carried by oral tradition, they were so materialized that the original experiences were almost entirely obscured. But an empty tomb could never be proof of a resurrection; there are too many other ways of explaining why a body was not found there.

Matthew further changes Mark by saying that, as the women ran to deliver their message, Jesus appeared to them in person; and that he instructed them to tell the disciples to return to Galilee, where they would see him. Then Matthew tells of a final appearance in Galilee (Matthew 28:9–20), thus indicating something of what the original conclusion of Mark contained.

Appearances of the Risen Christ

Mark's version of the resurrection implies that the appearance to Peter has a special importance. When he reports that the young man said to the women, "But go, tell his disciples and Peter that he is going before you into Galilee; there you will see him as he told you," he indicates that Peter had a decisive connection with the origin of the resurrection faith. He does not specifically say there will be a separate appearance to Peter, but that could be inferred. Paul says categorically that the first appearance was to Cephas, that is, Peter (I Corinthians 15:5), but provides no details. But Mark's statement (16:7-8) clearly implies that "the disciples and Peter" did in fact return to Galilee—a distance of about 70 miles from Jerusalem, about three days by foot as the disciples traveled—before they were convinced by one or more visions of Jesus in Galilee, or nearby, that he had risen. This much we have a right to take as historical fact. The first vision could have occurred on or near the third day in Galilee, the disciples' place of rendezvous. However, by the same token, Peter and the disciples could not have been in Jerusalem on the third day. All the stories in the Gospels which locate the first appearance of Jesus to disciples in Jerusalem should probably be regarded as modifications of the earlier tradition preserved in Mark.

First to Peter

Matthew says Jesus appeared first to the women in Jerusalem (28:9) before appearing finally to all the disciples in Galilee. Luke, on the other hand, has completely abandoned the tradition that appearances occurred in Galilee; he has moved them all to Jerusalem; yet he is the only one to record the appearance to Peter. First he tells how Jesus appeared to the two disciples walking to Emmaus, and states that, after Jesus revealed himself during supper and then vanished, the two astonished men rushed back to Jerusalem to report what had happened. But when they got to Jerusalem they found the amazed disciples there saying,

> The Lord has risen indeed, and has appeared to Simon! (Luke 24:34).

This fragment is the only specific account of the appearance to Peter (that is, Cephas or Simon) that has survived. Moreover, Luke says this occurred on the very day of the resurrection (24:13). He says further that after the two disciples from Emmaus had joined the others in Jerusalem Jesus himself appeared to them all. First he ate food with them to demonstrate that he was not a disembodied spirit; then he briefly explained to them what was happening. After that he led them out to Bethany and parted from them, apparently meaning that they were to see him no more (24:36-53).

The Gospel of John tells first of appearances of the risen Christ in Jerusalem, but concludes in chapter twenty-one with a final appearance on the Sea of Galilee. To all of these traditions should be added those in Acts 1:1-11, that Jesus remained with the disciples forty days after the resurrection, until finally, after he had given them his last instructions, on the Mount of Olives, the disciples were permitted to see him ascend in bodily form up into heaven.

Visions Then and Now

These appearances of the risen Christ to his disciples are powerful illustrations of the difficulties modern persons have of really understanding the Bible. The basic trouble is that these stories were written nearly 2000 years ago. So they represent forms of thought, ways ancient people understood their spiritual life, which have become strange if not incomprehensible to us. The rise of philosophy and science, now familiar in a general sense to every person who has been through college or even high school, has introduced a way of thinking about religion at complete odds with that reflected in the Bible. The new forms of thought have created a gulf between our generation and that of the time of Christ which is almost impossible for us to bridge. It is hard for us to comprehend what first-century men said about their spiritual life. We no longer believe that the spirit of a dead person may reappear in physical form and be seen by living persons, engaging in conversations and demonstrating in various ways that he is still alive. There is a natural tendency to discard all such stories as legends.

But after the popular embellishments are stripped away, we can see and admit that what those ancient stories relate still happens, or can happen, to us. To achieve this insight, we must first learn to understand what those ancient persons were saying. Then it is fully as important to recognize our own religious experience when it occurs. It is true that we no longer see the physical forms of persons who return from their graves. Nor do we converse with them. Yet we have our own ways of apprehending the presence of our departed loved ones and friends. We need to keep in mind that all of the appearances of Jesus were to persons who had known him during his life, to whom he was close and precious. The appearances were therefore real things which happened in the minds and hearts of persons who had known and loved Jesus while he was with them in bodily form.

The Letters of Paul, who was closer to Jesus in time than any other biblical writer, reflect an intense awareness of the continued presence of the living Christ with his disciples. He lived in their hearts, their minds, their souls. Paul could say,

It is no longer I who live, but Christ who lives in me (Galatians 2:20).

The wonder of this spiritual apprehension of Christ also pervades the Gospel of John (cf. 6:45–58). This author interprets apprehension of the living Christ in the hearts of believers as a present participation in immortality. Mystical, intuitive apprehension of this type, so clear in both Paul and John, can lay a bridge of understanding over the chasm which yawns between our generation and the one which wrote the traditions about the resurrection of Jesus. Christ still lives in the same way and makes himself known to those who love him; but he appears in forms of our own understanding and experience, not in apparitions and visions like those in the Gospels.

The Christian Meaning

The resurrection of Jesus can be fully understood only as the other side of the crucifixion. One is incomplete without the other. This is a paradox of the Christian faith. Standing alone, the crucifixion of Jesus would be the greatest tragedy in human history, with no single feature to relieve it. It appears to be a complete repudiation, refutation and defeat of an incomparably gentle and good man by the malignant forces of evil he challenged. But Christian faith has always seen the cross of Christ as a victory; as the fullest revelation of God man has received. Here is revealed the truth, not that the tragedy which pervades all life is a refutation of the moral order of the universe, but that it may become a gateway to life eternal.

The Easter story—however much its details may vary in the Gospels—affirms the reality of the resurrection of Jesus, but only after he had experienced desertion by his friends and rejection by the people he loved, and had endured the cruelest form of dying evil men ever devised. Because of the experience of Jesus, the cross, which inevitably belongs to life, came to be enshrined in Christian faith as its symbol of immortality. Christianity is not a naive optimism; it is aware of the tragedy of the world, but it knows that faith can transcend it.

We must translate the cross into terms all can understand. When Jesus said to his disciples,

If any man would come after me, let him deny himself and take up his cross and follow me (Mark 8:34), as so often, he was using figurative language. He did not mean that all of his disciples would be literally nailed to a cross What he is talking about is the tragic element in all life. He means frustration and loneliness; he means suffering of the good, the weak, the helpless; he means business failure and loss of the ones we love; he means sickness and old age; he means death; he means the sensitive conscience troubled by the loss of integrity in our human relations, the cruel and evil things men do to one another. Moreover, he means anxiety about all of these things. In this sense all of us bear a cross. No one escapes it. We verify this in our own experience. These are things life is made of.

Jesus is saying that his story may become our story. He shows us how to live, how to die, and also how to live again. So he continues,

> For whosoever would save his life will lose it; and whosoever loses his life for my sake and the gospel's will save it (Mark 8:35).

Jesus does not say that faith can remove the cross from life; nothing can do that. What his colorful metaphors affirm is that real faith in God can give eternal meaning to the cross everyone bears; that it can transform death itself into life.

Appendix: The Sources of Our Knowledge of Jesus

Most readers of our time hardly need to be told that Jesus himself was not a writer. He left behind no autobiography, no written collection of his sayings and parables, no manuscripts of any kind. But this should not be surprising. Jesus was an active public leader, a teacher, a healer, a reformer of the religion of his time. These activities consumed both his time and his energy. What we know about Jesus is therefore confined to what his disciples remembered about what he said and did. They eventually wrote down a record of these things or passed along orally what they could remember to others.

What is true of Jesus in this respect was characteristic of many other great religious figures of antiquity, such as Moses and the Hebrew prophets, Zoroaster and Gautama Buddha, and Mohammed at a later time. These men put little if anything into writing.

We need to bear in mind that much of what we now have about Jesus in written form in the New Testament had to be carried in the memory of the disciples during the years between his lifetime and the writing of the oldest records about him. This allows the possibility that interests and activities in the life of the disciples, while they were struggling to establish churches among both Jews and Gentiles, had an influence not only on things they remembered about Jesus, but also on the literary form the records finally assumed.

But this does not necessarily imply that the records of Jesus are inaccurate. On the contrary, one of the main features of Jewish education at the time was training the memory. As few books were available, education consisted to a great extent of what could be carried in memory. Students were trained to memorize great writings and important traditions. At the time of Jesus, Jewish traditions were almost as important as their Scriptures, but they had to be passed along entirely by memory. They were finally written down in the Mishnah, the oldest part of the Talmud, about A.D. 200.

The Letters of Paul

The primary records of our knowledge of Jesus are of course the four Gospels, but the letters of Paul were written considerably earlier. We might therefore expect to learn about the life of Jesus from Paul, but in this respect he is disappointing. Probably Paul's earliest surviving letter, I Thessalonians, was written about twenty years before Mark, the earliest Gospel. In the decade and a half that followed, Paul wrote numerous other letters, and about ten of his letters have survived and been accepted as genuine. As the oldest records of Christianity, these letters are in some respects the church's most precious documents. Yet they afford us little historical information about Jesus.

Paul wrote his letters as a way of dealing with the problems of his new churches. When he could not visit them in person, he either sent a messenger or wrote a letter; sometimes he did both. In the nature of the case, these letters had a practical character. Yet in every letter, after discussing various problems in the life of the church, including theological matters, Paul inserted a section on Christian moral conduct. In these sections we would expect him to quote sayings of Jesus, like the Sermon on the Mount and the parables; but not once does he do so. Aside from references to the death and resurrection of Jesus, two or three possible allusions to his sayings, and his account of the origin of the Lord's Supper (I Corinthians 11:23–26), itself taken by Paul from oral tradition, he writes as if he were uninformed about details of Jesus' life. Indeed he probably was. Certainly he was not one of the twelve apostles; he had not even been one of the personal disciples of Jesus; and it is doubtful that Paul had ever seen Jesus except in a vision several years after Jesus died (Galatians 1:16; Acts 9:1–19). Moreover, he not only wrote before any of the Gospels we know were in existence, but he gives no indication that he had or knew any written sources about Jesus whatever. In fact he took pride in his independence of those who became Christians before him, affirming that he had received his gospel directly from God, not from men (Galatians 1:11–24). This drives one to conclude that actually Paul did not know the life and sayings of Jesus as well as we do. What we do find in Paul instead is his remarkable apprehension of the spirit and presence of the living Christ, which has inspired him to become the most outstanding, the most influential single person in the ancient church after Jesus himself.

Dates of Paul's Life

Although the main events recorded in the New Testament rest on evidence historians consider trustworthy, it is difficult to establish exact dates either in the life of Jesus or in that of Paul. The reason for our uncertainty is that authors of the New Testament were not primarily interested in writing a history as we understand that word. They had a religious purpose in mind, and when they did attempt to date some event, they often used a method of dating we have no way of confirming.

Fortunately, however, archaeology has provided us with one pivotal date of great importance.[1] Some years ago in the Greek city of Delphi, site of the famous oracle of Apollo, fragments of a letter of the emperor Claudius to that city were found. The proud officials of the city had inscribed the letter on a public monument for all to read. On one fragment of that letter the emperor refers to information his friend Gallio, proconsul of Achaia, has sent him. This was evidently the Gallio before whom Paul was dragged by angry Jews of Corinth (Acts 18:11). From statements Claudius makes we are able to date the letter in A.D. 51–52. So we know that Gallio was proconsul of Achaia at that time. From Paul's own statement in I Thessalonians 3:1–2 and information in Acts 18:5, it is clear that Paul wrote I Thessalonians shortly after he arrived in Corinth; and as he had been in Corinth about eighteen months before he was brought before Gallio, we can date the letter about A.D. 50. This date now makes it possible to construct a chronology of Paul's life with some confidence, combining with it what he says about his travels in Galatians 1:11—2:21, along with additional bits of information from his imprisonment letters and Acts.

The Gospel of Mark

We are able to determine with strong probability that Mark was the earliest Gospel. Early tradition relates that Mark wrote his Gospel in Rome after the death of Peter, which on good evidence is dated during the persecution of Christians by Nero, about A.D. 64–65. Tradition records that Roman Christians urged Mark, who had been Peter's interpreter, to write down what he could remember of all that Peter had said about Jesus. So we would not be far wrong in dating the Gospel of Mark about A.D. 70.[2]

The Synoptic Gospels

Critical study of the Gospels has been carried on with vigor for about two centuries. Perhaps no subject of Western culture has engaged the prolonged attention of so many scholars. Today uncertainty remains

[1] Jack Finegan, *Light from the Ancient Past*, Princeton University Press, Princeton, N. J., 1946, p. 282.

[2] Morton S. Enslin, *Christian Beginnings*. Harper & Brothers, New York, 1938, pp. 373–388.

about details, but there is almost universal agreement about the central questions.

Among the first big advances was the recognition that Matthew, Mark and Luke have a close similarity in literary style as well as in general outline, and that John is different from the other Gospels not only in style and outline, but even in contents. The similarity of the first three causes them to be called the Synoptic Gospels. This means that they have the same outline; that they see Jesus from the same point of view. The great problems scholars have grappled with concerning the Gospels are their efforts to explain the over-all similarity and, at the same time, the interior dissimilarities of the Synoptic Gospels one to another; and also to account for the unique character of John, which sets it apart from all the others.

The solution of the Synoptic problem that fits the evidence best is that Mark was written first, and that Matthew and Luke are revised, enlarged editions of Mark. Both use Mark's chronological framework. Mark is much shorter than Matthew and Luke, and lacks many of the great sayings of Jesus, like the Sermon on the Mount and some of the parables; and Mark has no account of the birth and infancy of Jesus. Matthew and Luke contain almost all of Mark, and this is explained by assuming that both of them had Mark before them when they wrote, and that they copied most of it. Indeed if Mark should perish, very little we know about Jesus would be lost, for we could still read it in Matthew and Luke, though we would miss Mark's distinctive view of the person of Jesus.

The Q Document

Then it was observed that Matthew and Luke contain numerous extensive sections not found in Mark, in which they agree with one another almost word for word. This phenomenon is explained on the assumption that Matthew and Luke had before them as they wrote another document as old or possibly older than Mark, and that both of them copied from this document, each selecting from it and arranging the material on the Marcan framework according to his own purposes. This great common document is designated by the letter Q, an abbreviation of the German word *Quelle,* source.

Other Sources

In addition, Matthew contains many parables and sayings not found in either Mark or Luke; and Luke likewise contains much unique material. Therefore scholars conclude that each had sources not possessed by the other. These personal sources could have been either written or oral, but as the authors followed written documents in the case of Mark and Q, it seems likely that some of the private sources were also written ones which have not survived. Since Matthew contains excellent material which Luke does not have, and vice versa, it is best to assume that these two worked independently, neither being acquainted with the work of the other.

Editorial Freedom

From the way Matthew and Luke have dealt with Mark and Q—which can be observed when the three Gospels are placed in parallel columns, as in a harmony—it is obvious that these authors used editorial freedom to select the material they wanted, to arrange it, to make slight modifications in its style, sometimes even changing statements of fact, in accordance with what they considered more accurate information.[1]

The Gospel of John

The fourth Gospel presents a more difficult problem. It is so unlike the Synoptic Gospels that little is to be gained by comparing it with them. It differs so radically in both style and contents that it seems to come from another world. Here one finds few sayings in the style of the Sermon on the Mount, and not a single parable. It seems incredible that a Gospel could be written without including some of the great sayings and parables so well known from the other Gospels, yet this is true of John. In the Synoptics Jesus speaks the language of contemporary Jewish sages. He is a master of the brief epigrams characteristic of the wisdom writers. In his hands the parable, already a standard literary form among the Jews, reaches its highest excellence. But on occasion, when the subject and his own mood call for it, Jesus turns to the spectacular symbols of the apocalyptic writers. With all of these forms, in the Synoptic Gospels, Jesus is at home; but in John all three of them have almost completely vanished.

In the Synoptic Gospels, as an adult, Jesus makes only one journey to Jerusalem for the celebration of Passover. He arrives there on Palm Sunday near the end of his career, and is crucified the following Friday. But according to John, he makes three or possibly four trips to Jerusalem for the Passover, and his ministry spans at least three years instead of one as suggested by the Synoptics.

[1] This analysis of the Gospels is conveniently summarized in my book *The Religion of the Bible*, Thomas Y. Crowell Co., New York, 1960, pp. 225–233. Good harmonies are *A Harmony of the Synoptic Gospels*, by E. D. Burton and E. J. Goodspeed (English edition: Charles Scribner's Sons, New York, 1917; Greek edition: University of Chicago Press, 1920); and *Gospel Parallels*, by B. H. Throckmorton, Thomas Nelson and Sons, New York, 1949. The former uses the American Standard Version; the latter, the Revised Standard Version.

We derive a feeling that John is based on a different tradition, with real substance of some kind, but we are not able to penetrate fully into its mystery. However, it was probably written later than the other Gospels. If Mark was written around A.D. 70, and Matthew and Luke in the decade of 85–95, John was written still later, perhaps A.D. 100–110. Whereas in the Synoptic Gospels Jesus speaks the language of a Palestinian sage, or rabbi, or apocalyptic prophet, in John he speaks the language of a different religious culture. This Gospel comes from some area where the faith of Judaism and the new Christian tradition are merging with the symbolical, mystical and philosophical thought of Greeks and Romans, far from the native Galilee of Jesus.

Jesus is a different person in John. Here he is presented as an incarnation of God; he is the eternal Word; he is God's agent in creating and sustaining the universe; and he has now appeared in the world as flesh, as a human being (John 1:1–18). So he moves through John, speaking the language of Hellenistic piety, standing in sharp contrast to the Jewish sage whose words come down to us in the Synoptic Gospels.

The author of John appears to have been familiar with Paul's ideas about the resurrected and living Christ. Perhaps he had read Paul's letters and thus learned to appreciate the great apostle's mystical apprehension of Christ as a real presence, both above and within him. He appears to have taken Paul's insights and given them a much fuller elaboration (compare Galatians 2:20 with John 6:56 and 15:4). If Paul was the first Christian theologian, the author of John was certainly the second. He probably got from Paul his idea of the pre-existent Christ and his role in the creation and control of the world (Colossians 1:15–20; John 1:1–14). These ideas John sets in the framework of the Hebrew sages who wrote the wisdom literature (see Proverbs 8:22–31). At the same time he adopts the Logos concept (i. e., "Word") so popular in Roman Stoicism, where it means the rational order and energy of the universe. The new element in John in this respect is that the eternal wisdom of the Hebrew sages and the eternal Logos of the Stoics is the same divine being, which has now appeared as a man, indeed as Jesus of Nazareth.

John even discards most of the miracle stories found in the Synoptic Gospels. Then he introduces some extraordinary deeds of Jesus not found elsewhere. But his miracles turn out to be allegories of the truth of the new Christian faith; and they appear to have been chosen deliberately to replace the parables of the Synoptic Gospels.

These conclusions make it difficult to use John as a historical record of the same type as the Synoptic Gospels. Yet we can hardly fail to recognize that this Gospel possesses a reliability of its own, which has its contribution to make to an understanding of Jesus. Here we have the work of a brilliant Christian of possibly the third generation, who freely selects, rearranges, and reformulates whatever he finds in the traditions of Jesus coming down to him. He has as his goal not to write a conventional history, but to present for his own generation the meaning of the Christian faith in a new literary form and in a vocabulary better suited to the time and the region in which he lived. At any rate, all through the centuries the Gospel of John has been highly cherished by most Christians, leading them to an intuitive, mystical apprehension of God, and this remains true today. But it also means that John finds its true place at a fairly advanced stage of an emerging early Christian theology, rather than as a simple historical chronicle of the life of Jesus. Yet in some places I have not hesitated to rely on John, usually indicating my reasons for doing so.

But to give a complete explanation of why I have selected certain passages and not others would place too much of a burden on the reader. Often my reasons are intuitive; they are at times literary, based on the conviction that the words of Jesus have a characteristic style; but my decisions may also be based on complex considerations, including documentary, historical, psychological and other factors.

While I judge certain passages to be legends, they occur more often in the narratives than in the words of Jesus. Large bodies of his sayings have been well preserved, and many things he did are faithfully recorded. As scholars have held for many years, the Synoptic Gospels also reflect a theological interpretation of Jesus. But this has by no means erased his historical figure from their pages.

Form Criticism

Form criticism is a type of study developed by German scholars, cultivated especially during the two decades of 1920–1940. Recognizing that both the words of Jesus and the stories about him were carried by oral tradition during the period between his lifetime and the writing of the Gospels, its aim was to go beyond the sources, or documents incorporated in the Gospels, and deal with the material while it existed only in oral form. It attempted to show that the Gospel of Mark, for example, was composed of separate units, each of which had assumed essentially its present form before it was written down, and that the author of the Gospel was only an editor, who had arranged the individual units into a sequence, supplying enough introductory and transitional statements to give the entire collection of traditions the impression of a continuous narrative.

In addition, form criticism takes each separate fragment and seeks to show the different interests and activities in the life of the early church which caused it to assume its present form. Such interests may have been celebration of the sacraments, missionary preaching, instruction of converts, arguments with the Jews, collection of Messianic passages from the Scriptures, and the like.

Form criticism has much to contribute to our understanding of the Synoptic Gospels, but it has not been so successful with John. Yet, in any case, it remains only a specialized literary method, with little right to pass judgment on the historical accuracy of the traditions. Martin Dibelius and Rudolf Bultmann are two of the best known form critics.

Environmental Criticism

Form criticism was not fully accepted by either British or American scholars, both of whom felt that it needed to be supplemented by other forms of study. Its counterpart in America was the more broadly conceived environmental criticism practiced by Shirley Jackson Case and his colleagues. Along with literary considerations, this method sought to understand and evaluate the Gospels by studying them against the background of all elements in the environment, both Palestinian and Greco-Roman, of Jesus himself and the rising churches after his time. These scholars stress the entire complex of life: political, economic, social, military, educational, artistic, religious, philosophical. They also make use of the history, psychology and philosophy of religion, both Christian and non-Christian.

The Return of Theology

During the last four decades there has also been a definite rebirth of interest in theology. The leaders have been Karl Barth of Switzerland, Rudolf Otto and Rudolf Bultmann of Germany, the German-born and trained—but now American—Paul Tillich, the Jewish Martin Buber, and the American Reinhold Niebuhr.

This return of theological interest has been reflected in biblical criticism under the name of *biblical theology*. As applied to the New Testament, especially the Gospels, the key technical word for it is *kerygma*, a Greek word for the proclamation or preaching by the early church of its faith in Christ: what he was, what he did, what he was now doing and would do, in implementing God's work of salvation. *Kerygma* is a testimony; it expresses the faith of the person presenting it. The main point in this particular approach is that the early Christian writings are primarily theological documents; they affirm the faith of the church. They do not deliberately violate historical standards; but history as such is secondary.

Key figures in this most recent trend are Rudolf Bultmann again—certainly one of the most stimulating New Testament scholars of his generation; C. H. Dodd of England; and James M. Robinson of this country, whose *A New Quest of the Historical Jesus*[1] gives an incisive survey of this latest development in New Testament studies.

Nonbiblical Sources

There is no information of any consequence specifically about Jesus outside the New Testament.

The now famous manuscripts from the Essene community of Qumran, commonly known as the Dead Sea Scrolls, which began coming to light in 1947, are Jewish.[2] Their main value is the light they throw on the Essene movement in Judaism just before and during the time of Jesus. But indirectly they also throw light on John the Baptist and Jesus and the early Christian churches. They demonstrate numerous common elements between the Essenes and early Christians. These range from similar ways of interpreting the Scriptures to similarities of vocabulary along theological lines, ceremonial practices and organization of their communities. But early Christianity had greater affinity with the normative Judaism of the time; and there were vast differences between both faith and practice of the Christian churches and the Essene communities. The precise nature of the influence of the Essenes on early Christians remains to be clarified.

The apocryphal Gospels, such as the Gospel of Peter and the Gospel of the Hebrews, fragments of which have long been known, are obviously legendary and contribute nothing of certain historical value.[3]

This negative historical judgment appears to apply also to the more recently discovered Coptic Christian documents found in Egypt, but these do provide important evidence of certain aspects of Egyptian Christian thought about Jesus during the second and third centuries.[4]

[1] Alec R. Allenson, Inc., Naperville, Ill., 1959.

[2] Millar Burrows, *The Dead Sea Scrolls*, The Viking Press, New York, 1955; Frank Moore Cross, Jr., *The Ancient Library of Qumran and Modern Biblical Studies*, Doubleday and Co., Inc., Garden City, New York, 1958; William H. Brownlee, *The Meaning of the Qumrân Scrolls for the Bible*, Oxford University Press, New York, 1964.

[3] M. R. James, *The Apocryphal New Testament*, Oxford, 1924.

[4] A. Guillaumont, H. Puech, G. Quispel, W. Till and Yassah 'Abd Al Masih, *The Gospel of Thomas*, Harper & Brothers, 1959; also, Kendrick Grobel, *The Gospel of Truth*, the Abingdon Press, Nashville, 1960

Bibliography

This selected bibliography calls attention to only a few of the good books about Jesus, but each book listed will usually contain a special bibliography of its own.

I. Geography

E. J. Kraeling, *Rand McNally Bible Atlas*, Rand McNally, Chicago, 1956. This atlas combines convenient size with good maps.

G. E. Wright and F. V. Filson, *The Westminster Historical Atlas of the Bible*, Westminster Press, Philadelphia, 1956. Large and good maps, with useful introductions.

L. Grollenberg, *Nelson's Atlas of the Bible*, Thomas Nelson and Sons, New York, 1956. Unequaled in number of good pictures and unique for its annotated maps.

II. New Testament Introductions

E. J. Goodspeed, *Introduction to the New Testament*, University of Chicago Press, 1937. Scholarly and readable.

M. S. Enslin, *Christian Beginnings*, Harper & Brothers, New York, 1938. Combines a good historical survey of the Maccabean and Roman background with a competent and vivid account of the New Testament literature.

S. V. McCasland, *The Religion of the Bible*, Thomas Y. Crowell Company, New York, 1960. An untechnical introduction to the literature and religion of the entire Bible, intended for college students and other general readers.

III. The Times

S. J. Case, *The Evolution of Early Christianity*, University of Chicago Press, 1914. Interprets the origin of Christianity as response to natural forces resident in the environment.

―――― *The Social Origins of Christianity*, University of Chicago Press, 1923. A further development of the above-stated thesis.

―――― *Experience with the Supernatural in Early Christian Times*, The Century Company, New York, 1929. A Discussion of supernatural phenomena presented in the literature and religion of the Hellenistic period.

H. R. Willoughby, *Pagan Regeneration*, University of Chicago Press, 1929. Interprets the ceremonials and sacraments of the Hellenistic mystery cults.

M. S. Enslin, "Palestine in New Testament Times," *The Interpreter's Bible*, the Abingdon Press, Nashville, 1951, vol. 7, pp. 100–113.

S. V. McCasland, "The Greco-Roman World in New Testament Times," *op. cit.*, pp. 75–99.

———— "Ships and Sailing in the New Testament." *The Interpreter's Dictionary of the Bible*, the Abingdon Press, Nashville, 1962, vol. 4, pp. 335–337.

———— "Travel and Communication in the New Testament." *op. cit.*, pp. 690–693.

———— "Education in the New Testament." *op. cit.*, vol. 2, pp. 34–38.

F. C. Grant, *Roman Hellenism and the New Testament*, Charles Scribner's Sons, New York, 1963. Interprets the New Testament as a response and literary record of Hellenistic religious life.

Robert H. Pfeiffer, *History of New Testament Times, with an Introduction to the Apocrypha*, Harper & Brothers, New York, 1949.

Jack Finegan, *Light from the Ancient Past*, Princeton University Press, Princeton, N. J., 1946.

IV. The Gospels

E. D. Burton and E. J. Goodspeed, *A Harmony of the Synoptic Gospels*, Charles Scribner's Sons, New York, 1917. Based on the American Standard Version. The same book in Greek, University of Chicago Press, 1920.

B. H. Throckmorton, *Gospel Parallels*, Thomas Nelson and Sons, New York, 1957. A harmony based on the Revised Standard Version.

B. S. Easton, *The Gospel before the Gospels*, Charles Scribner's Sons, New York, 1928. A useful introduction to form criticism.

Martin Dibelius, *From Tradition to Gospel*, Charles Scribner's Sons, New York, 1935. Translated from the German of 1919, one of the pioneers of form criticism.

Rudolf Bultmann, *History of the Synoptic Tradition*, Harper & Row, New York, 1962. From the German of 1921, another classic of form criticism.

H. J. Cadbury, *The Making of Luke-Acts*, The Macmillan Company, New York, 1927. A scholarly introduction to this two volume work.

B. H. Streeter, *The Four Gospels*, The Macmillan Company, New York, 1925. An authoritative analysis of the documentary structure of the Gospels.

E. F. Scott, *The Fourth Gospel*, T. & T. Clark, Edinburgh, 1908. Perceptive of the basic meaning of the Gospel. Authoritative.

F. C. Grant, *The First Gospel*, The Abingdon Press, Nashville, 1943. Covers general introduction along with discussion of original language of this Gospel, roles of Jerusalem and Galilee, etc.

E. C. Colwell and E. L. Titus, *The Gospel of the Spirit*, Harper & Brothers, New York, 1953. An exposition of the uniquely spiritual character of this Gospel.

D. M. Beck, *Through the Gospels to Jesus*, Harper & Brothers, New York, 1954. A comprehensive introduction to the four Gospels.

Joachim Jeremias, *The Parables of Jesus*, Charles Scribner's Sons, New York, 1955. The parables were set forth in relation to specific situations and must be interpreted in that light. From German editions of 1947 and 1952.

C. H. Dodd, *History and Gospel*, Charles Scribner's Sons, New York, 1938. The Gospels are pervaded by an early theology, expressed in an accepted tradition, *kerygma*, and teaching, *didaché*.

—— *Interpretation of the Fourth Gospel*, Cambridge University Press, 1953. An erudite analysis of this Gospel; continues elaboration of the above ideas in John.

E. G. Kraeling, *The Four Gospels*, McGraw-Hill Book Company, Inc., New York, 1962. Trenchant commentary by an eminent linguist.

V. Apocryphal Sources

R. H. Charles, *The Apocrypha and Pseudepigrapha*, 2 vols., Oxford, 1913. Still indispensable.

M. R. James, *The Apocryphal New Testament*, Oxford, 1924. Still good, but needs revision and expansion.

William H. Brownlee, *The Meaning of the Qumran Scrolls for the Bible*, Oxford University Press, New York, 1964.

Millar Burrows, *The Dead Sea Scrolls*, Viking Press, New York, 1955. Excellent introduction and translation of main documents.

John Marco Allegro, *The People of the Dead Sea Scrolls*, Routledge and Kegan Paul, London, 1959. Introduction and good pictures.

Frank Moore Cross, Jr., *The Ancient Library of Qumran and Modern Biblical Studies*, Doubleday & Company, Inc., Garden City, New York, 1958. Incisive comments by an authority.

A. Guillaumont et al., *The Gospel According to Thomas*, Harper & Brothers, New York, 1959. Text and translation of a Coptic Gospel from the second or third century A.D. Recently found in Egypt.

Kendrick Grobel, *The Gospel of Truth*, The Abingdon Press, Nashville,

1960. Another Gnostic Coptic Gospel from Egypt of around the second and third century.

VI. *The Historical Jesus*

S. J. Case, *The Historicity of Jesus,* University of Chicago Press, 1912. States and refutes the arguments of those who hold that Jesus never lived; that his story is only a myth.

——— *Jesus, a new Biography,* University of Chicago Press, 1927. One of the best critical evaluations of the Gospels against their social environment, presenting Jesus as a prophet.

F. C. Grant, *The Gospel of the Kingdom,* The Macmillan Company, New York, 1940. Holds that the religious movement led by Jesus was more widespread than indicated in the Gospels and Acts.

Rudolf Bultmann, *Jesus and the Word,* Charles Scribner's Sons, New York, 1958 (German, 1926). This famous scholar interprets Jesus from the point of view of the philosophy of existentialism.

M. Dibelius, *Jesus,* Westminster Press, Philadelphia, 1949. From the point of view of form criticism.

E. J. Goodspeed, *The Life of Jesus,* Harper & Brothers, New York, 1950. A most readable life of Jesus by a famous translator.

V. Taylor, *The Life and Ministry of Jesus,* The Abingdon Press, Nashville, 1955. By a leading British scholar, well informed, up to date.

W. E. and M. B. Rollins, *Jesus and His Ministry,* Seabury Press, Greenwich, Conn., 1954. Beautifully written, by a scholarly man and his scholarly wife.

John Knox, *Jesus: Lord and Christ,* Harper & Brothers, New York, 1958. A theological study of Jesus in the contemporary mood.

G. Bornkamm, *Jesus of Nazareth,* Harper & Brothers, New York, 1960. A German work which sees that in spite of the fragmentary character of the Gospels it is still possible to write a life of Jesus.

M. S. Enslin, *The Prophet of Nazareth,* McGraw-Hill Book Company, Inc., New York, 1961. A competent presentation of a thoroughgoing scepticism of the possibility of writing a real life of Jesus.

A. Schweitzer, *The Quest of the Historical Jesus,* second English edition, The Macmillan Company, New York, 1936. A brilliant account of the efforts scholars made from about 1750 to 1900 to write a critical life of Jesus.

James M. Robinson, *A New Quest of the Historical Jesus,* Allenson, Inc., Naperville, Ill., 1959. Analysis of the last three decades of German research in the Gospels, with emphasis on Bultmann and scholars under his influence.

Heinz Zahrnt, *The Historical Jesus,* Harper & Row, New York, 1963. Although brief, a promising beginning of a life of Jesus, translated from the German.

VII. Some of My Own Researches

S. V. McCasland, *The Resurrection of Jesus,* Thomas Nelson and Sons, New York, 1932. From the perspective of form criticism, this study traces the development of the narratives of the resurrection, beginning with the vision of Peter, the first seen.

—— *By the Finger of God,* The Macmillan Company, New York, 1951. A study of demon possession in the New Testament in the light of modern views of mental illness.

    The following papers in the *Journal of Biblical Literature:* "Christ Jesus," Dec., 1946, pp. 377–381; "Some New Testament Metonyms for God," June, 1949, pp. 99–113; "Abba, Father," June, 1953, pp. 79–91; "Signs and Wonders," June, 1957, pp. 149–152; "The Way, Sept., 1958, pp. 222–230.

"Miracle," in *The Interpreter's Dictionary of the Bible,* vol. 3, pp. 392–402.

"Miracles," in *Hastings Dictionary of the Bible,* rev. ed., Charles Scribner's Sons, New York, 1963, pp. 663–666.

"Religious Healing in First-Century Palestine," in *Environmental Factors in Christian History,* edited by McNeill, Spinka and Willoughby, University of Chicago Press, 1939, pp. 18–34.

"The Black One," in *Early Christian Origins,* edited by Allen Wikren, Quadrangle Books, Chicago, 1961, pp. 77–80.

VIII. Philosophy of Religion

William James, *Varieties of Religious Experience,* Longmans, Green & Company, New York, 1903. A pioneer in this field, still informed and readable. Houghton Mifflin Co., New York, 1910.

E. S. Ames, *The Psychology of Religious Experience,* A scientific method and pragmatic philosophy oriented with reference to anthropology.

—— *Religion,* Henry Holt & Company, New York, 1929. Elaborates the above approach with reference to social and aesthetic symbols.

    Rudolf Otto, *Das Heilige,* 1917; tr., *The Idea of the Holy,* Oxford, 1923. As the Holy One, God has elements of awe, mystery and terror; he destroys as well as creates; judges as well as loves.

Martin Buber, *I and Thou,* T. & T. Clark, Edinburgh, 1952. The thesis that while science and philosophy know reality as impersonal, religion apprehends it as personal.

Paul Tillich, *The Courage to Be,* Yale University Press, New Haven, 1952. Courage is a central element in healthy personality.

—— *Biblical Religion and the Search for Ultimate Reality,* University of Chicago Press, 1955. Confronts biblical revelation with the rational demands of philosophy, showing how they may be reconciled in the framework of existentialism.

———— *The Dynamics of Faith*, Harper & Brothers, New York, 1957. Faith of intelligent persons always carried the possibility of doubt, which it can transcend.

———— *Christianity and the Encounter with World Religions*, Columbia University Press, New York, 1963. Analyzes the reasoned encounter of Christianity with Buddhism as one example of its encounter with other religions of the world.

Index of Scriptures

Index